I am very respectfully,
Your obedient, &c.
Saml. Prentiss.

HISTORY

OF THE

TOWN OF MONTPELIER,

FROM THE TIME IT WAS FIRST CHARTERED IN

1781 TO THE YEAR 1860.

TOGETHER WITH

BIOGRAPHICAL SKETCHES OF ITS MOST NOTED DECEASED CITIZENS.

Written in accordance with a vote of the Town in March Meeting, 1859.

BY D. P. THOMPSON.

MONTPELIER:
E. P. WALTON, PRINTER.
1860.

TO THE

NATIVE CITIZENS OF MONTPELIER,

OF THIS AND COMING GENERATIONS,

WHO MAY BE DESIROUS OF KNOWING

THE INCIDENTS CONNECTED WITH THE ORIGIN OF THEIR TOWN:

HOW THEIR FATHERS AND MOTHERS OF THE EARLY TIMES LIVED

HOW THEY TOILED; HOW THEY STRUGGLED,

AND HOW THEY CONQUERED THE WILDERNESS AND ITS DIFFICULTIES,

TO LEAVE FOR THEIR DESCENDANTS

THE PLEASANT VILLAGE HOMES AND CULTIVATED FARMS

THEY NOW ENJOY,

This Work is Respectfully Dedicated,

BY

THE AUTHOR.

PREFACE.

A PREFACE, which can only be necessary for explanation of matters which otherwise might not be clear to the reader, or of matters which might not otherwise be so fully appreciated, to be good for anything, should never be touched till the last line of the book to which it is attached has been written. And having completed our task of writing a History of Montpelier, according to the best of our humble abilities, with our means of information and the time we could bestow upon it, we now sit down to write a brief preface, both explanatory and apologetic—to explain and designate our means of information on the subjects introduced and discussed, and render our excuse for having performed the literary part of our task so imperfectly.

Having, when Zadock Thompson had his Gazetteer of Vermont in preparation, undertaken, at his request, to furnish a brief history of Montpelier, we visited, for the purpose of collecting materials for that task, the most intelligent survivors of the first settlers of Montpelier and the neighboring towns, and made minutes of the facts and incidents which we condensed into the brief sketch of the town that appears in that work, together with many more which the space allowed us would not permit of being introduced. Among the best informed of the men thus consulted were JAMES SAWYER, Col. CYRUS JOHNSON, ZACHARIAH PERRIN, and others of the first settlers of Berlin ; Hon. SETH PUTNAM of Middlesex, and JOHN TAPLIN, Esq., CLARK STEVENS, and Gen. PEARLY DAVIS of Montpelier, who were considered the best historians of the first settlement then living. And to the facts and representations then derived from these well-informed and reliable men, and especially General Davis, Judge Putnam and Esquire Taplin, who had been leading men in the public affairs of the early times, we have been indebted not only for much correct information, which, as they have all since passed away, could not now have been obtained, but for our conceptions of the true character of those times, and of the characters, habits and springs of action of the hardy men who figured therein.

With these important advantages we commenced the present work. But feeling that we had only entered the field to be explored, we begun our investigations anew. And besides examining all the written and published evidence to be found, which had any reference to the subject on hand, we at once commenced a series of personal visits to all the still remaining survivors of the first settlement in Montpelier and the neighboring towns, that we might take down from their own lips that oral testimony of general facts, particular incidents, personal descriptions and the current opinions and notions of the men and times of which they spoke, and which could alone enable us to give a true and just picture of those men and times. Among the principal persons thus visited and consulted are Thomas Davis, Jonathan Shepard, Mrs. Marsh, the widow of the late William Marsh, Mrs. Brooks, widow of the late Lemuel Brooks, and Mr. Levi Humphrey, who died September 1859, about a fortnight after our interview with him,—all of Montpelier, Mr. Elisha Cummins of East Montpelier, Rev. James Hobart, Simeon Dewey, Esq., and Mrs. Hannah Jones, widow of the late Major Jones, of Berlin, and Captain Holden Putnam and Mrs. Warren, widow of the late Lovell Warren, of Middlesex. From these persons, all bordering the age of ninety, and several of them from two to five years older, we have gained much of the additional information we needed to make out a full and reliable account of the first dozen years of the settlement. And for much we have embodied connected with the period immediately succeeding 1800, we acknowledge our indebtedness to the Hon. Geo. Worthington and Mrs. Clarissa Worthington, the venerable Capt. Jewett, the Hon. Daniel Baldwin, the Hon. Joseph Howes and Mr.

Samuel Goss, of Montpelier. And to these we should, perhaps, add Gen. Sylvester Churchill of U. S. Army, who, having resided here at the time the first State House was built, has furnished some interesting incidents of that period.

Thus it will be seen, the sources and means of our information have been good, and we have spared no time or pains in availing ourself of them to the best advantage.

But we cannot say as much for the manner in which we have elaborated and brought out the materials of the work. There was scarcely a day during the time we were engaged in the composition of the work, in which we were not compelled to drop our pen and go abroad to ascertain from old living witnesses, family records or books, or pamphlets out of print, some fact, circumstance or date, which we found it necessary or desirous to introduce. This not only greatly limited the time we had to bestow on the composition of the book, but had the tendency to disturb the keeping, ease and harmony of the style, and in many instances to cause it to be left imperfect. For these reasons, we must ask the indulgence of the reader in making all the allowance for the literary execution of the work, to which the circumstances may entitle him.

In regard to the biographical sketches, which are now made to constitute a considerable portion of the work, it may, perhaps, be proper to remark, that they have been extended in number, and in the length of most of them, much farther than we oginally designed: For, on investigating the facts and events connected with the public and private lives of the individuals whose characters have been sketched, we found many matters of historical interest which, had we discovered them before, we should have inserted in the body of the work, and which, deeming our history incomplete without them, we have taken this method to add to it.

D. P. THOMPSON.

MONTPELIER, August, 1860.

CONTENTS.

CHAPTER XI.

CHAPTER XII.

CHAPTER XIII.

CHAPTER XIV.

BIOGRAPHICAL SKETCHES.

ERRATA.

Besides a few typographical errors which the eye of the reader will naturally correct, there are two so much affecting the sense that we are unwilling they should pass without being pointed out:

Page 155, about midway, on the subject of floods, &c., read *quantity*, not *quality*.

" 224, top line, in the sketch of Judge Ware, read *fertile*, not *futile*.

The christian name of General Davis was always written, by himself and others of his times, *Par*ley, and was intended so to have been put in type in this work, till too late to make the change.

HISTORY OF MONTPELIER.

CHAPTER I.

ORIGIN OF THE NAME OF THE TOWN. — THE NAMES OF THE RIVERS BORDERING IT. — THE PHYSICAL AND GEOLOGICAL FEATURES OF ITS LOCATION.

On the sinuous banks of the upper portion of the mountain-born Winooski, amidst the clustering confluences of its chief tributaries, in latitude 44° 17′, longitude 4° 25′ from Washington, and at an altitude of 540 feet above the level of the ocean, lies, snugly embosomed among the hills, in the heart of the Green Mountains, the flourishing and important interior town of which I have undertaken to give the history, under the unusual name of MONTPELIER.

As enquiries respecting the origin of a name so peculiar as the one bestowed on this town will here very naturally arise in the mind of the reader, and some explanation as naturally be looked for in a work of this character, I will endeavor to meet this, and other anticipated queries of the kind, at the outset.

The name in question was bestowed by Colonel Jacob Davis, a leading proprietor, and the first permanent settler of the town. The Colonel being a man of an independent and originating mind, and consequently one of those who are not to be led by the examples and customs of others any farther than found consonant with their own notions, had noticed, with dislike, the propensity of the proprietors of most of the townships of the State to bestow on their respective grants the names of the towns in the old States where they resided, or with which they were in some way associated; and he, therefore, resolved to have a new name for the township in which *he* was interested—one which should not be obnoxious to the imputation of such servility as had been shown in the naming of other towns in the new State, and one, at the same time, which should obviate the inconvenience and confusion that he foresaw must some day arise in consequence of having so many places of the same name in one confederacy. And in casting about for such a name as he would be willing to appropriate for the purpose, he thought of the city of France bearing the name of *Montpelier*, a word originally compounded, perhaps, of *Mont*, a hill or mountain, and *peller*, bare or shorn, and first bestowed on account of some bare elevation at or near the site of that city. But however that may be, the name, the more particular applicability of which for the name of a town among the mountains was suggested by the first part of the word, seemed to strike the fancy and meet the requirements of the Colonel; and proposing it to his fellow petitioners for the proposed grant of a township here, it was at once adopted, the name of *Montpelier* inserted in the petition to the Legislature, and the grant made accordingly.*

Next to the name of the town, the name of the important river that bounds or passes through the borders of more than half the town, together with those of the four of its principal tributaries which enter it within the limits of the town, or during its long, winding course around it, demands from us, we think, something more than a passing notice. This river, previous to the settlement of the part of the country through which it runs, was mostly known to people abroad by the name of *French River*. This fact we not only learn from tradition, but from the terms used in bounding the other towns bordering on this stream, in whose charters, issued by the royal Governor of New Hampshire, nearly twenty years before that of Montpelier, the words "*French* or Onion river" may be found. The name was doubtless derived from the well known fact that, during the old French wars in this country, the French and Indians made the valley of this stream their principal route in their predatory excursions from Canada to the frontier settlements of New Hampshire and Massachusetts; while the hunting and trapping stations which the French subsequently established along the banks of the river, in consequence of their knowledge of the localities thus obtained, and to which they, for years after, continued to resort, contributed to confirm and prolong the use of the appellation among the English colonists of New England. But when this section began to be explored with the view of settlement, the explorers found everywhere growing along the banks of this river great quantities of leeks, or wild onions, which soon led to the discovery of the Indian name of the river, or rather the land bordering upon it, *Winooski*, a name composed of two words of the Algonquin language, *winoos*, onions, and *ki*, land. The true signification of the term, therefore, as applied to the stream,

* My authority for this statement respecting the naming of the town is derived from the Hon. George Worthington, who married Clarissa, the youngest daughter of Col. Davis, and the first child born in the town. Mr. W. well remembers being in company among others with the Colonel, when the latter was asked how the town came to be named Montpelier, and that he then, by way of reply, made the statement I have, in substance, above given.

would be *Onion Land River*. The French, through whom we obtained the word, pronounced it *Wenooskee*, the *i* taking the sound of our *e*. But as the Indians would give the same sound to the *i* that we do, I do not perceive the propriety of our following the French pronunciation of the name, especially while the original Indian pronunciation must be nearly or entirely consonant with that of our own language. There is a literary snobbishness of our times that affects the French sound of the vowels in all possible cases. It is proper, perhaps, that we should retain the French pronunciation in all the words we *adopt* from that language, but that is no reason why we should try to Frenchify everything.

I cannot forbear, in passing, to express a regret that the practical tastes and common-place notions of our first settlers should have so far governed them, in respect to this name, as to have led them generally to adopt the homely translation instead of the poetic original. The Indian names are not like most of ours, arbitrary and inexpressive, but ever have their significations. This of itself is a beauty. It ensures, also, the applicability of the name to the thing. And as the appropriation of these aboriginal appellations would have furnished us with sonorous and expressive names for our streams, lakes, mountains, &c., besides obviating the inconvenience ever experienced from duplicating our common ones, it is much to be regretted, we think, that they had not been more generally ascertained and scrupulously adopted. The writer of these pages well remembers having had, more than twenty years ago, a conversation with his friend and namesake, though no relative, the late Zadock Thompson, on this subject generally, but in reference more particularly to the name of the river now under consideration, when we mutually agreed that we would do what we could towards restoring the Indian name. That eminent historian and naturalist, of whom the State may well be proud, has done much towards effecting this object, especially among the people of Chittenden County, embracing the lower portion of the river, where it is now very generally called Winooski; shall not the surviving party to the agreement be aided in completing that object, by restoring the name also among the people of Washington County, within which the stream collects the great body of its waters? Let its name never more be written otherwise than *Winooski*.

Of the four tributaries of the Winooski, before mentioned, the first, when taken in order, in ascending the main stream, is *Dog River*, which, rising in Roxbury and Northfield, enters it from the west part of Berlin, about a mile below Montpelier village. The name grew out of the fact that one of the white pioneer hunters had the misfortune to catch his dog in a trap set for beaver or otter in the edge of the stream, when the animal, in his struggles to escape, was drowned. The manner by which this name was derived from the circumstance just named was certainly not quite so forced as that by which the wit derived the name of the British orator, Fox, from rainy day—"*rainy day—rain hard—reynard—Fox.* But the process by which the subjugates, varying and abreviated from time to time, finally settled down into the name seems, nevertheless, to have been a little awkward. It probably began and proceeded somewhat thus: *The river where the hunter lost his dog—the river of the lost dog—the lost dog river*—DOG RIVER. It could have been wished that this river had received a more appropriate and dignified name. It is surely deserving of one; for it is undoubtedly one of the most beautiful streams, of its size, in the whole country, being surpassed by no other for the coolness, purity and crystal clearness of its waters, which have ever made it, from the earliest settlement of the country to the present day, the favorite resort of the fastidious trout.

The next tributary in order is the *Little North Branch*, which, coming in on the opposite side, gathers most of its waters in Worcester, gains some additions in East Middlesex, and passes through the midst of Montpelier village, within which it enters the river. The reason why this was called the *Little* North Branch is not now very apparent, for it is *not* the *least* North Branch of the Winooski, the lesser one coming in about seven miles further up the river. It was probably so called, however, in contrast with the principal stream, which here begins to wind round the town from a northerly direction. But the impropriety of the term has latterly been obviated by the now more generally used name of the Worcester Branch.

The third tributary in order is *Stevens Branch*, which, starting within the borders of Williamstown, Washington and Orange, and draining the town of Barre and the east part of Berlin, enters the river, in the last named town, at the great northern bend about two miles above Montpelier village. The name of this quiet stream was derived from a singular casualty, which may well be ranked among the incidents composing the romance of our early history. A reputable young man by the name of Stevens, residing in Corinth, when that was a frontier town bordering the great wilderness thence to Lake Champlain, was engaged in marriage to a girl of the same town, who, from fickleness or some unwarranted freak of jealousy, broke her plighted faith, and suddenly married another. This so wrought on the mind and feelings of Stevens that he soon resolved to banish himself from society into the lone forests, never more to return. Accordingly, throwing up his business, which was that of a house-carpenter, he provided himself with gun, traps, and other things composing the hunter's outfit, and having made his way to the nearest part of the Winooski, established his camp on the east bank of the stream that subsequently took his name, about a quarter of a mile from its mouth, on the farm occupied, for the first forty years of the present century, by Daniel Thompson, the father of the writer of these pages. This was, as has been supposed, in early autumn; and nothing more was heard from him until the following spring, when two hunters, passing that way, found his dead body near his camp, in a situation which pretty plainly indicated the circumstances which must have attended his melancholy exit. An old tree had fallen lengthwise the bank of the stream, so as to form a sort of wharfing to the deep, circular eddy here formed by an abrupt turn of the current above. A few feet in the rear of this fallen tree the body was found, with one hand resting on a fishing-pole, with a half rotted fish-line attached, and extending across the log over the waters. Within about a rod of the body stood a hunter's camp, containing a gun, hatchet, traps, and a blanket spread over the usual bough-bed. Before the camp lay the charred remains of a fire, over which was suspended, from a cross-bar or pole lying in upright crotches, a camp kettle half filled with herbs and water; while on a sharp knot, projecting from a spruce tree standing near by were found hanging a few mink skins, and other small peltries. He had evidently been seized with sickness, superinduced probably by despondency, and here, in a last effort to procure a fish to sustain life, while his herb tea was steeping, his strength had entirely failed him, and, with none to aid or nurse him, and no friendly eye to witness his death struggles, he had breathed his last alone in the dark wilderness. The exact spot where the hunters buried him was not known till about the year 1806, when Mr. Thompson, in plowing up a spot from which he had removed an old hedge fence, turned out his bones. I, then a small boy, was present on the occasion, and the sensation which the sight of these remains, as they were thrown out by the deep furrow that was made lengthwise through them, with the rust-eaten jack-knife lying in the midst, palpably to view, caused it to become one of the most vivid of my early recollections, and subsequently led me to make minute enquiries of the oldest settlers in all that related to the unfortunate hunter. And it was from their concurrent testimony, and particularly that of Grandmother Fowler, as she was called, who was the wife of Jacob Fowler, the old hunter and first permanent settler of Berlin, and who, when a girl, lived in the same neighborhood with young Stevens, that these particulars were derived.*

The fourth and upper great tributary of the Winooski is *Kingsbury's Branch*, which, after draining most of the numerous ponds of Woodbury and Calais, enters the river in the north-easterly corner of the town. Its name was derived from that of an early settler living on the stream. And for the particulars of the naming I am more especially indebted to A. J. Sibley, Esq., of North Montpelier, who, having investigated the subject, writes me: "There was once a man who lived in Woodbury, (but now lives in Goshen Gore,) very near this branch, and used to fish in it a great deal, and call it *his* branch; and after calling it *his* branch for many years, it became a name for everybody, who thenceforward called it *Kingsbury's Branch*."

This completes our account of the four great tributaries that enter the Winooski in and around Montpelier, more than doubling it in size. These four streams, except the one last described, which is perceptibly smaller than the three others, are so nearly alike in size that it is very difficult to decide which discharges the greatest average volume of water into the main river.

Here the Winooski, after having wound, like a serpent, round half this town, and gathered in its course the tribute of these streams, seems to start off direct, in its accumulated strength, and sweep on, in an almost straight line, to the beautiful border lake, into which it disembogues its mountain waters. This river is the largest, and, considering its course almost through all the central portion of the State, and the immense number of mill privileges it furnishes, quite the most important river of the State. The Vermont Gazetteer ranks the four largest rivers of the State, with their relative sizes computed from the number of square miles they respectively drain, as follows: The Winooski draining 970 square miles, the Otter 900, the White 680, and the Missisco 582 square miles. This method of computing the size of rivers might not be very accurate when comparing the rivers of one country with those of another, since some rivers flow through a long stretch of country after gaining nearly their full size, which would, of course, greatly increase the area they may be said to drain; while others terminate almost as soon as they acquire their greatest volume, and therefore draw their water from a much smaller compass. But it is the

* The Vermont Gazetteer, under the head of Berlin, states, in regard to this incident, that the bones of Stevens were discovered by Mr. Thompson in 1812, in digging a ditch. There are two errors in this statement: the bones were found about a half dozen years earlier; and they were plowed out of a dry piece of ground from which an old log and bush fence had just been removed. They were reinterred near, but the exact place is again lost.

most accurate method yet known; and, so far as regards our Vermont rivers, must give their comparative sizes with a very close approximation to exactness. I have measured over the areas drained by these rivers, on our best maps, and cannot but think that, in case of the Winooski, the author of the Gazetteer, who probably computed by right line parallelograms, must have omitted the measurement of several irregularly shaped gores of land shooting out considerably beyond the general outline of the tributaries, such as those drained by the upper portions of Huntington and Waterbury rivers; and he thereby made the area drained by the river in question at least thirty square miles too small. I cannot make the true area drained by this stream to be less than one thousand square miles. Its length, from its mouth to the head of its most distant source, in the town of Walden, is, when measured on the stream, nearer ninety miles than the seventy given for it in the Gazetteer. By the travelled roads nearest the stream, the distance between these two points is about seventy-five miles, and nearly ten more should be allowed, probably, for the short turns and windings of the river. The true head of this river, however, is in the Peacham, or Winooski Pond. Those who will go to the junction of the Cabot branch and the outlet of Peacham Pond, cannot fail to perceive, after a few fairly made observations, that the latter discharges the greatest average volume of water, and should therefore be considered the main stream, and bear the name of Winooski to its true head in Peacham Pond, which should also take the same name. From the source of the inlet of this pond, through the pond, down the tortuous outlet, and then down the river to its mouth, would probably be about seventy-five miles.

The geological formation of the township of Montpelier is mainly slate and limestone, prevailing separately and wholly in a few localities, but perhaps more generally alternating on the same piece of ground, and mingled with other substances, such as talc, mica, hornblend, &c. The crumbling and pulverization of intermingled slate and lime compose, perhaps, the best and most durable soils to be found; and this will account for the excellence of the soil of the town of Montpelier, and that of the other towns in Washington County of like formation.

The site of Montpelier was evidently once the bed of a lake over one hundred feet deep. The well defined strata of earth marked on all the surrounding hills, and showing the gradual subsidence of the waters, are too palpable to leave any rational doubt of the fact. A lake of this depth here would send its waters up the valley of Dog River to Northfield or Roxbury; up the Little North Branch to the further part of Worcester; up

Stevens Branch nearly to the borders of Williamstown; and up the main river to Plainfield; while its downward or western limit was probably the rocky barrier at the place now known as Middlesex Narrows. This would make a branchy lake, measuring through its longest extremities nearly twenty miles in length, of a breadth varying from one to two miles, and forming a body of mountain waters which must have been singularly irregular in outline, and highly picturesque in appearance. The summit level of this lake was doubtless the sandy plain above the village of Montpelier, now generally known by the designation of the Washington County *Fair Ground*. This plain, or plateau, as may be read in the strata on its borders, dipping at a small angle to the north and to the south, on the corresponding sides, was thrown up by the meeting here of the opposing currents, one coming down the northern branch of the lake from Worcester, and the other coming down the south-eastern branch from Barre. These opposing currents were created by the east wind, which, owing to the differently situated mountain barriers over which it passes, is often found to be blowing down the river from Barre, and, at the same time, to be blowing down the branch from Worcester; when, meeting here from almost opposite directions, they unite and pass down the river. The southern current, having a longer and less confined sweep, and being therefore a little stronger, would naturally be forced some distance along the basin-formed hills to the north, and there being brought round to the direct current from that direction, would form another and smaller plateau; and just such a plateau, or sand shelf, is found one mile up the branch, above the Poor Farm, on what is called the Somerby Place. If there was a small side current on the other, or south-western side of the lake, it must have struck across on to Col. Reed's farm, at the lower end of the village; and there, also, we find a small sand or loam shelf to confirm the supposition, in the shelfy hill rising from the back of Col. Reed's house. Two miles above Montpelier village, on the old Jacob Davis Jr.'s farm, and on the part now owned by Mr. J. Douglass, there is another distinctly marked sandy plateau, of about the same dimensions as that of the Fair Ground. This plateau is situated at the exact point where the currents from the Barre and Plainfield branches of the lake would meet, and it was undoubtedly formed by them in a similar manner. There would likewise naturally be something of the same effect produced where the Dog River, or Northfield branch of the lake, united with the main body of the water. But owing to the angular manner in which this branch would come in, and the shape of the surrounding hills, the current must have shot obliquely across the present bed of the river, and struck the opposite hills more than a mile down stream; and here yet again, on the Erastus Camp farm, rising from his saw-mill on the brook below, is to be found another corresponding sand plain, formed in the same manner as those already described. And what would seem to be a demonstration of this theory is the fact that the summits, or surfaces, of all these remarkable plateaus are almost exactly on the same general level, which, as the earth would not be likely to be thrown much above the surface of the water, may safely be set down, also, as the highest level of the lake, whose average depth was not far from one hundred feet above the present beds of the rivers, some miles back each way from its central point on the site of Montpelier village.

The manner in which this lake, and those also below it, were drained off, can now only be read on our leaf of the great volume of Nature, where earth's great changes in the past are all unerringly recorded, for the reading of any Geologist who has thoroughly mastered her language.

There is much geological evidence to warrant the belief that, within a comparatively moderate period, a great change has taken place in the altitude and extent of Lake Champlain ; and that, consequently, all the lower parts of Rutland, Addison, Chittenden and Franklin Counties, must have once been covered by its wide spreading waters, which, on this supposition, would have flowed back to the foot of that lowest natural pass in the great western range of the Green Mountains, which is to be found at Bolton Narrows. From this pass to Middlesex Narrows, there was probably an intermediate lake, covering the lower grounds of Waterbury, parts of those of Duxbury, Middlesex and Moretown, and setting up the valley of Mad River into Waitsfield, making this lake, at Waterbury, somewhat deeper than the one above, as may indeed be found indicated by the greater height of the sand hill east of Waterbury village.

Now, the falling away of the waters of Lake Champlain must have produced a powerful suction current and falls at Bolton. This would, sooner or later, in proportion to the depth of earth and the looseness and depth of rocks to be removed, cut down a channel, which would drain off this intermediate lake up to the next great separating barrier at Middlesex. And here the same process would be passed through, until the upper lake, centering at the prospective site of Montpelier, would be drained off, in another and later period of time, like the one below.

The natural position of Montpelier village, which was the part of the town first settled, and which, in point of population and trade, has ever since continued to maintain its ascendency over all other parts, is, in almost all respects, an unusually central one—more so, perhaps, than that of any other interior village in New England. Besides the numerous hill roads, the great thoroughfares of five or six productive vallies centre at this favored location—the first coming in along the Winooski upward from Middlesex, where it is united with Mad River valley, and thus made the conduit for the products and trade of seven good agricultural townships; the second passing down the valley of Dog River, and bringing in those of a territory equalling at least three good townships; the third coming in down the Worcester branch, with those of two or more townships; the fourth entering from the valley of Stevens Branch, with those of about five towns, some of which are among the best farming towns in the State; and the fifth coming down the valley of the Winooski, from the borders of Danville, with those of five or six more towns of almost equal thrift and productiveness. These vallies are not limited to Washington County, but, extending into the borders of Orange, Caledonia and Lamoille Counties, form natural inlets to this village, radiating out from the place to an average extent of nearly twenty miles in every direction around, and comprising an area of about seven hundred square miles of highly productive agricultural territory, whose trade Montpelier must always mainly control. These great natural advantages sufficiently account for the steady and healthful growth of this village, from its first settlement to the present time. And they well warrant the expectation of an equally unvaried continuance of its increase and progressive prosperity, until it shall become one of the most populous and important interior towns in the whole country.

The natural site of this village, comprising a level plain of nearly two hundred acres of the richest alluvial land to be found anywhere in Vermont, and being everywhere sheltered from the winds, so as to make it comparatively warm and comfortable, and being, moreover, situated near the confluence of so many streams, favorable for hunting or fishing, must have made it, as it doubtless was, the favorite residence, or resort, of the original inhabitants of the forest, who, at the time of the first discovery of Vermont by the French Nobleman, Samuel Champlain, in 1609, and probably for a considerable time afterwards, were a part of the powerful Iroquois, or Six Nations, though the latter were probably trespassers on the territory of the Abenaqus, or Canadian Indians, who eventually expelled them. Evidence, indeed, of its aboriginal populousness does not rest wholly on tradition. Indian mounds, tomb-stones, and other memorials of aboriginal life and death, were found here, or in the vicinity, by the first settlers, and traces of some of them still remain. On the meadow of the old Collins Farm, about two miles below Montpelier, was found what was evidently an Indian mound. Two miles above Montpelier, on one of the lake-made plateaus before described, were found the remains of rude Indian pottery; and about a mile and a half east of the village, in the woods, on the old Boyden Farm, a large, upright, blue lime-stone which was found standing, where it still stands, by General Davis when he first made lines into the forest in laying out the town. It was obviously wrought and shaped by human hands, and so closely resembles the Indian monuments for graves to be seen in the illustrations of Schoolcraft as to leave little doubt that it was originally erected as a tomb-stone, or to commemorate some mournful or important event. And historical evidence, indeed, of the aboriginal populousness and savage thrift of the valley of the Winooski River is by no means wholly wanting. When Champlain, who, as before intimated, was the first white man to set eyes on the territory now known as Vermont, and who virtually gave it its name, by pointing it out to his companions, from their boat in the mid-lake, with the exclamation, "*Verd Monte!*"—when that enterprising explorer was making these observations, his red attendants, pointing up the gorge between Camel's Hump and Mansfield Mountain, said to him: "*Big river come that way—plenty of Indians there, and raise much corn.*" Thus it would seem that the meadows and flats of the Winooski River were as well known among the natives for corn-raising capacities as they have since been among the succeeding race of white men.

Here, then, we may all be daily treading on the long buried generations of the Red Men. For here, doubtless, passed, one after another, for unknown ages, their successive generations, with no chronicler to note their comings and goings. Here they planted their corn, hunted, lighted their council lodges, planned their tribal wars, wooed, wed, and wasted away in age and death, as much unheeded and unknown by the civilized world as the successive growths of the dark and gloomy forests they inhabited. Yes, here,

"Their wigwams stood on every plain,
Through every wood they sought their game,
And up the mountain climb'd;
For free they roam'd, and made their home,
Where'er their will inclin'd.

But, ah, the land the Indian lov'd,
Where they invok'd the Red Man's God,
Hath many a time-worn mound,
Where lie entombed their mouldering bones,
O'ergrown with moss and trees around.

For, one by one, a mournful band,
They all have sought their Spirit Land,
Whence none shall e'er return.
Full well they strove, till, spark by spark,
Their camp-fires ceased to burn."

CHAPTER II.

PROPRIETARY HISTORY OF THE TOWNSHIP.

SOMETHING like one hundred and sixty townships of Vermont had been granted by Governor Wentworth, of New Hampshire, previous to the organization of its civil government, in March, 1778. The State Legislature then took the power of making these grants into their own hands, and, both for the encouraging of settlement, and the swelling of the much needed State revenues by assessments of several hundred pounds for each grant made, except those for public services, rapidly continued its exercise until the whole State was granted. The process of procuring and making these grants seems to have been a simple and speedy one. A company of resident and non-resident men, of some means, got up a petition to the Legislature for the grant of a township in a given locality; the Legislature thereupon appointed a standing committee to act on such petition; when, if the committee reported favorably, as was generally the case, a simple resolve was passed making the grant in question, and the Governor, if the required fees were paid, issued the charter accordingly.

In pursuance of these forms, Timothy Bigelow and fifty-nine others, including Colonel Jacob Davis and his two minor sons, Jacob and Thomas, presented to the Legislature, at the October session, 1780, their petition for the grant of a tract of unappropriated land, in the locality therein specified, under the name of Montpelier; when, the usual committee having been appointed for the purpose, the following action, as appears by the House Journal of that session, was taken in the premises:—

"HOUSE OF REPRESENTATIVES, 21st of October, 1780.

"The committee appointed to take into consideration the ungranted lands in this State, and the several Pitches on file in the Secretary's office, &c., brought in the following report, viz:

"'That, in our opinion, the following tract of land, viz: lying east of and adjoining Middlesex, on Onion river, and partly north of Berlin, containing 23040 acres, be granted by Assembly to Col. Timothy Bigelow and Company, by the name of MONTPELIER.

'PAUL SPOONER, Chairman.'

"The foregoing report was read and accepted, and

"*Resolved*, That there be, and hereby is granted unto Col. Timothy Bigelow and company, being sixty in number, a township of land, by the name of MONTPELIER, situate and lying in this State, bounded as follows, viz: lying east of and adjoining Middlesex, on Onion river, and partly north of Berlin, containing 23040 acres: And the Governor and Council are hereby requested to issue a Grant or Charter of incorporation of said township of Montpelier, under such restrictions, reservations, and for such considerations, as they shall judge best for the benefit of the State."

"SATURDAY, IN COUNCIL, 21st of October, 1780.

"The Governor and Council, to whom was referred the stating the fees for the grant of land made this day, by the General Assembly of this State, having had the same under consideration, have stated the fees aforesaid at four hundred and eighty pounds for said land, being one township by the name of MONTPELIER, in hard money, or an equivalent in Continental Currency; to be paid by Col. Timothy Bigelow or his attorney, on the execution of the Charter of Incorporation, on or before the 20th of January next.

"Attest, JOSEPH FAY, Secretary.

"£480."

For some reason unknown, though probably because the required fees were not paid in, the charter above authorized was not issued till the succeeding August; when the following one was issued:

"CHARTER OF MONTPELIER."

"[L. S.]" "*The Governor, Council and General Assembly of the Freemen of the State of Vermont, to all people to whom these presents shall come*, GREETING:

"KNOW YE, that whereas Timothy Bigelow and his associates, our worthy friends, have, by petition, requested a grant of unappropriated lands within this State, in order for settling a new Plantation, to be erected into a Township—

"We have therefore thought fit, for the due encouragement of their laudable designs and for other valuable considerations us hereunto moving, and do, by these Presents, and in the name, and by the authority of the Freemen of the State, give and grant the Tract of land hereafter described and bounded, unto him, the said Timothy Bigelow and the several persons hereafter named, his associates, in equal shares, viz:—Bethuel Washburn, John Washburn, Elijah Rood, Thomas Chittenden, George Foot, Elisha Smith, Jedediah Strong, James Prescott, Jacob Brown, Gideon Ormsbee, James Mead, John W. Dana, Timothy Brownson, Gideon Horton, Matthew Lyon, Samuel Horsford, Ithamer

Horsford, William Smith, Jacob Spear, Jonas Galusha, Mary Galusha, Noah Smith, Moses Robinson, Moses Robinson Jr, John Fasset Jr, Jonas Fay, Abiathar Waldo, Thomas Tolman, Timothy Stanley, Joseph Dagget, Ira Allen, Lyman Hitchcock, James Gamble, Alanson Douglas, Adam Martin, the heirs of Isaac Nash, Jonathan Brace, Howel Woodbridge, James Brace, Henry Walbridge, Jr., Joseph Fay, William Goodrich, Sybil Goodrich, Thomas Matterson, Amos Waters, David Galusha, Jacob Davis, Ephraim Starkweather, Shubael Peck, Jacob Davis, Jr., Thomas Davis, John Ramsdell, Issachar Reed, Isaac G. Lansingh, Ebenezer Davis, Levi Davis, Asa Davis, Ebenezer Stone, and Samuel Allen,—

"Which, together with the five following Rights, reserved to the several public uses in manner following, viz :—

[Read the Charter of Ripton, in which are the same words with this, for disposing of the five Public Rights.]

"Which Tract of land, hereby given and granted, as aforesaid, is bounded and described as follows, viz :

"Beginning at

and the same be, and hereby is incorporated into a Township by the name of MONTPELIER, and the inhabitants that do, or shall hereafter, inhabit said Township, are declared to be enfranchised and entitled to all the privileges and immunities that the inhabitants of other towns in this State do, and ought, by the laws and Constitution thereof, to exercise and enjoy,—

"To have and to hold the said granted premises, as above expressed, with all the privileges and appurtenances thereto belonging, unto them and their respective heirs and assigns forever, upon the following conditions and reservations, viz :

"That each proprietor in the Township of Montpelier aforesaid, his heirs or assigns, shall plant or cultivate five acres of land, and build an house at least eighteen feet square on the floor, or have one family settled on each respective Right, within the term of three years next after the circumstances of the war will admit of a settlement with safety, on penalty of the forfeiture of each respective Right, or share of land, in said Township, not so improved or settled; and the same to revert to the Freemen of this State, to be by their Representatives regranted to such persons as shall appear to settle and cultivate the same.

"That all Pine Timber suitable for a Navy be reserved for the use and benefit of the Freemen of this State.

"*In testimony whereof we have caused the seal of this State to be affixed, in Council, this* 14*th day of August, A. D.*, 1781, *and in the* 5*th year of our Independence.*

"THOMAS CHITTENDEN.

"*By His Excellency's command,*

"THOMAS TOLMAN, D. Sec'y."

Under this imperfect Charter, without any definite boundaries, and with exacting and absurd conditions imposed, was Montpelier settled and organized. It had been hard enough for the settlers to have forfeited their Rights because they had not, in just so many years, cleared just so many acres, and built log houses just so large; but to forfeit them because they cut the needed pine trees, that might be suitable for a Navy, when they were forty miles from any navigable waters, was the height of absurdity. The clause reserving all pine timber suitable for a Navy seems to have been introduced by the Royal Governor of New Hampshire in all his grants of Vermont lands; and the Legislature of our State, on assuming the power, seem, strangely enough, to have kept along the form, at least, in the charters they caused to be issued, till about 1783, when it appears to have been suddenly dropped.

Under other circumstances, it would be difficult to conceive how a township could be correctly and safely surveyed, allotted and deeded, without legally defined boundaries. But in the present instance, the difficulties were mainly obviated by the known boundaries of several of the surrounding towns, which had been previously chartered. By these guides, the township was doubtless very correctly surveyed and divided. And so far as regarded forfeitures, little attention was paid to the subject, and as little apprehension of incurring them entertained, probably, by the proprietors and settlers; for many were the Rights on which the specified improvements were not made within the time prescribed. And a general onslaught on all the pine timber was among the first movements of the resident proprietors. The uncertainties and dangers involved in the defects and conditions of the first charter at length, however, began to be realized by the interested; and they therefore applied to the Legislature for a new charter; when that body, at the heel of an adjourned session, held at Windsor, January, 1804, passed a special act for the purpose; and, under the prompt action of Secretary David Wing, Jr., in whose beautiful chirography the document appears, within five days from the passage of the act, was duly issued a new charter of the township, which, for the sake of having both charters in connection, we here insert.

"THE CHARTER OF MONTPELIER."

" *The Governor of the State of Vermont, to all*
" [L. S.] " *People to whom these Presents shall come,*
" GREETING:

" WHEREAS, the Legislature of the State of Vermont, at their adjourned session, holden at Windsor, on the first day of February A. D. 1804, was pleased to pass an act entitled 'an act authorizing the Governor of this State to issue a new charter of Montpelier,'—

"*Now therefore Know Ye*, that I, *Isaac Tichenor*, *Governor* within and over said State, and in the name, and by the authority of the same, and in pursuance of, and by virtue of the act aforesaid, Do, by these presents, give and grant the tract of land hereafter described and bounded, unto *Timothy Bigelow*, and to the several persons hereafter named, his *associates*, in equal shares, viz:

Ebenezer Waters, Ebenezer Upham, Elisha Wales, Elisha Smith Wales, Joel Frizzle, Bethuel Washburn, John Washburn, Elijah Rood, Thomas Chittenden, George Foot, Elisha Smith, Jedediah Strong, James Prescott, Jacob Brown, Gideon Ormsbee, James Mead, John W. Dana, Timothy Brownson, Gideon Horton, Matthew Lyon, Samuel Horsford, Ithamer Horsford, William Smith, Jacob Spear, Jonas Galusha, Mary Galusha, Noah Smith, Moses Robinson, Moses Robinson, Jun., John Fassett, Jun., Jonas Fay, Abiathar Waldo, Thomas Tolman, Timothy Stanley, Joseph Dagget, Ira Allen, Lyman Hitchcock, James Gamble, Alanson Douglass, Adam Martin, the heirs of Isaac Nash, Jonathan Brace, Howell Woodbridge, James Brace, Henry Walbridge, Jun., Joseph Fay, William Goodrich, Sybil Goodrich, Thomas Matterson, Amos Waters, David Galusha, Jacob Davis, Ephraim Starkweather, Shubael Peck, Jacob Davis, Jun., Thomas Davis, John Ramsdell, Issacher Reed, Isaac G. Lansingh, Ebenezer Davis, Asa Davis, Levi Davis, Ebenezer Stone, and Samuel Allen,—

"Which, together with the five following Rights, reserved to the several public uses, in manner following, include the whole of said tract or township, to wit: One Right for the use of a Seminary or College, one Right for the use of County Grammar Schools in said State, lands to the amount of one Right to be and remain for the settlement of a Minister or Ministers of the Gospel in said Township forever, lands to the amount of one Right for the support of the social worship of God in said Township, and lands to the amount of one Right for the support of an English School or Schools in said Township,—which said two Rights for the use of a Seminary or College, and for the use of County Grammar Schools, as aforesaid, and the Improvements, Rents, Interests and Profits arising therefrom, shall be under the control, order, direction and disposal of the General Assembly of said State forever.

"And the proprietors of said Township are hereby authorized and empowered to locate said two Rights justly and equitably, or quantity for quantity, in such parts of said Township as they, or their committee, shall judge will least incommode the general settlement of said Tract or Township.

"And the said proprietors are further empowered to locate the lands aforesaid, amounting to three Rights, assigned for the settlement of a Minister or Ministers, for their support, and for the use and support of English Schools, in such, and in so many places, as they, or their committee, shall judge will best accommodate the inhabitants of said Township when the same shall be fully settled and improved, laying the same equitably, or quantity for quantity,—which said lands, amounting to the three Rights last mentioned, when located as aforesaid, shall, together with the Improvements, Rights, Rents, Profits, Dues and Interests, remain inalienably appropriated to the uses and purposes for which they are respectively assigned, and be under the charge, direction and disposal of the inhabitants of said Township forever.

"Which tract of land, hereby given and granted as aforesaid, is bounded and described as follows, to wit:

"Beginning at a Basswood Tree on the North Bank of Onion River marked MIDDLESEX CORNER, JULY 13, 1785; thence North 36° East, six miles to a Beech Tree marked MONTPELIER CORNER, JUNE 14, 1786; thence South 54° East, six miles and an half, to a Maple Straddle marked MONTPELIER CORNER, JUNE 17, 1786; thench South 36° West, five miles and five chains, to a Basswood Tree in Barre North line, marked JUNE 19, 1786; thence North 67° West, one mile and sixty-seven chains, to Onion River; thence down said river as it tends to the first bound.

"And that the same be, and hereby is incorporated into a TOWNSHIP by the name of MONTPELIER.

"And the inhabitants that do, or shall hereafter, inhabit said Township, are declared to be enfranchised, and entitled to all the privileges and immunities that the inhabitants of other towns within this State do, and ought, by the laws and Constitution thereof, to exercise and enjoy.

"TO HAVE AND TO HOLD the said granted premises, as above expressed, with all the privileges and appurtenances thereunto belonging, unto them and their respective heirs and assigns forever.

"*In testimony whereof I have caused these letters to be made patent, and the seal of your State to be hereunto affixed.*

"*Given under my hand at Windsor, this* 6*th day of February, A. D.* 1804, *and of the Independence of the United States the twenty-eighth.* ISAAC TICHENOR.

"By His Excellency's command,

"DAVID WING, JR., Secretary of State."

4

The first thing noticeable, on comparing this Charter with the old one, is that it fully supplies the omitted boundaries of the town, and properly embodies the provisions for the Rights set apart for public uses, which were before supplied by reference to the Charter of another town; and the second, that in it the objectionable conditions and forfeitures of the old one are entirely discarded, leaving the town unencumbered by the vexatious liabilities thereby to be incurred, and wholly free to appropriate what timber they chose, and clear their lands and build their houses as they saw fit. It will also be noticed that in this new Charter five new names, not found in the former one, viz:—Ebenezer Waters, Ebenezer Upham, Elisha Wales, Elisha Smith Wales, and Joel Frizzle,—are inserted after the name of the leading proprietor, Timothy Bigelow. But, as the other proprietors would never have suffered this to be done to the lessening of their own shares by making a greater divisor, unless the men whose names were thus inserted were really among the grantees, it is but reasonable to attribute the omission of these names, in the first Charter, to the mistake of Tolman, the Deputy Secretary of State, who recorded the Charter, the original of which is not now to be found. This view of the subject, indeed, finds confirmation in the fact that Tolman was one of the proprietors of the township in question, and the Clerk of the proprietors' first meeting, and in the book of their records, in transcribing the Charter, inserted all the omitted names, with the continued acquiescences of all concerned. And yet it is singular that a similar mistake should have been made in the count of the petitioners, at least by the Legislature, who really made the grant only to sixty men, while sixty-five subsequently found their way into the Charter.

It was about three years after the proprietors had obtained their Charter before they appear to have made any movement towards surveying their township, with a view of settlement. At the expiration of that period, however, the following circular, or warning, was issued:—

"THE WARNING FOR THE FIRST PROPRIETORS' MEETING OF THE TOWNSHIP OF MONTPELIER.

"STATE OF VERMONT.

"WHEREAS application hath been made to me by more than one-sixteenth part of the Proprietors of Montpelier, in this State, to warn a meeting of said Proprietors;—these are, therefore, to warn the Proprietors of said Township to meet at the house of Eliakim Stoddard, Esq., Innholder, in Arlington, on Tuesday, the 17th day of August next, at 9 of the clock, in the forenoon, to act on the following articles, to wit:—1. To choose a Moderator—2. A Proprietors' Clerk—3. A Treasurer—4. To see what the Proprietors will do respecting a Division of said Township, and to transact what other business shall be thought necessary when met.

" (*Signed*) ELIAKIM STODDARD, Just. Peace.

" ARLINGTON, June 11th, 1784."

In pursuance of this warning, the Proprietors held their first meeting, organized, and transacted the following business, as appears by their Book of Records, which, being prefaced by a certified copy of their Charter, and the above copied warning, were then commenced; which are still preserved in the Town Records of Montpelier, and from which we copy *verbatim:*

" ARLINGTON, Tuesday, August 17th, 1784.

" Agreeably to the foregoing warning, the Proprietors met, and the meeting was opened at the house of Eliakim Stoddard, Esq., and the Proprietors proceeded to the business of the meeting, agreeably to warning, as follows, viz:—

" 1. *Voted*, Major Gideon Ormsby Moderator of this Meeting.

" 2. *Voted*, That Thomas Tolman, Esq., be, and is hereby appointed Clerk of this Propriety.

" 3. *Voted*, That Jonas Galusha, Esq., be, and he hereby is chosen and appointed Treasurer of this Propriety.

" 4. *Voted*, That we will lay out a First Division of lands in said Township.

" 5. *Voted*, That 150 acres be the quantity of the First Division in said Township, to be laid out as soon as circumstances will admit.

" 6. *Voted*, That we will appoint a committee of six, four of whom shall transact the business, to lay out said Division.

" 7. *Voted*, That Thomas Tolman, Esq., Mr. Samuel Horsford, Major Gideon Ormsby, Jonas Galusha, Esq., Mr. Joseph Dagget, and Lieut. Samuel Beach be, and are hereby appointed our said committee.*

" 8. *Voted*, That this meeting stand adjourned to the first Monday in April next, which will be in the year 1785, then to meet at the house of Thomas Tolman, Esq., in this town, at two of the clock, in the afternoon; and the meeting was accordingly adjourned.

" Attest, THOMAS TOLMAN, Propr's Clerk."

---

* *Note by the Clerk on original Records:*—

" This committee were all Proprietors but the Surveyor, Lt. Samuel Beach.

" N. B. The Proprietors, present at this meeting, who acted for themselves, and others by power of Attorney, were,

" His Excellency, Thomas Chittenden, Esq., Hon. Timothy Bownson, Esq., Maj. Gideon Ormsby, Jonas Galusha, Esq., Thomas Tolman, Esq., Mr. Joseph Dagget, and Mr. John Ramsdell."

By the records, it next appears that the foregoing " *Meeting*," which was adjourned to the first Monday of April, 1785, " *was*," to use the words of the Clerk, " *lost by not attending to the adjournment*." Therefore, on application of the required number of Proprietors, a new warning was issued for a meeting at the house of Eliakim Stoddard, in Arlington, on the second Wednesday of January, 1786, to organize anew, and see if the Proprietors would lay a tax to defray the expenses already incurred, and those that might arise from laying out a Division of said Township. And, accordingly, the Proprietors, in larger numbers than at the first meeting, it is to be inferred, convened at the time and place specified in the warning; when the following business was transacted, which we again copy *verbatim* from the records :—

" THE SECOND MEETING OF THE PROPRIETORS OF MONTPELIER.

" ARLINGTON, Wednesday, January 11, 1786.

" Agreeably to the foregoing warning, the Proprietors met, and the meeting was opened at the house of Eliakim Stoddard, Esq., and proceeded to business as follows, viz :—

" 1. *Voted*, That Col. Timothy Brownson be, and he is hereby chosen Moderator of this meeting.

" 2. For want of a convenient room for business,

" *Voted*, That this meeting stand adjourned fifteen minutes, to meet, at the end of that time, at the house of Mr. James Hawley, in this town, for the convenience of a room.

" At the house of Mr. James Hawley, agreeably to adjournment, the meeting opened again, and proceeded to business, and

" 1. *Voted*, To ratify the vote of the last meeting appointing Thomas Tolman, Esq., Clerk of this Propriety.

" 2. *Voted*, To ratify the vote of last meeting for laying a first Division in said Township of 150 acres to each Right, with the addition of five acres to each Lot as an allowance for Highways. And that said Division be laid out in good form—the lines of said Lots to be parallel with the Town Lines; turning on Square Angles; no Lot to exceed 200 rods in length, and to be all in one body; to lie as near the centre of the Town as may be.

" 3. *Voted*, That the said Division be surveyed, and a complete Survey Bill thereof, with a correct plan of the whole, according to act—the Survey Bill specifying the Bounds and Corners of each Lot, the Lots in number 70, including 5 Public Rights—be made out and returned to this meeting, to be held by adjournment in this town on the 2nd Tuesday in January next.

" 4. Colonel Jacob Davis made the following proposition, viz :

that he will complete the survey of the First Division of said Township, agreeably to the above votes, for the sum of *One Pound* 3*s* 10*d* per Right, counting 65 Rights; Whereupon,

" *Voted*, That the Proprietors accept of the proposal of the said Davis, and shall depend upon his performing the service accordingly.

" 5. *Voted*, That the former committee for laying out said Division be discharged, and that the following persons be, and hereby are appointed a committee to lay out said Division, viz: Colonel Jacob Davis, Mr. Ebenezer Waters, (or in case of his failure, Mr. Caleb Ammadon,) Mr. Samuel Horsford, Col. Samuel Robinson, and Capt. Abiathar Waldo.

" 6. *Voted*, That this meeting stand adjourned to the 2nd Tuesday in January next, then to be holden at the house of Thomas Tolman, Esq., in this town, at 10 o'clock in the forenoon.

" Attest, THO. TOLMAN, Propr's Clerk."

" ARLINGTON, January 9th, 1787, (Tuesday.)

" The meeting opened according to adjournment, at the house of Thomas Tolman.

" 1. *Voted*, That, as Colonel Timothy Brownson, Moderator of this meeting, is absent, Colonel Jacob Davis be Moderator in his absence.

" 2. *Voted*, That, for the convenience of a room for business, this meeting stand adjourned to the house of Capt. Elisha Wales, in this Town, to meet at one of the clock, this afternoon.

" THO. TOLMAN, Propr's Clerk.

" At the house of Capt. Elisha Wales, the meeting opened according to adjournment.

"The Committee, viz: Jacob Davis, Abiathar Waldo and Samuel Horsford, were sworn before His Excellency to the faithful discharge of their trust. Mr. Nathan Waldo, Chairman, was also sworn.

" 1. *Voted*, That the Proprietors do accept of the Return, Plan and Survey Bill brought in by our Committee, as satisfactory and agreeable to the direction of this Propriety, in their votes of January last, for a first Division in said Township.

" 2. *Voted*, That the Plan of the 1st Division, as now brought in by the Committee, be entered in this Book, on a convenient Scale, and also that the Survey Bill of each Lot in said Division be recorded."

Here follows a Plan of the Division; when the meeting further

" 3. *Voted*, That we will proceed to make a Draft of said 1st Division, which being attended to and completed as the law directs, in the presence of the meeting, is as follows:—"

Next follows the Draft, above mentioned, of the first Division Lots, containing one hundred and fifty-five acres each, with numbers affixed to them respectively, and the names of the proprietors, or grantees to whom they were assigned, together with the Survey Bill bounding each Right; when it was still further

"4. *Voted*, That the following accounts against this Propriety be allowed, viz:

"To Col. Jacob Davis, for laying out said 1st Division,	£77 9 2
"To Thomas Tolman, Clerk, as per his acct. on file,	£ 5 0 0
"To the Collector of this Propriety, for the expense of the first advertizement of the tax to be levied,	£ 0 15 0
	" £83 4 2

"5. *Voted*, That, for the discharge of the above account, a tax be laid on each Right (public Rights excepted) of One Pound 5s 8d, and that the same be immediately collected, paid into the Treasury, and paid out to the several persons as the law directs.

"6. *Voted*, That the vote of the Proprietors in Aug., 1784, appointing Jonas Galusha, Esq., Treasurer of this Propriety, be and it is hereby ratified, and the said Treasurer is directed, on receiving the above tax of the collector, to pay out the above accounts immediately, on the receipt of the several persons to whom the same are made up.

"7. *Voted*, That Mr. Joseph Dagget be, and is hereby appointed Collector for the collecting of said tax; and that he be directed to proceed in the collection of the same according to law, so as to hold his Vendue for the sale of delinquent Proprietors' lands, if any there should be, in this town, on the 2nd Tuesday of June next, and that he thereupon immediately settle in full with the Treasurer.

"8. WHEREAS, Joel Frizzel has become an actual settler in the Township of Montpelier, previous to a first Division in said Township, and represents to this Meeting that he made his Pitch by virtue of owning the original Right of James Gamble in said Township, and requests that he may be confirmed in his Pitch, in lieu of his after Drafts, excepting a Pine Pitch; Whereupon,

" *Voted*, That the following Pitch be, and hereby is granted and confirmed on the Right of James Gamble, in said Township—to contain one hundred acres, and three acres as an allowance for Highways, and to be in lieu of all other lands and after Drafts on said Right, excepting the first Division Lot, and a Pine Pitch, if any be made by Draft to the Proprietors; and also that said Right be subject to pay an equal proportion of taxes for laying out future Divisions, cutting roads, &c., viz:—Beginning at the South Westerly corner of the town, being the South Easterly corner of Middlesex, on Onion River—thence up said river 50 rods on a Right line—then extending this breadth back North Easterly parallel with the North Westerly line of the Town, so far as to contain the said quantity of 103 acres.

"9. *Voted*, That we will lay out a second Division of lands in said Township, to contain 120 acres, and an allowance of four acres to each Lot for High Ways, which said Division shall begin 165 rods from the North Westerly line of the town and the South Easterly line of Middlesex; to extend South Easterly and then North Easterly, taking in all the now vacant lands between the river Onion and the South Easterly line of the Township, and the first Division of lands in the Township, and, if the same should require, to extend as far as need be, North Westerly between the North Easterly line of the Township and the said first Division—

"That the said Division contain sixty-six Lots, (the Rights of James Gamble, Jacob Davis, Jacob Davis, Jun., and Thomas Davis excluded.)

"10. *Voted*, That Col. Jacob Davis have the privilege of pitching (within the lands above described for a second Division previous to said second Division being laid out) the quantity which he would have in the said 2nd Division on the Rights of Jacob Davis, Jacob Davis, Jun., and Thomas Davis, viz:—186 acres, in good form, and not more than double the length of the breadth, where he shall judge is a convenient place for building a Saw Mill; and 186 acres more, in like good form, where he shall judge is a convenient place for a Grist Mill,—which lands are to be in lieu of the 2nd Division Lots on the Rights of the said Jacob Davis, Jacob Davis, Jun., and Thomas Davis,—on condition that he build a good Saw Mill, which shall be ready to do business within the term of two years; and a good Grist Mill, which shall be ready to do business within three years from this time. And, on failure of building said Mills, as above said, then said pitches to revert as undivided lands to the Propriety, and the said Davis to be subject to receive the said quantity of land of said pitches in other undivided lands in said Township, as the Proprietors may hereafter direct.

"11. *Voted*, That a *Third* Division of lands be made in said Township, which shall be called the 3d or *Pine Pitch Division*, and shall be laid in the following manner, viz:—The parcel of pine land in the South Westerly corner of the Township, lying between the Pitch of 103 acres voted on the Right of James Gamble in consequence of the settlement made thereon by Joel Frizzel, and the beginning of the 2nd Division, shall be examined and a Division of 70 equal Lots laid thereon, as large as the quantity of the said pine timbered lands shall be found to admit on such examination—the lots to lie in square form, and to be as nearly equal for timber as may be.

"12. *Voted*, That the 2nd and 3d Divisions be laid out and surveyed according to act, and correct Plans and Survey Bills thereof be made out and returned to our next adjourned meeting, to be holden in this town, on the 2nd Tuesday of June next.

"13. *Voted*, That the proposal of Col. Jacob Davis, viz: that he will perform and complete the Survey of said 2nd and 3d Divisions, and make regular returns thereof, agreeable to the foregoing votes, for the sum of £1 8 0 per Right, (public Rights excepted,) be, and it is hereby accepted by this Meeting; and we depend upon his performing and completing the said service accordingly.

"14. *Voted*, That the following persons be, and are hereby appointed a Committee to lay out said 2nd and 3d Divisions, viz: Mr. Ebenezer Waters, Surveyor, Col. Jacob Davis, Mr. Pearly Davis, Mr. Nathan Waldo, and Mr. Joel Frizzel.

"15. *Voted*, That the Proprietors' Meetings of the Propriety be, in future, warned by the Proprietors' Clerk, upon application of one-sixteenth part of the Proprietors.

"16. *Voted*, That the adjournment of this Meeting be notified in the papers by the Proprietors' Clerk.

"17. *Voted*, That this Meeting stand adjourned to the 2nd Tuesday of June next, at 11 o'clock, in the forenoon, then to meet at this house, (Capt. Elisha Wales's, Arlington.)"

"ARLINGTON, June 11th, 1787.

"Agreeably to an adjournment of the 9th of January last, the Proprietors of Montpelier met at this place, (at the house lately occupied by Capt. Elisha Wales, now by Lieut. Abel Aylesworth,) and proceeded to business, Col. Timothy Brownson in the chair.

"1. Mr. Ebenezer Waters, Surveyor, and Col. Jacob Davis, and Nathan Waldo, Chairman, were sworn before the Hon. Timothy Brownson, Esq., Assistant, that they have faithfully discharged their office and trust as a Committee in laying out the 2nd and 3d Divisions in the Township of Montpelier.

"2. Our said Committee, appointed to lay out the 2nd and 3d Divisions in said Township, brought in and laid before the

Meeting their Returns and Plans of said 2nd and 3d Divisions, and the same being examined,—

"*Voted*, unanimously, that the doings of our said Committee, in laying out of the 2nd and 3d Divisions in said Township, and their Returns and Plans thereof, be accepted.

"3. *Voted*, That this meeting will immediately proceed to make a Draft of the said 2nd and 3d Divisions, and that Mr. Ebenezer Waters be appointed the person to draw the Numbers, and the same being done deliberately, correctly, and in Open Meeting, the Drafts of the 2nd and 3d Divisions are as follows:—"

Here follow the names of the Proprietors and the numbers of the Lots drawn to each respectively, together with the Survey Bills and Plans of said Divisions.

The next day, the accounts of Jacob Davis for laying out these two Divisions were allowed, and payment provided for by a proportionate tax on each Right. Jacob Davis and Pearly Davis were appointed a committee to lay out and make all the necessary public roads in said Township, at the expense of the grantees, and with orders to make their returns to the next meeting, which was then fixed on, by adjournment to the 2nd Tuesday of the next January.

A public vendue, previously appointed and notified, to sell so much of the Rights of Proprietors, found delinquent in paying their proportion of the sums assessed to pay expenses, as should meet the same, was holden at the same time and place, and records duly made of the sales, and conditions of redemption established.

The meeting, pursuant to the last adjournment, again met at Arlington; when Col. Davis requested, and was allowed, the further time till next June to complete the roads in the Township, which he and Pearly Davis had been authorized to lay out and build by the vote of the previous meeting. And the assessment of three shillings per Right was voted to defray the expenses of the same; when the meeting, after allowing the accounts of its officers, further adjourned to the first Wednesday of the next June, to meet at the house of Jonas Galusha, in Shaftsbury.

At the adjourned meeting at Shaftsbury, on the 4th of June, little appears to have been done but to accept the report of Jacob Davis and Pearly Davis, the committee to lay out and build the roads in said Township, allow their accounts, and make an additional assessment of nineteen shillings per Right, to defray the expense of the roads, made and projected, in the Township. And when this was done, these important meetings, which had been protracted through so many adjournments, were brought to a close.

All but a small remnant of the Township, on its Western and Northern borders, having now been surveyed, allotted, and the roads built or authorized to be built, the Proprietors held no other meeting for over four years; when a new meeting, on the warning of David Wing, Jr, .Justice of Peace, was duly called and holden at Montpelier, on the 28th of August, 1792.

At this Meeting, Mr. Clark Stevens, of Montpelier, was chosen Moderator, and David Wing, Jr., Esq., of Montpelier, Proprietors' Clerk; and it was

"*Voted* to make Division of the undivided lands in said Town; and lay out the whole of the undivided lands in said Township into *seventy equal parts or shares.*"

And it was also

"*Voted*, That a Committee of One be chosen to make such Division, and that Col. Jacob Davis be that Committee; to perform the service, and make his returns at the next adjourned Meeting, to be holden at the house of said Col. Davis, in Montpelier, on the 2nd Tuesday of May, 1793."

At the adjourned meeting, May 14, 1793, Col. Jacob Davis made due returns, as directed, of his doings, consisting of a completed Plan of a Fourth Division of Montpelier, which was examined, and unanimously accepted; when, a vote therefor having been obtained, and Rufus Wakefield appointed to draw the numbers, an allotment was made and recorded, consisting of seventy equal parts or shares, being one share to each Proprietor's and Public Rights, as in all previous allotments. The meeting then, after allowing the account of Col. Jacob Davis, at £11 5 0 for laying out said Division, and those of his assistants and the officers of the meeting, adjourned to meet at the house of David Wing, Jr., Esq., in Montpelier, on the 14th of May, 1795.

At the adjourned meeting last named the following is the brief record of the proceedings:

"MONTPELIER, May 14, 1795.

"Agreeably to the adjournment of May 14th last, the Proprietors of Montpelier met; and there appearing no business before the Meeting, *Voted*, that this meeting be dissolved; and it was dissolved accordingly.

"Attest, DAVID WING, JR., Pr. Clerk."

This completes the Proprietary history of Montpelier. But as the Plans of the surveys and several Divisions of the Township have not been here given, it may be well, perhaps, to state, for the information of the general reader, how these Divisions were relatively located in the town, and of what they were made to consist.

The *First Division*, consisting of seventy lots, of one hundred and fifty acres each, commenced one hundred and sixty-five rods from the dividing line between Montpelier and Middlesex, and two hundred rods from Calais line, and preserving those distances from Calais and Middlesex lines, so laid as to make nearly a square body of land, extending about three miles each way, coming within about one mile of the Winooski River at Montpelier village, and embracing all the central parts of the town.

The *Second Division* embraces an average of about three tiers of lots lying along the Winooski, below and above the village, up to where the river becomes wholly within the town, above the Goodenow Mills, and then widening into four tiers of lots, and embracing all the Eastern parts of the town, between Plainfield and a part of Marshfield, and the First Division.

The *Fourth Division*, about one-third the size of the First and Second Divisions, lies along the whole border of Middlesex, and so far along that of Calais as the First Division extended East, and embracing a tract of the width of one hundred and sixty-five rods along the Middlesex, and two hundred rods along the Calais line, being the border tract, for some now unknown reason omitted in laying out the First Division. And the Third Division, which was intended for a Division of pine lumber rather than lands, embraced but seventeen and a half acres of land, and lay near the Winooski river, within about one hundred rods from the Middlesex line, and on the high swell below our Cemetery, on a part of what has since been called the old Walton Farm. This tract, which was entirely covered with valuable pine trees, was divided into seventy equal parts, making one-quarter of an acre to each Proprietor and Public Right, the Proprietors at large deeming it, as it would appear, much too valuable to be suffered to fall to the share of any one of them. Simeon Dewey, Esq., one of the first settlers of Berlin, and now nearly ninety years old, has recently informed us that he worked in Col. Davis' Saw Mill, the first year after it was erected, on the falls of the North Branch, within Montpelier village; and that he sawed, during the time, the greatest part of the pine growing on this tract, for the Colonel, who had bought in most of the shares; and Mr. Dewey assured us that he had never since seen, in Vermont, New Hampshire, or even Maine, a more splendid lot of pine trees, growing on so small an area, than the one covering this little Third Division of Montpelier. And yet, curiously enough, not a single pine tree of the whole collection was found which was deemed suitable to be used for a Navy!

Col. Davis' first pitch embraced what is now the village of Montpelier, from the river against Colonel Reed's house, near the lower end of the village, extended up the river to the Old Arch Bridge, and back from the river, parallel with town and lot lines, far enough to embrace the Waterman Falls on the Branch and contain one hundred and eighty-six acres. His second, or upper pitch, embraced the same number of acres within the great bend of the river, two miles above, and was long known as the Jacob Davis, Jr., Farm.

In the great controversy between New York and New Hampshire, for the jurisdiction of Vermont and right to grant her lands accordingly, New York does not appear to have very persistently interfered, as on the other side of the mountain, for the control of any part of this central portion of the State, and not at all for that of such townships as had been granted by the Governor of New Hampshire, such as Berlin, Moretown, Middlesex and Worcester, granted by the latter in 1763. But when, in 1764–5, New York laid claim, under a new grant of Charles II. to the Duke of York, to the whole territory as far East as Connecticut River, and Governor Wentworth mostly ceased making grants therein, there appeared to be a large tract, lying South-Easterly of the towns above mentioned, and between them and the first two tiers of towns west of Connecticut River, remaining ungranted; and it *does* appear that a movement was made by the Governor of New York to appropriate this section of the ungranted wilderness. There has been preserved, in the Historical Collections of the Colonial History of New York, an old map of the disputed territory, designating with the letter *y* the townships previously granted by New Hampshire, and marking off and putting names of new townships on the rest, as having been recently granted by New York. On this map we find marked off a large tract westerly of Corinth, which is designated with the name of Kingsboro, (the same, doubtless, afterward called Kingsland,) and which was made to embrace the present town of Washington as its central point. And there is record evidence to show that *this* township was taken possession of by the New York authorities in 1770, Judges and a Sheriff appointed for holding courts, consisting of John Taplin and Samuel Sleeper, Judges, and John Taplin, Jr., Sheriff, (the latter becoming afterwards one of the first settlers in Berlin, and its first Justice of Peace); and that, in the winter of 1781, they went through the woods and deep snows till they supposed they were "at Kingsland" Centre, when they opened a court in the woods, and adjourned to the last Tuesday of the next May; and at that time came again, drummed up a case of bastarday, disposed of it, and never met there again, though they subsequently did so for two or three years afterwards at Newbury, to act for the same Kingsland, and built a log jail at Washington, still designed for the seat of justice, as soon as it could be settled.

On the north-west of this Kingsboro, or Kingsland, there appears, on the old map before mentioned, another and smaller, oblong tract, lying immediately south and east of Middlesex and Berlin, marked off by lines, and designated by the name of "Kilby." And this last named tract, called Kilby, must have embraced the whole of Montpelier, part or all of Barre, and perhaps Plainfield. And that such a tract hereabouts was granted by New York, and that, under color of the grant, sundry New Yorkers made an attempt to survey it, with the view of sales and settlement, finds confirmation in the papers left by Ira Allen, the noted pioneer surveyor of the State, and the indefatigable foe of the Yorkers in their attempt to get possession of our lands. In Ira Allen's Field Book, or rather Journal of his surveys and excursions through the unsettled parts of the State, which was left in manuscript in the hands of his son, the present Hon. Ira Allen, of Irasburgh, and which we had an opportunity of perusing a few years ago, he makes the entry, under date about 1772, that "learning that the Yorkers were running lines on the upper part of Onion River," he headed a party to go in pursuit of them; and, passing up the west side of the river, through Moretown and Berlin, (then already granted and known by name,) they crossed over Stevens' Branch; when, after having proceeded up the river four or five miles, to an extensive piece of meadow—the one next east of Lightning Ridge, probably—they came to the camp of the Yorkers, who, as was judged by the live embers of their fire, had, but an hour or two before, fled, never more to make their appearance in this section—they, as he thinks, having been warned by a hunter whom he had met on the way, and who must have been in the interest of the intruders, and took a short cut to their camp, to apprise them of the approach of the dreaded Green Mountain Boys.

Thus, it would appear that Montpelier was once claimed as a New York grant, and that but for the spirit and resolution of Ira Allen, backed by his indomitable brother, Ethan, it would very likely have been settled by the Yorkers, instead of the Massachusetts men to whom it was subsequently granted and sold.

CHAPTER III.

THE FIRST SETTLEMENT OF THE TOWN AND ATTENDING INCIDENTS.

On the 3d day of May, 1787, Col. Jacob Davis, late from Charlton, Worcester County, Mass., in company with his hired man, and his cousin, Pearly Davis, with one horse among them, and each loaded down with as much as he could well carry, with flour, salt pork, beans, salt and a few other common condiments, tools, cooking utensils, spare clothing, blankets, and a set of Surveyor's instruments belonging to Pearly Davis, the afterwards noted Surveyor in this region, all started from Brookfield in this State, to which the Colonel had a short time before removed his family, for their prospective home in Montpelier. Their rough, half-made road, which was the first one cut out to this section, led them over Williamstown heights, down the valley afterwards occupied by the Old Paine Turnpike, to the flats near where now stand Sproat's Mills on the inlet to Berlin Pond, then along the slope of the hills on the west side of the Pond and down the central ridge in Berlin to the old Tilley Hubbard place, next south of the Phelps farm, then down the westerly side of what is called Campbell's hill, over the Allen farm, and then down over the Martin and Shepard farms, onward to the mouth of Dog River. Here they waded through the Winooski, at the rapids, or rather shallows, about twenty rods above the mouth of Dog River, and proceeded down the river about a mile, to the residence of Seth Putnam, within the border of Middlesex—he, a brother, Thomas Mead, Jonah Harrington and Lovel Warren, having effected openings in the forest, built their log houses, and taken up their abode there as the first settlers of that town. The next day, Colonel Davis and his party employed themselves in cutting a passable bridle way up along the banks of the river from Putnam's opening to the Hunter's Camp, situated on the west bank of the Little North Branch, forty or fifty rods above its mouth, on the site now occupied by Washington County Jail, in the village of Montpelier. And having accomplished that object, and brought forward their luggage during the day, they took up their temporary abode in this primitive shanty, which, having evidently been constructed with considerable labor and care by previously sojourning trappers and hunters, and composed of a frame work of strong crotches and poles, well roofed and walled on three sides by the thick bark peeled from the elms of the surrounding meadows, was found to be weather proof, and sufficiently spacious for their immediate purposes.

Thus was effected the first permanent settlement of Montpelier, on the 4th of May, 1787, about four years after the virtual close of the Revolutionary War, about nine after the organization of the Civil Government of Vermont, and about four before her admission as a State into the Union.

It appears, it is true, that, in the spring of the year previous to this settlement of the township by Colonel Davis, one Joel Frizzle, a trapper and hunter, who, from the fact that he had got his name inserted among those of the Proprietors several years before, may be safely supposed to have been, for a considerable period, an occasional sojourner in his calling somewhere in this section of the wilderness, squatted on the banks of the river, in the south-west corner of the township, on what was afterwards known as the Old John Walton Farm. Here he felled the trees on the space of an acre perhaps, burned it over, planted corn among the charred logs, in the manner of the natives, erected a small log hut, and removed into it with his wife, a small, red haired French woman, whom he brought from Canada. On the strength of this little opening, which he had made previous to the survey for the First Division, in the summer of 1786, he had prevailed on the Proprietors to vote him the right of making a pitch, including his opening, fifty rods wide, and running back from the river along the Middlesex line far enough to embrace one hundred acres, with the extra allowance of three acres for roads. Here he was found by Col. Davis, who had spent a good part of the summer previous to his settlement in making surveys for the First Division of the township, as authorized, as will be recollected, by the vote of the Proprietors. And it seems probable that the Colonel employed Frizzle as an axe-man in the surveys of that summer, since we find his name added at the next meeting of the Proprietors, as a sort of supernumerary member of the committee appointed with the Colonel, to act under and with him, in laying out the Second and Third Divisions of the town, for which he had also contracted. This is about the last we hear of Frizzle. He doubtless, however, acted in some capacity in the laying out of the Second and Third Divisions of the town, and remained on his place perhaps a year or two longer; when, having squatted and obtained his pitch only, as is probable, for the purpose of disposing of his lands to better advantage, he sold out, left this part of the country, and returned, it was said, to his former residence in Canada. He could not properly be called the first settler, nor properly, indeed, any kind of settler, but was one of those roving, half savage men who are ever to be found near the borders of civilization, and who yet ever flee before its approach.

As soon as Colonel Davis had established himself and his party at the camp, it was his first care and business to make preparations for erecting a large, substantial log house. Accordingly, with his accustomed energy, he at once went to work in smoothing off a spot for the contemplated fabric, adjoining the camp, cutting and drawing in the trunks of the nearest suitable trees, and peeling bark for the roofing. Then followed the process of rolling up and fitting the logs, raising the rafters, ribbing them with poles, and putting on the bark covering. And so rapidly was all this performed that, within eight or ten days, a log house, thirty-two feet long and sixteen feet wide, stood ready for summer occupancy. By this time the two sons of Colonel Davis, Jacob, aged nineteen, and Thomas, aged fifteen, arrived from Brookfield, with another horse, to augment the laboring force of the company; when they all commenced an onslaught on the surrounding forest, and continued their labors till a square tract, extending south to the mouth of the Branch, and down the present State Street to the site of the Pavilion Hotel, was prostrated and drying in the summer's sun, preparatory to the next step in the process of subduing the wilderness—that of burning the *slash*.

Colonol Davis, having thus provided a house, and put the work of clearing up his land in good progress, left it to be continued by his hired man and his two sons, and repaired to Arlington to attend a Proprietors' meeting, which had been adjourned to come together again at that place on the 11th of June, 1787; while Pearly Davis, in the meantime, proceeded with the unfinished surveys of the township, and located himself on a tract of about three hundred acres of land, at what soon became known as Montpelier Centre, where he permanently settled, and passed the remainder of his days.

At the meeting of the Proprietors just named, as will be seen by their records, copied in the preceding chapter, Colonel Davis, after having made returns of his surveys and plans of the Second and Third Divisions of the township, and had his accounts allowed, was appointed, with Pearly Davis, a committee to lay out and construct all the public roads of the town, as fast as needed by settlers, at the expense of the grantees. And the commencement of this heavy and long to be protracted job, together with prosecuting the work of clearing the extensive meadow on which he had begun, occupied him and his employees for the remainder of the summer and fall seasons of that year. Among the improvements made during this season, was the making of a comparatively good road from the bank of the Branch, near the new log house, down round the foot of the hills to the lower end of the meadow, then along the river to Middlesex line, and also the cutting out of a road from the Tilley Hubbard place, on Berlin ridge, at the point where the road diverged westward towards the mouth of Dog River, directly down the east side of the hill, to the Winooski River, by the Andrew Cummings farm, in the same place where the road has ever since been maintained. The object of making this road being to save the unnecesary distance occasioned by going down round by the mouth of Dog River in journeys from the Davis opening to Brookfield, it was brought down the Berlin side of the river below the falls, where the Langdon Mills now stand, to about the point now occupied by the Gas Works, where the river could generally be forded. The river here, however, was considerably deeper than at the old ford near the mouth of Dog River, and it required a good knowledge, in the traveller, of the state of the stream, to enable him to ride a horse through with safety. And to guard against the dangers which strangers, or the unobservant, might incur by attempting to ride through the river when it was too high to be safely forded, a resort was had to one of those simple expedients that characterize the settlement of all new countries—a post, or large stake, was driven down firmly into the bottom of the river, at the place of fording, the top of which was made to come just to the surface of the water at the highest stage of the swolen stream in which a horse could pass without swimming, and without, consequently, at that rapid place, being swept away by the current. And then it was given out, and soon understood by all, that so long as they could see the top of the stake it would do to attempt to cross, but that if the top of the stake could not be seen from the shore, then no attempt was to be made at fording. Nearly twenty acres of forest had been felled, burnt over, logged off, and planted by hoes, with Indian corn, a fine and, near the streams especially, a heavy crop of which came to maturity the same season. And all this had been accomplished by the energetic Colonel, his two sons, and his one steadily employed hired man, with such occasional help as he could obtain from transient land lookers and hunters. In the labors of the forest, indeed, the Colonel was himself a host; and he was known, as some of his surviving cotemporaries have told us, to have felled, with his own hands, trimmed out and cut into logging lengths, all the trees on an acre of forest of average growth, in one day, and to have accomplished the same task for many days in succession.

This beautiful meadow, which embraces, in its whole length

and breadth between the Branch and its lower extremity at the old Parson Wright house, and between the river and the hills, nearly fifty acres, was found covered by a thrifty growth of tall and shapely maple trees, constituting, it is said, one of the most magnificent pieces of forest land ever beheld in this or any other country. And its fertility, on clearing it up, was found equal to its beauty as a forest ground. This was sufficiently shown by the facts that Colonel Davis raised on this meadow ten successive crops of Indian corn, without putting on a shovelfull of manure, while each crop yielded from sixty to one hundred bushels to the acre. Potatoes were raised at the rate of four hundred bushels per acre; and one crop of wheat, on a part of these bottoms, is mentioned, among the other generally abundant ones, which was computed to have yielded the extraordinary amount of eighty bushels per acre, and all of the most superior quality.

The manner in which Colonel Davis and his party lived that summer, though not quite savage, was yet certainly rather primitive. They slept under blankets, laid on beds of the boughs of the hemlock spread on the ground along the walls of their yet unfloored log house. At first they had no fire-place within the house, for, no ledges or loose rock then being visible along the rock-woven and moss-covered hills, within carrying distance, they knew not where they could find stone to build one. At length, however, as one of them happened to be passing up one of the ravines of the present State House hill, he made the agreeable discovery of a loose ledge of slate-stone, which might be dug out and made available for the desired object; and all hands turning out, they dug out and drew down enough stone to construct, as they then soon did, the lower part of a rude chimney, placed in the middle of the house, with two fire places opening on opposite sides, so as eventually to serve for each of the two large rooms into which the house was to be divided. This chimney was carried up to where the chamber floor was to be, while from the top of the funnel thus raised the smoke was left to find its way up through an aperture left in the roofing above. Their cooking utensils consisted of one iron pot, a frying-pan and bake-kettle, in which they boiled their vegetables, stewed or baked their beans, boiled or fried their pork, fish and wild meats, and baked johnny-cakes and some of their bread. Most of the latter article, however, as they had no oven, they procured to be baked by Mrs. Seth Putnam, they carrying down the flour to her and bringing back the bread.

All these cool, pure, mountain streams were then found swarming with trout, in their highest condition of flavor and richness as an esculent. And the forest was richly stocked, in every direction, with moose, deer, bear, and all other wild quadrupeds common to our northern latitudes. Jacob Davis, the elder of the two sons of Colonel Davis, whom we have mentioned as soon following their father to his new encampment, informed us, during his life time, that the next morning after he and his brother arrived at the camp, he took a fish-line and hook he had brought with him, some raw pork for bait, with a half-bushel basket to hold the fish, and went down to the nearest bank of the Branch, a few rods distant, when he cut a pole, tied on his line, baited, and threw in towards the middle of the stream to await the result. The instant the bait struck the water, he said, the trout, in astonishing numbers, darted forward from every direction, and like a flock of hungry chickens, commenced a keen tussle for the unwonted prize thus suddenly dropped among them. He then had no lack of business for the next half hour, at the expiration of which, though he had thrown back into the water all the little ones as fast as he hooked them against his will, he yet had filled his basket with trout of the weight of a half pound and upwards to two pounds, when he returned to camp to cook and enjoy, with his company, the luscious breakfast he had so easily supplied. Thomas Davis, the younger of the two brothers, who still survives in full possession of his faculties, at the advanced age of nearly 90, has, also, very recently told us that many a morning, that same summer, has he gone down on the trunk of a tree that they had fallen into the stream, near their house, and caught a pailfull of fine trout in time to cook them for breakfast. "I once," he added, "caught a cunning old stager that, even in those days, was considered an extra large one. He would bite at nothing, till tearing from my waist a bit of my red flannel shirt, I put it on to my hook, threw in, and the next moment laid him floundering on the bank." Subsequently to this, trout weighing four and five pounds were frequently caught in the larger streams of this section of the country.

Bears were nearly as plenty in those times as woodchucks are at the present day, and quite as fearless, too, of the approach of man. As Thomas Davis, who, being the youngest, was made the errand-boy of the party, was, one evening just at dark, during the summer of which we have been speaking, returning on horseback from Putnam's, with the usual number of loaves of bread the good wife had baked for them, he encountered one of these animals on the road near the place now occupied by William S. Smith's Butchery. There was then a deep, muddy brook which made out of the hills and crossed the road at that place, so large that they had been compelled to build a pole bridge over it before they could get along with a horse. As young Davis came up at a brisk trot, a large bear rose up, and throwing itself on to his haunches, took his stand upon this bridge, as if to dispute the passage of the horse, when the lad, having little time and probably quite as little inclination for a tilt with Bruin, gave his horse the lash, dashed over, or by the ugly customer, and galloped home to supply the waiting supper-table with bread, and enliven it, doubtless, with a recital of his adventure with a bear in the dark. And Mrs. Marsh, whose husband, the late William Marsh, settled on their farm, a mile up the Branch, in a few years after Col. Davis came, has told us that, in the absence of the men folks, she was sometimes compelled to sally out, with club and outcry, to prevent the bears from seizing their hogs or young cattle. Moose also were quite plenty. This gigantic animal of the deer family was much hunted by the early settlers, for its highly relished and valuable meat, which furnished them with an excellent substitute for beef. Colonel Davis shot one in a place afterwards known as Eames' Beaver Meadow, about two miles northerly of Montpelier Centre, and, with the help of his sons, backed it home, a distance of nearly five miles, all the way through the pathless forest. They were often slain in all parts of this and neighboring townships. But the most singular capture of this animal, mentioned in those times, was that of the taking of a large one, on the shore of Berlin Pond, by Jacob Fowler, who settled on what is now a part of the Martin farm, on Dog River, about a half mile from its mouth, and who made hunting his main business. He borrowed a large bear trap, weighing thirty pounds, with teeth an inch long, of one of the Davis boys, and having set it in a path where the moose came down to the pond to drink or crop the wild grass, and chained it securely to a sapling, went there the next day, and found he had caught a monster. The long, murderous teeth of the trap had clinched by each other right through the fetlock of one of the animal's feet, and held him so fast that he was easily knocked on the head and slain. The mode of preserving the meat of the moose, when slain at too great a distance from home, or when the snow was too deep for transportation, as was often the case, was quite unique and curious, as the following instance will exemplify. During the first or second winter the Davis family passed here, two men, coming from Waterbury over Worcester mountain, when the snow was four or five feet deep, struck on to a yard of five moose that were so completely shut in by the impassable crusted snow walls that the whole were easily slain. The men brought down to the Davis family as much as they could travel with on their snow shoes, and told the boys they might have the rest by going and securing it; whereupon Thomas Davis proceeded to the spot on snow shoes, with a bag of salt on his back, dug out a deep trough from a hemlock log, salted down the moose, securely fitted into the top a basswood slab, and left it till the spring opened, when returning with a horse and a large pair of panniers, he found his moose beef all safe, and transported it homeward through the woods, and thus furnished the family with a supply of good corned meat for most of the summer season.

Deer do not appear to have been very numerous in this section during the first years of the settlement, nor so much so as they were afterwards. This seems to confirm what has been said by old hunters, that deer are rarely found in any considerable numbers in any locality much frequented by the moose, but that as the latter recede before the approach of civilization, the former, for a time, take their place.

Of the strictly ravenous wild animals, wolves were the most numerous, and the most destructive to the cattle and sheep, that for years could be only safely protected from their ravages by being yarded, at night, in strong and very high log enclosures near the house. The panther, the largest and most dangerous, but fortunately the least numerous, of all the wild cat family, were occasionally encountered here, as they were everywhere else by the first settlers of all these northern latitudes. And when one of these much dreaded animals was encountered and slain, the adventure always formed an exciting theme for fireside recital.

A singular story of an adventure with a panther, within the limits of this very village, is told of Jacob Fowler, which must have occurred on one of that hunter's excursions to this part of the wilderness, some time before he came here for permanent settlement. Fowler, as he used to relate the story, was one day passing along up the banks of the Little North Branch, and when he had arrived at a point near the upper end of our old grave yard, and a few rods below a small sand island which had been thrown up in the middle of the stream, and which remained there within the memory of many of our oldest inhabitants, his attention was suddenly arrested by the noise of some heavy animal rapidly making for the stream a short distance above him. Quickly concealing himself in a covert near the edge of the water, he peered out up stream, and beheld an old bear rush furiously down the bank, dash through the water, and fall to digging, with hot haste, a hole in the sand on the island. When she had excavated a hole sufficiently large to receive her body, she threw herself on her back within it, leaving her strong, fending paws stiffly projecting upward above the surface. Scarcely had this been effected before a large panther, following hard on the trail, appeared on the bank, bounded through the stream, and leaping high, came down on the face and paws of the bear. For a minute or two the sand flew so as nearly to conceal from view the terrific struggle, and the woods rang with the mingling yells and roars of the combatants. Shortly, however, the exertions of the panther relaxed, and then he soon feebly crawled off on to the sand, completely disembowelled, when the hunter's bullet finished him on the spot, while the bear jumped up, apparently unharmed, and quickly made off into the forest.

If this story is true, and it appears to have been believed to be so by the old settlers to whom it was imparted, it shows a remarkable instinct for self-preservation in the bear against the attacks of its formidable natural enemy. For a while after hearing the story related we were much disposed to doubt its truth, but subsequent enquiries of old woodsmen and hunters, or of those who have often listened to their experiencies, have led us to conclude that the incident might have occurred as related. They say that the bear, whenever beset by the panther, always seeks the best hollow place it can make or find, in the permitted time and place, and throws itself on its back to receive its assailant, that being the only way it can successfully defend itself in the encounter, though it is not often its good fortune to be able to reach in time a sand bank, out of which to make so good a citadel as did the fortunate bear whose feat we have been describing.

CHAPTER IV.

THE FIRST SETTLEMENT AND ATTENDING INCIDENTS, CONTINUED.

After Colonel Davis had harvested his first crops, and as the autumn was drawing to a close, he again turned his attention to his imperfectly finished house, and commenced fitting it up in the best manner the circumstances would permit, to make it a more comfortable receptacle for his family, the whole of whom he intended removing into it, from Brookfield, the following winter. An oven was to be built, a cellar to be dug or otherwise constructed, the chimney to be topped out, and some kind of floors to be contrived and supplied to the house. In building the oven, a stone platform was laid up against the house outside, to the height of an ordinary window-sill, then an aperture made on a level with it into the house, by sawing out a piece of one of the logs of the walls, and then an oven laid up of stones in clay mortar, so built that the mouth opened into the room designed for the kitchen. A cellar was constructed by setting a low, log frame-work a foot or two into the ground, placed also against the outside wall of the house, opening into the kitchen in the same manner as the oven, and made impervious to the frost by deeply banking the whole frame-work over with earth. The chimney was topped out by building it up with split sticks of the required length, laid in clay mortar, and so laid and plastered as to prevent any of their surfaces from exposure to the accidental blaze, or the sparks of the fire, when ascending the flue of the structure. To provide floors for the two rooms of the house was a more difficult undertaking, for, there being no saw-mills yet built within twenty miles of the place, the use of boards or plank for the purpose was, at this time, entirely out of the question; but a substitute for the latter was soon found in the free-splitting basswood. Long, straight-grained trees were selected, felled, cut into lengths corresponding to the width of the rooms, carefully split, with a series of wedges through the whole length and breadth, into pieces of the thickness of bridging plank, evened and straightend with the axe, brought in, laid on sleepers, and so fitted in their places as to make a tight, smooth, white floor, of a uniform surface, and of a very neat general appearance.

Having accomplished all this to his mind, Colonel Davis gave up work for the season, and, with his sons, returned to Brookfield, for the purpose of getting the family in readiness for removal, and then removing them all, with their goods, with the fall of the first snow of a depth sufficient to make passable sledding.

The Colonel's family consisted, at this time, of himself, his vigorous and provident wife, his two sons already named, and four very fair and promising daughters, who, as might be expected from their worth and personal attractions, as well as from the influential position of their father, were destined soon to become the wives of the leading men of the now rapidly increasing settlements in this section of the country. Rebecca, the eldest, married the Hon. Cornelius Lynde, of Williamstown; Hannah, the second, married the Hon. David Wing, Jr., of Montpelier; Polly, the third, married Captain Thomas West, then of Montpelier, but subsequently removed to the Western country; Lucy, the third, married Captain Timothy Hubbard, of Montpelier; and Clarisa, the fifth, born the next year after the family came here, married the Hon. George Worthington, of Montpelier,—all of whom, and their numerous descendants, have taken either high or respectable positions in society, and filled important spaces in our town history.

A snow sufficiently deep for their purposes having fallen the last of December, Jacob and Thomas Davis, with two of their sisters, Rebecca and Polly Davis, and with as much of their furniture as could be brought at one load, came over, and were all left here, except Jacob who returned with the team for the rest of the family. But before the latter were prepared to start, there commenced such a series of blocking snow-storms as to prevent their removal until the following March, Thomas and his two sisters having remained here the whole intervening time, during which not another human face made its appearance at their lonely, snow-hedged and forest-girt cabin. At length, however, the anxious trio, weary of waiting and watching, were relieved of their loneliness by the welcome arrival of the rest of the family.

The appearance of Colonel Davis in the settlement was, as everywhere else where he appeared in those days, the signal for active business. Previously engaged hired laborers soon followed him from Brookfield, while every transient man, or new coming settler, that could be enlisted, was drawn in to swell the laboring force, which amounted sometimes, it is said, to nearly twenty men ; when the efforts of all were variously directed to the accomplishment of the contemplated enterprises of the season. These enterprises were the felling and clearing of further tracts of forest on the different pieces of bottom land adjoining the domicile, and the building of a saw-mill. And so vigorously were they prosecuted that, besides the planting and harvesting of the greatly increased crops of that summer, most of the remainder of the lower, or State Street meadow, was cleared, considerble inroad made on the forest on the easterly side of the Branch, and the meadow on the westerly side mainly cleared up to and around the first falls on that stream, a good saw-mill built on those falls and got to running ; and all accomplished before the end of the working season of that busy year. Early the next spring—that of 1789—Colonel Davis commenced, and during the summer completed the construction of a grist-mill at the same falls, which, considering the distance and the extremely rough roads over which the mill-stones and heavy gearing had to be transported, was an enterprize, at that day, of no ordinary magnitude to be accomplished in one season. The sun had now been let in on forty or fifty acres of land, which was now yielding crops not only sufficient for home consumption, but affording considerable surplus for those not yet able to raise their own supplies. But another want was by this time experienced by Colonel Davis and his family—that was, the want of a larger and more convenient house. The family proper now consisted of nine persons. In all the working season, at least, he kept many hired men, while his house, at all seasons, was almost continually thronged by land lookers and freshly arriving new settlers, who had already begun to flock into this and the other adjoining townships, and who evidently regarded this central establishment as a sort of head-quarters, where accommodations for the traveller could be found, land purchased of the Colonel, or information obtained from him where and how it could be purchased of others. And it is difficult to conceive, at this day of domestic comforts and strangely altered customs of living, how so many variously assorted people could be accommodated, in any manner, in one log house, with only two rooms and a low attic chamber. To obviate these inconveniences, Colonel Davis therefore decided on the immediate erection of a large frame house. And accordingly, early in the spring of 1790, the timber for the frame was got out, boards sawed, shingles made, a brick-yard opened under the hill in the rear of the present Cadwell house, and a team dispatched to Massachusetts for all the lime and nails required in the construction. As soon as the materials could be collected, carpenters were put in requisition, and a frame thrown up calculated for four spacious square rooms on the ground floor, the same number in the second story above, and a large attic extending over the whole. And without being suffered to rest here, the business was prosecuted with so much spirit that before the next cold weather the whole structure was completed and occupied by the family. This building was what has long since been known as the old Jail House, which in 1858, to make room for the new brick Jail House, was removed to the bank of the Branch some distance above, where it may still be found, in wondrous strength of frame, and in a remarkable state of preservation. This was the first frame house ever built throughout in Montpelier. The bare frame of a large one story dwelling house had, however, been got out, and raised a few days before that of the Davis house, located about a mile from the village, on the road leading by Mr. Henry Nutt's, and afterwards known as the old Silloway house. But the work was not immediately prosecuted, and the Colonel's was the first frame house ever finished in town. The house on the hill, which was built by James Hawkins, the first Blacksmith of the town, and finished the next year, was the second frame house built in the town; while the old house still standing near the paper mill and Arch Bridge, and formerly known as the Frye house, and also built by Hawkins, the same or the next year, was the third; and the first Union House, built by Colonel Davis, and the old Cadwell house, built also by Hawkins and still standing, were probably the fourth and fifth.

From this time the settlement proceeded apace. During the years 1789, 1790 and 1791, over twenty families had moved into town; so that at the taking of the first U. S. Census, in 1791, the population of the town numbered one hundred and thirteen persons, including twenty-seven legally voting freemen; while additional numbers were constantly arriving to increase this now fully established and prosperous settlement.

Thus far we have almost wholly connected our descriptions of the early settlement of the town with the action and movements of Colonel Davis and his family. This we have done because, for the first two years after he came, his was the only permanently resident family here, and his history consequently became the history of the town during those two first important years of its existence; and also because by his energy and judicious calculation was the first great impetus given to the settlement, and its rapid subsequent progress insured; while his opinions and examples continued, it is evident, long and largely to operate on cotemporary and succeding settlers, in imbuing them with his own qualities, in giving a healthy tone to coming society in regard to frugality, industry and perseverance, and in keeping up in it those invaluable traits and that spirit of enterprise which made the town what it subsequently became in individual thrift and general prosperity. But the town had now become sufficiently populous to warrant, and even require, a municipal organization, which, by the consent of all, was about to be effected. Individual description and accounts will, therefore, henceforth mainly be merged in the general history of the settlement, and of the town in its corporate capacity.

Before proceeding with this, however, we should relate several characteristic or noted incidents which occurred at different periods during the first four years of the settlement, and without the relation of which our picture of the times would hardly be complete; and having heretofore found no convenient place for them, we will here introduce them, as properly constituting the closing part of this chapter.

We have noted the construction of the first frame house as constituting a marked era in the progress of the settlement. But of scarcely less practical importance, perhaps, was the event of the introduction of the first wheel carriage, which was effected, in the face of what would now be considered insurmountable difficulties, during the second summer after Colonel Davis made here the first opening in the forest. The Colonel, in a journey to the other side of the mountain—probably a journey to attend one of the Proprietors' meeting at Arlington—had heard of, and purchased, a stout wagon at Vergennes; but the question was how it could be got home to Montpelier, from which, down the river to Williston, none other than a bridle path, or at best a rough, winter sled road had, as yet, been opened. Thomas Davis, however, then a strong, resolute boy of sixteen, volunteered to enter alone on the arduous undertaking. Accordingly, taking a horse, some kind of a harness and an axe, he repaired to Vergennes, fitted in a rude pair of thills, and commenced his slow journey homeward. He found but little difficulty in getting along to Governor Chittenden's at Williston; but dubious enough appeared the prospect of working his way through from that place up to Montpelier. By frequently stopping to cut away logs and trees to make the path wide enough to permit the passage of the wagon, he at length, however, made out to reach the then formidable rocky pass, or rather precipice, afterwards known as Rock Bridge, on the old turnpike, about a mile above Waterbury bridge, on the Moretown side of the Winooski. This pass, on the subsequent opening of the road, and especially on the construction of the turnpike, was blasted down, and the gulf on the east side filled up as much as possible, without incurring enormous expenses. And, even at that, it was far the most precipi tous and dangerous part of the whole road from Montpelier to Burlington. It was then a high, steep, rough ledge, around or above which, winding among the rocks and fallen trees, a path had been blocked out barely passable for a single horse. But the persevering lad was not to be balked in his purpose even at this difficulty. Having first taken out and led his horse down round to the flat below, and rolled up the wagon to the brink of the ledge, he contrived, by means of a pole and withes, to fasten or connect it to the top of a young tree, and then, by the momentum of the wagon and his own exertions, he bent forward the tree and thus let down the wagon fifteen or twenty feet. Here he secured it on the side of the ledge, by shoring it up with poles or rocks, as he best could, released the first tree and fastened to another, by which he let down the wagon another space, and so proceeded till he had got the ponderous vehicle to the bottom of the precipice; when he again put in his horse, made his way up the river, forded it below the mouth of Mad River, crossed over into the better road in Middlesex, and at last reached home in safety.

There were no extraordinary floods during the first few years of the settlement; but there had evidently been one not long before, in which the Winooski rose higher than it has from that day to this. When Colonel Davis and his men were felling the trees on the spot where the Pavilion Hotel now stands, which was a knoll many feet higher than any part of the meadow lying south and east of it, and which has never since been overflowed, they found the sand in the moss on the northern side of the trunks, at the height at which they wished to make their incisions, so thick that, even on that knoll, they had to clear away the moss to save their axes from dulling. This sand had obviously been lodged there by the water, and as obviously marked the height to which that great flood attained. This was confirmed by a living withess of both that flood and the great flood of 1830, which last, by most people, was said to be the highest that ever occurred. That witness was Judge Seth Putnam, of Middlesex, who, being alive in 1830, affirmed that the first year he came into that town, about two years before the coming of Colonel Davis, there was a remarkable flood, which reached to a certain tree or rock on his farm, and which, by comparison, was found to be considerably higher than the highest water mark of the flood of 1830.

But though there were probably few *great* floods in those early times, the streams were yet, when compared with those of the present day, almost continually very flush of water. The evaporation from forest lands is comparatively small; while their thick mosses, leaves, rotting wood and loose soil take up the heavy rains like a sponge, and leave them to drain off slowly; so that, through the operation of both these causes, the streams, admitting the yearly fall of water to be the same, would be far less liable to sudden and great fluctuations, but would be, at the same time, generally kept flush and full, as they were almost invariably found to be while the country was covered with forests. Indeed, there can be but little doubt that the average quantity of water then discharged by our rivers was very nearly double that discharged by them now. But still it is to the rivers of a cleared country that we are to look for the highest and most dangerous floods. It must have been indeed a tremendous rain that produced the great flood we have just noticed as occurring here about the year 1785. Such an one now would convert the whole site of Montpelier into a lake deep enough to be navigated by a light draft steamboat. And the same causes that so equalized the water in summer, probably had considerable effect in modifying and equalizing the temperature in winter, admitting of fewer thaws, but, at the same time, of fewer days of intense coldness. At any rate, the snows commenced early, covered the ground continuously through the winter, but gradually melting away in the spring, at length brought out the earth, like a fever patient from a wet blanket, smoking, warm and renovated, with all the circulating fluids in full play to quicken and push forward an exuberant vegetation. The absence of thaws of course left the snows to accumulate steadily through the winter, and often to become piled up to an enormous depth before spring. This, on account of turning out, rendered travelling inconvenient on all the roads, while on the unfrequented roads it was often wholly discontinued. This difficulty of the turning out of meeting sleighs was pleasantly illustrated in an incident which occurred to two of the early settlers of this region, and which, as it not only serves our present purpose, but shows the peculiarly strong traits of one who afterwards became one of the most noted characters of this part of the country, we will take the liberty here to relate:

While the settlements of this and the neighboring towns were yet in their infancy, Josiah Benjamin, Esq., one of the early settlers of Berlin, whose old farm lies within about a mile and in sight of our village, set out, with a two horse sleigh deeply loaded with wheat, for the market of Boston; and when he reached Williamstown, he was joined by Elijah Paine, the first settler of that town, with a similar load and bound to the same destination. "The snow," said Mr. Benjamin, from whose lips, in his lifetime, we had the account, "was, at that time, quite solid, and nearly five feet deep on the level, making it utterly impossible to turn out, unless we were lucky enough to hit on some place where the snow had been beaten down for that purpose. In going through Brookfield, and while in one of the worst places, we met a team loaded with salt; when, finding there was no possibility of getting by each other, except by unloading all our sleighs and then turning them up sideways on each side of the snow-walled path, and so running them by each other empty, we all fell to, unloaded the three sleighs, run the man's sleigh past ours, and, as it happened, first loaded up his sleigh and got him ready to start. Judge Paine and myself then turned back for the purpose of loading up our own teams, expecting, of course, that the stranger would assist us. But the next instant we heard the loud crack of his whip, when looking round, we saw the fellow mounted on his sleigh and lashing his horses into a run, to escape and leave us to do our own work. The Judge looked after the pitiful fugitive an instant, with eyes that fairly flashed fire; when, suddenly dashing off his hat and great-coat, he gave chase on foot, running as I think I never saw any one run before, till he overtook the team, leaped like a tiger upon the load, seized the shrinking puppy by the collar and made a flying leap with him sideways into the snow. He then drew his prisoner into the road and led him back to our loads; when, giving him a mighty significant push towards our bags of wheat, still lying untouched on the snow, he coolly, and with that sort of curt, dignified politeness which, even in moments of anger, rarely ever forsook him, observed—'*There, friend, if you will take hold of those bags, and load up both of our sleighs, we will be much obliged to you—very much obliged to you, sir.*' And the fellow sheepishly did so, to the last bag, while we both looked on, the Judge not permitting me to lend the least assistance; when we drove on, leaving him to sneak back after his own team, with all the comforting reflection which the incident was calculated to suggest to him."

During the continuance of the deep snows, at this period, travelling was mostly performed on rackets, or snow-shoes; while hand-sleds were used for drawing all the various kinds of light luggage. In this manner Abijah Wheelock and Samuel Twiss, two of the first settlers of Calais, having arrived at Colonel Davis', from Massachusetts, in the winter season of 1789, travelled, with their wives, one child, some bedding, &c., to their previously erected log houses in that town, a distance of ten miles. But the greatest feat of female racket travelling ever told us was accomplished by a young girl of the neighboring town of Waterbury, on a mournful occasion, which, as it was connected with the fortunes of one of our early settlers, it may not perhaps be out of place here to relate, as well as the remarkable feat we have just mentioned.

James Marsh, who was the first settler of Waterbury, undertook, in the month of March, 1785,—the winter season after he removed to that town, with a wife and eight children,—to go to mill on rackets, with a bag of grain on his back, to Jericho, through the then unpathed forest, a distance of about twenty miles. After getting his grist ground, and coming with it two or three miles up the river homeward, he crossed over the stream on the ice, to a settler's house on the west side, for the purpose of running some pewter spoons for the use of his family, in the spoon mould the settler was known to have. When he had run his spoons, and borrowed or bought a brass kettle which he found he could obtain of the settler, to do his sugaring with, he attempted to recross the river, with the kettle swung over his head or neck, but broke through the ice into an undetected, thinly covered glade in the stream, and, incumbered as he was with his grist, kettle and rackets, was unable to extricate himself, and after beating out an open place a dozen rods down the glade, in his terrible struggles for life, was swept under the ice before those whom his cries for assistance had attracted could reach the spot. His body was soon recovered, but, as it was so difficult to get it home, it was decided to bury him in that neighborhood; and his oldest daughter, the only member of his family which circumstances would permit of attending, went seventeen miles on rackets to the funeral, on the morning of the day of his burial.*

William Marsh, a son of the unfortunate man, subsequently, in consequence of the breaking up of the family by this sad casualty, came to live with Colonel Davis; and with the forty pounds paid him as wages, at the age of twenty-one, purchased the farm near the village, up the Branch, where he ever continued to reside, an industrious and thrifty farmer, until his death, which was occasioned by the falling of a tree, some years ago. His widow, an unusually smart and intelligent old lady, from whose lips we recently obtained the particulars of the incident above related, is now residing with one of her sons in this village.

An event occurred during the first winter after Colonel Davis moved into his new house, which afforded the settlers the unexpected opportunity of setting their eyes on embodied royalty, in the person of Prince Edward, on the occasion of his passage through this part of the country from Montreal to Boston. The Prince was, of course, the son of the bigoted and muddy brained George III., and must have been, if all accounts of him were correct, a true chip of the old basswook block. At all events, his sayings and doings, as he passed through these settlements, furnished the people with food for many a merry commentary on his astuteness. Reaching here from Burlington in one day, he and his suit put up with Colonel Davis over night. Full of the notion that the Americans, especially on the border settlements of the North where his countrymen in the then recent war had received several costly lessons, were little better than savages, and probably still hostile in spirit, he at first was evidently keenly apprehensive of personal danger from assassination or poison. And to guard against the former, he had brought along with him a band of fifteen or twenty armed attendants; while, to ensure his safety from the latter, he had provided several of what our people called his *tasters*, who must examine, taste and eat a por-

* James Marsh moved, with his family—wife and eight children—into Waterbury, June, 1784, and during that whole year was the only settler in town. The late venerable Philip Sprague, father of the Hon. Worcester Sprague, of Montpelier, while on a visit to his son, the year before his death, which occurred at the age of about ninety-three, but two or three years ago, related how, to his surprise, he found, on a foot journey through this part of the State, this solitary family in Waterbury, in a little opening in the wilderness, with no other resident within thirty miles south, and scarcely less that distance in any other direction, living on game and what breadstuff Mr. Marsh brought on his back from Jericho.

tion of every meal prepared for him before he would venture to touch it himself. He was so far reassured, however, the next morning, by a long talk with Colonel Davis, who greatly enlightened him respecting the intelligence and moral sense of our people, and who told him he was far safer here than in the streets of London, that he consented to dismiss the greater part of his armed retainers to return to Montreal; and he then resumed his journey in much better spirits. His next stop was at Judge Paine's, of Williamstown, for his dinner. Here he began to be himself again, and seemed disposed to become quite chatty and jocose. "I suppose, madam," he said to Mrs. Paine, among other of his witty efforts, "that you here never read anything but your Bible and Psalm Book?"

"O, yes, we do," promptly replied Mrs. Paine, "we are all quite familiar with the writings of one Peter Pindar."

Those who have read the scorching satires of Pindar on the character and capacities of the then Royal family will readily appreciate the keenness of the Lady's retort.

Still another incident has always been related by our old people, of his journey through Vermont, which occurred at the house of a shoemaker on the road, where, for some purpose, he had made a short call. By this time he had become so much like himself at home, that he rudely stepped up and kissed the shoemaker's wife, observing, by way of soothing her evident resentment: "O, never mind it—you now can tell your people you have had the honor of being kissed by a British Prince."

"O, never mind," exclaimed the incensed husband, as he unceremoneously sent the Royal puppy from the house by a kick in the rear—"O, never mind, sir; you can now go home and tell *your* people you have had the honor of being kicked out of doors by an American cobbler."

But the most striking, because the most melancholy event that ever transpired here, happened on the night of the 3d of December, 1791, and became doubly memorable in all this region by its saddening character, and its association with the first Thanksgiving ever held in the settlement. Yes, it was on the then novel occasion of a first ball, on a first Thanksgiving. Animated by the anticipated pleasures of the day, the young men and maidens of this and the neighboring settlements, for many miles around, assembled, in mutually chosen and happy pairs, at the house of Colonel Davis, to while away the golden hours in the lively dance. Here everything went on as merry as a marriage bell; and the festivities were prolonged nearly through the night by the joyous company, who little dreamed that the next repose of one of the most loved and loving pairs of their gay and happy assemblage would be the repose of death, in the cold, watery bed of the dark and turbid Winooski. A little before daylight, however, the company broke up and departed for their respective homes. Among this light-hearted party were two fair and blooming sisters, the daughters of Captain James Hobart, one of the first settlers of Berlin, who then resided on what was subsequently known as the old Maj. Jones' farm, near the river, about three miles below Montpelier village. Betsey Hobart, one of these sisters, and a young lady everywhere respected for her virtues and personal attractions, was attended by Theophilus Brooks, of Montpelier, her affianced lover. The other sister was attended by the afterwards well known Captain Isaac Putnam, then one of the most herculean and resolute young men among the Montpelier settlers. There being at that period no bridges across the river, and the stream being unfordable, the party, on going from Montpelier, passed down the same side of the river to a canoe landing in the borders of Middlesex, nearly opposite to the home of the young ladies. Here they all embarked in a log canoe which was used for crossing at this place. The river was swolen by recent rains, and the current was strong and rapid ; and this circumstance, and the nervous alarms of the females, which probably prevented them from preserving the balance of their rolling vessel, caused the canoe to upset, when the four were precipitated into the deepest part of the high, wintry stream. By almost superhuman exertions, Putnam at last succeeded in righting the boat, and placing within it not only the two girls, but Brooks, who, being unable to swim, was equally helpless. But the three latter had how lost all their self-possession, and the canoe being partially water-logged, which rendered it far more unsafe than before, they were all again upset and plunged into the stream. By this time Putnam had become so much chilled and exhausted as to prevent him from attempting to save them all ; and seizing his own partner, he barely succeeded in swimming with her to the Berlin shore ; while the despairing outcries of the fated Brooks, and the shrieks of his fair companion in death, as well as in life, were soon lost in the rushing murmurs of the dark and angry flood, beneath which they now disappeared forever. The body of Miss Hobart was recovered the next day, but that of Brooks was not found till the breaking up of the ice months afterwards.

CHAPTER V.

THE ORGANIZATION OF THE TOWN, AND ITS MUNICIPAL HISTORY FOR THE FIRST TWELVE YEARS.

ON the 4th day of March, 1791, was made the first movement among the inhabitants of Montpelier towards effecting a municipal organization of their town. On that day the following petition of three of the freeholders of the town of Montpelier was presented to John Taplin, Esq., a resident of Berlin, but a Justice of the Peace of Orange County, to which both Berlin and Montpelier then belonged:

"*To John Taplin, Esquire:*

"The Petition of the subscribers, inhabitants and freeholders of the town of Montpelier, prays your Honor to issue a warrant for calling a meeting of the inhabitants of said town, for the purpose of organizing said town.

"JACOB DAVIS,
"CLARK STEVENS,
"JONATHAN CUTLER.

"March 4th, 1791."

A statute of one of the first Legislatures of Vermont, then in force and ever since retained on our Statute Book, required the petition of *four* respectable freeholders as the initiatory step in the organization of new towns; and it cannot now be ascertained why that requirement of the law was not complied with in this first step towards the organization of Montpelier. But it is probable enough that Colonel Davis, who must have known the law, drew up the petition, signed it and sent it to Mr. Stevens, with directions to pass it round till the required number was obtained; that the last signer, through some misapprehension or inadvertency, neglected to procure a fourth signer, and passed it at once to the Justice, who either took no exceptions to it as it was, or expecting some other person would call and sign it to justify him in the procedure, thereupon issued the following warrant:

"ORANGE, SS. } *To Clark Stevens, one of the principal inhabitants of the town of Montpelier,*

"GREETING:

"By the authority of the State of Vermont, you are hereby required to warn all the freeholders, and other inhabitants of the town of Montpelier to meet at the dwelling-house of Jacob Davis, in said Montpelier, on Tuesday, the 29th day of March instant, at 9 of the clock, in the morning, to act on the following articles, viz :—

"1st. To choose a Moderator to govern said meeting.

"2nd. To choose a Clerk, Selectmen, Treasurer, and all other Town Officers.

"3d, To see if said town will choose some proper person to remove the Proprietors' records into said town.

"*Given under my hand, at Berlin, this 8th day of March*, 1791.

"JOHN TAPLIN, Jus. Peace."

And on the same day Mr. Stevens, in pursuance of the foregoing, posted the following notice probably at the house of Colonel Davis, at his Grist-mill, and perhaps at some other place of public resort in the central part of the town, viz :

"By virtue of a warrant to me directed by John Taplin, Esq., this is therefore to notify and warn all the freeholders and other inhabitants of the town of Montpelier to meet at the dwelling-house of Jacob Davis, in said Montpelier, on Tuesday, the 29th day of March, instant, at 9 of the clock in the morning, to act on the following articles :

"1st, To choose a Moderator to govern said meeting.

"2nd, To choose a Clerk, Selectmen, Treasurer, and all other Town Officers.

"3d. To see if said town will choose some proper person to remove the Proprietors' records into said town.

"CLARK STEVENS,

"An Inhabitant of said Town.

"March 8th, 1791."

And, in pursuance of the foregoing warning, all the freeholders, and other legally voting inhabitants of Montpelier, assembled at the appointed time and place, and effected the objects of their meeting in the following transactions, from the old record of which we copy *verbatim :*

"At a town meeting of the inhabitants of Montpelier, legally warned and met at the dwelling-house of Col. Jacob Davis, in said Montpelier, on the 29th day of March, 1791,—

"Proceeded to choose a Moderator, &c., &c.

"1st, *Voted*, and chose Col. Jacob Davis Moderator to govern said meeting.

"2nd, *Voted*, and chose Ziba Woodworth Town Clerk.

"3d. *Voted*, and chose James Hawkins 1st Select Man.

"4th, *Voted*, and chose James Taggart 2nd Select Man.

"5th, *Voted*, and chose Hiram Peck 3d Select Man.

"6th, *Voted*, and chose Jonathan Cutler Town Treasurer.

"7th, *Voted*, and chose Pearley Davis Constable and Collector.

"8th, *Voted*, and chose Josiah Hurlburt,
"9th, *Voted*, and chose Benj. I. Wheeler,
"10th, *Voted*, and chose Solomon Dodge } Highway Surveyors.

"11th, *Voted*, and chose Col. Jacob Davis,
"12th, *Voted*, and chose Benj. I. Wheeler,
"13th, *Voted*, and chose Clark Stevens } Listers.

"14th, *Voted*, and chose Col. Jacob Davis Fence Viewer.

"15th, *Voted* to adjourn said meeting till the 1st Tuesday of September.

"The aforementioned officers were duly sworn and affirmed to the faithful discharge of their respective offices, before John Taplin, Justice of the Peace for said County.

"ZIBA WOODWORTH, Town Clerk."

Accompanying this record, we find the names of the voters who acted in thus organizing the town, and who, as the record leads us to infer, constituted the whole number of its freemen at that time, as follows, viz:

BENJAMIN I. WHEELER,
DAVID PARSONS,
PEARLEY DAVIS,
EBENEZER DODGE,
SOLOMON DODGE,
NATHANIEL PECK,
DAVID WING,
LEMUEL BROOKS,
CLARK STEVENS,
JONATHAN SNOW,
HIRAM PECK,
JAMES HAWKINS,
JAMES TAGGART,
JOHN TEMPLETON,
ELISHA CUMMINS,
JONATHAN CUTLER,
CHARLES McCLOUD,
COL. JACOB DAVIS,
ISAAC PUTNAM,
NATHANIEL DAVIS,
ZIBA WOODWORTH,
JERAHMEL WHEELER,
SMITH STEVENS,
CHALES STEVENS,
EDMUND DOTY,
DUNCAN YOUNG,
FREEMAN WEST.

Of all this enterprising and intelligent band, twenty-seven in number, so distinguished by the circumstances as the founders and first freemen of Montpelier, but one,—it is sad to reflect,—but one, at the time we are penning this page, (November the 15th, 1859,) alone remains alive—the venerable Elisha Cummins, who, at the age of ninety-two, still resides with his family, consisting of several of his children and grand-children, on his original homestead, two miles east of Montpelier village. But they nearly all still live, and their wholesome examples of frugality and honest industry still live, in their numerous descendants, who now constitute, probably, a majority of the inhabitants of the united town of Montpelier.

Previous to the time to which the meeting above described had been adjourned the Selectmen called a special town meeting, to assemble on the 10th of May, to provide for the making of roads and bridges, procuring town record books, and such other business as should be deemed necessary when met. And at the meeting thus called David Wing, Jr., having been chosen Moderator, it was

" *Voted* to raise fifty pounds for the repairing of roads and bridges in said town.

" *Voted*, and chose Colonel Jacob Davis, Larned Lamb and Pearley Davis, a committee to superintend the business of repairing the river bridge.

" *Voted* to reconsider the vote for raising fifty pounds for the repairing of roads and bridges in said town. Likewise (*voted*) for each person to pay his highway tax agreeably to the statute.

" *Voted* to raise money by subscription to purchase town books.

" *Voted*, and chose the Town Clerk to collect said money and purchase suitable record books; likewise to collect the labor to repair the bridge.

" *Voted* to hold town meetings, for the future, at the dwelling-house of Pearley Davis."

At the adjourned meeting, on the first Tuesday of September, nothing appears to have been done except to choose and qualify Benjamin I. Wheeler a Town Grand Juror. From what next appears on the records, however, it would appear probable that some informal action was taken at this last meeting to insure a compliance with a statute which had been passed a year or two before by the Legislature, requiring the stock owners of each town to distinguish their respective animals by some peculiar mark on or around the ear; and when these marks were agreed on, adjusted and made by and among such owners, to cause brief descriptions of them to be entered on the town records, as notice to all concerned for the return of estrays to the proper owners, and as the means of discovering the owners of cattle *damage-feasant*. And as this feature of the early laws and municipal regulations of this State may prove something of an antiquarian curiosity to all, and be a matter individually interesting to the descendants of those who adopted it, we have concluded to copy entire the first record of the marks of the stock owners of the town, as follows:

"MARKS."

"David Wing's mark, a slit on the right ear.

"Pearley Davis' do., a slit on the left ear.

"Ziba Woodworth's do., a hole in the left ear.

"Daniel Woodworth's do., a square crop on the right ear.

"Caleb Bennett's do., a square crop on the left ear.

"Philip Wheelers do., a swallow-tail on the right ear.

"Jerahmel Bowers Wheeler's do., a swallow-tail on the left ear.

"Theophelus W. Brooks' do., two half-pennies on the left ear.

"Isaac Putnam's do., two half-pennies on the right ear.

"John Templeton's do., a square crop on each ear.

"Solomon Dodge's do., a hole in the right ear.

"Hiram Peck's do., two holes in the right ear.

"Nathaniel Davis' do., a cross-cut or slit on the upper side of the left ear.

"Chas. McCloud's do., two slits on the left ear.

"Nath'l Peck's do., a half-round or semicircle on the left ear.

"Jonathan Snow's do., a swallow-tail on the right, and square crop on the left ear.

"Benj. I. Wheeler's do., a crop and hole on the left ear. (Entered against this,) 'This mark flung up.'

"Elisha Cummins' do., a slit in the end and a half-penny in the right ear.

"Jacob Cummins' do., a crop and hole in the right ear.

"John Cutler's do., a half-crop on the under side of the left ear.

"James Hawkins' do., a half-crop under the right ear.

"ZIBA WOODWORTH, T. C."

To this record the enumerations of the marks of those who neglected to enter them at this time, and of those who were constantly moving into town, continued to be added, from year to year, even up to 1812, when the custom appears to have fallen into disuse. But having given this specimen, it will hardly be expected we should occupy the space required to insert the whole of the extended list.

The freemen of Montpelier, having thus effected their organization and successfully put its machinery in operation, thenceforward annually held their town March Meetings, resulting in the frequent change of town officers, and the transaction of the usual variety of town business, the most important of which, as affecting or indicating the growth and moral progress of the town, we shall note as we proceed.

No Freemen's Meeting, for the election of town representative to the Legislature and State officers, was held in 1791, or the September following the organization of the town. But on the

18th of August, 1792, Jerahmel B. Wheeler, the Constable of Montpelier, issued his warning notifying the freemen to meet at the dwelling-house of Pearley Davis, on the first Tuesday of September next, falling on the 4th day of said month, "to act on the following articles, viz:

"1. To elect and depute some person from amongst the freemen to represent said freemen at the next General Assembly of this State, to be held at Rutland on the second Thursday of the succeeding October, and so from day to day during their session or sessions.

"2. To give their votes for Governor the succeeding year.

"3. To give their votes for Lieutenant Governor.

"4. To give their votes for a Treasurer.

"5. To give their votes for Twelve Councilors."

And at the time and place specified in the warning, the legal voters of the town assembled for their

FIRST FREEMEN'S MEETING IN MONTPELIER.

Of the proceedings of this meeting, the following is a copy ot the record:

"At a meeting of the freemen of Montpelier, Sept. 4th, 1792.

"Pursuant to the foregoing notification, proceeded, and made choice of Colonel Davis to represent the freemen of said town at the General Assembly the ensuing year.

"And received 24 votes for Thomas Chittenden, Governor.

"And received 20 votes for Peter Olcott, Lieut. Governor.

"And received 12 votes for Samuel Mattocks, Treasurer.

"And the following names voted for as Councilors, viz:

Samuel Safford	20	Luke Knowlton,	20
Jonas Galusha,	20	Timothy Brownson,	20
John Strong,	20	Ebenezer Marvin,	20
Thomas Porter,	20	Colo. Kent,	18
Samuel Hitchcock,	19	Jerem'r Bailey,	1
Jonathan Hunt,	20	Eleazer Harvey,	1
Paul Brigham,	20	Ira Allen,	1
Jona. Arnold,	20		

"Recorded,

"CLARK STEVENS. T. Clerk."

At this meeting, as will be perceived, Colonel Jacob Davis was chosen unanimously as the first Representative of Montpelier. This was no more than was due to him, under the circumstances, if his character and capacity warranted the preferment; and that his townsmen believed they did is clearly shown in the fact that they gave him the next four successive elections, making him the Representative of the town he had shown so much energy and foresight in founding, the first five years of its organized existence.

The next public meeting held in town was also of a political character, and the first one ever called for that purpose, which was, in the words of the warning, for the freemen to meet at the dwelling-house of Pearley Davis, on the first Monday, the 4th of January then next,

"To give in their votes for a Representative to represent the Eastern District of Vermont, comprehending the Counties of Windham, Windsor and Orange, in the Congress of the United States."

And on said specified 4th day of January, 1793, the freemen accordingly met and gave their votes for a Member of Congress for the District to which they belonged, as follows:

For the Hon. ELIJAH PAINE, 2 votes,
For the Hon. PAUL BRIGHAM, 12 votes.

This was the first vote ever given in Montpelier for a Member of Congress; and, as that period was anterior to the reign of King Caucus, or the age of political drummers under pay of candidates for beating through the whole of their districts, it is not surprising that this vote was given for men not generally supported in other sections. Such at least appears to have been the case, since Nathaniel Niles of Thetford, was elected as the first Member of Congress for the then Eastern District, and at this time received his second election.

At the annual March Meeting of this year, 1793, the most noteworthy of the transactions perhaps, were the votes:

"To assess 20 pence on the pound of the Grand List for repairing Highways, the present year.

"That oxen be allowed two thirds the wages allowed to a man per day, in working said tax, viz: 2s 8d.

"That all town taxes be received in wheat, at four shillings per bushel, by the collector, of those who incline to pay their proportion of such taxes that way."

At this meeting also the freemen made choice, for their Town Clerk, of David Wing, Jr., a young man of unusual promise and capacity for public business, who held the office continuously to the time of his death in 1806, and who, thenceforward, seems to have put a new face on the records, reports, drafts and all other town transactions passing under his quick and ready hand.

On the 24th of June in the same year, at a meeting duly warned for the purpose, Col. Jacob Davis was elected a delegate to represent the town "in the Convention appointed to consider of, establish or reject, the amendments proposed by the Council of Censors in the Constitution of the State of Vermont."

A meeting also was called and held on the 3d day of September, the same day with the Freemen's Meeting of that year, "to see if the inhabitants will lease or dispose of the public lands in said town, as shall be most to the benefit of the public." But the proposition was decisively rejected.

At the Freemen's Meeting, the same day, the votes of the town were cast, twenty-three in number, for the old candidates for Governor and Treasurer, and for Jonathan Hunt, the new and successful candidate for Lieutenant Governor, and also for several new and successful candidates for Councilors, among whom was Cornelius Lynde of Williamstown.

At the annual March Meeting in 1794, a committee was appointed, with instructions to purchase and prepare two acres of land in some suitable place, to be established and consecrated as a public Burying Ground in the town.

Another town meeting was called and held on the 21st of July, this year, to try again the question of disposing of or leasing the public lands of the town; when the motion to sell said lands was once more negatived. But a vote was obtained to lease them out for the highest rent that could be procured; and David Wing, Jr., Esq., Major Pearley Davis and Mr. Ziba Woodworth were appointed a committee to act with discretionary powers in carrying the vote into effect.

Still another meeting for the transaction of town business was again called this year, to meet at the same time and place at which the annual Freemen's Meeting for the September election had been warned.

At this town meeting the committee appointed to purchase and clear a public Burying Ground made report that "they had purchased of Joseph Wing two acres of land for said purpose, at fifteen shillings per acre, lying on the road that leads from Col. Davis' to Calais, and have fell the timber on the same." The location of this Burying Ground, as we have ascertained from sources independent of this singularly indefinite description of the committee, was in the angle formed by the roads passing to North Montpelier and to Calais, as they divide on the swell beyond the brook about one hundred rods north-east of the Meeting House at Montpelier Centre. The report being adopted, the place was consequently forthwith prepared for use. And this was the first public Cemetery ever established in Montpelier.

At this meeting, likewise, was made the first movement ever taking place in the town looking to the establishment of Common Schools. A committee of five, consisting of John Templeton, Rufus Wakefield, Thomas McCloud and Ziba Woodworth, were appointed to divide the town into school districts, and report their doings to the adjourned meeting.

The first case of pauperism that ever occurred in town was also disclosed at this meeting. It appears that one John Marsh, a resident of the town, had become unable to support himself by reason of lameness, caused by the fall of a tree, and want of means; and that the Selectmen had employed medical attendance and provided for his support. The meeting voted their approval of the course of their Selectmen, and appointed a committee to audit the several accounts growing out of the case.

We further find among the new and note-worthy proceedings of this important meeting, a vote

"That this town will ensure to the *Minute Men*, now enlisted from this town, the wages, while in actual service, that the Governor and Council of this State have promised to recommend the Legislature to ensure them: *provided* that Congress nor said Legislature do not do it."

Why Minute Men should have been ordered to be enlisted and held in readiness for some emergency, at this period when we were threatened with no foreign wars, and when there was no longer any fear of Indian aggressions in this section of the country, we have not been able to ascertain. The order, however, may have grown out of the alarm occasioned by the somewhat formidable "*Whiskey Insurrection*" in Pennsylvania, in the summer of this year, to quell which the militia of Maryland were ordered into actual service, while the other States might have been requested to be on their guard.

At the adjourned meeting held on the first Tuesday of December of this year, the committee appointed to divide the town into School Districts made their report, which was adopted; whereby the town was divided into six districts, designated as follows:

"*First District*—Beginning at the south-westerly corner of the town, (Middlesex line on the river,) including the inhabitants from thence to Jacob Davis, Jr.'s, likewise all on the North Branch as far as Mr. Wiggins', and on the south road (the road now leading by Henry Nutt's) to James Hawkins.'

"*Second District*—On the south road, to contain all the inhabitants from Jonathan Cutler's to Caleb Bennett's, including Mr. Edwards, Mr. Doty, Elisha and John Cummins.

"*Third District*, or East Hill District—To include all the inhabitants in said town east of Onion River.

"*Fourth District*, or Centre District—To include all the inhabitants from Rufus Wakefield's to Elnathan Pope's, including David Wing, Esq., John Stevens, Capt. Doty, Barnabas Doty, Jr., Lemuel Brooks, Levi Humphrey, John Cutler and Mr. Woods."

"*Fifth District*—To include all the inhabitants from the aforementioned bounds to Joshua Peck's, and as far east as the Great Brook known by the name of Putnam's Brook, excepting Ensign Gilbert, taking in Robert Waugh and Francis West east of said Brook.

" *Sixth District*, or Eastern District—To include all the inhabitants east of the aforesaid brook, except Mr. Waugh and Mr. West, taking in Ensign Gilbert on the west side of said brook."

And Jacob Davis, Clark Stevens, Nathaniel Clarke, Pearley Davis, Thomas West and Enoch Cate were thereupon, on the nomination of the voters of their respective districts, appointed Committees of the same, "to be, with the Selectmen, Trustees of Schools in said town."

At this meeting, also, was presented and adopted the report of the committee appointed to audit the several accounts growing out of the medical attendance and support of John Marsh, who, it had been ascertained by David Wing, Jr., the agent appointed for the purpose, had his legal residence in Haverhill, N. H., and who was then ordered to be removed to that town.

Among the accounts was one on which it may be interesting to many to bestow a passing notice. It was the account of Rebecca Peabody, of seventeen pounds five shillings, for her medical services in the case, which account was cut down by the committee to nine pounds fourteen shillings, but finally raised to fifteen pounds and accepted. Miss Peabody was a daughter of Col. Stephen Peabody of New Hampshire, a Revolutionary officer, and a sister of Dr. Peabody, with whom she had studied and practiced, in cases of surgery principally, in Johnson, on the Lamoille River, in this State. She was from the intellectual and well known family of the New Hampshire Peabodys, many of whom had then won, and have since won, in one calling or another, much distinction for talents and enterprise. Her father was one of the most gallant and active of all the field officers in Gen. Stark's command at the Battle of Bennington, and was wounded by a bullet in the leg as he stood on a stump, giving orders to the troops in the heat of the Battle. Soon after coming to Montpelier to attend on the poor invalid, Marsh, she married General Pearley Davis, and, besides retaining through life a notoriety for surgical skill which continually brought her the visits of the unfortunate from every part of the State, she became truly one of the mothers of the town, not only diffusing blessings among the sick and afflicted, but acting well her part in social life, and at length leaving the numerous offspring, she had so well reared, to look back, as they justly may, with respect and pride on her memory.

At the Freemen's Meeting of the September of this year, the highest vote cast for State officers was thirty-seven, showing the number of freemen in attendance at this meeting to have been thirteen more than that of those who voted at the election of the preceeding year, and affording the best of evidence of the rapid progress the town was making in its growth and prosperity.

Among the municipal transactions of the next year (1795) we find several items which will probably be deemed note-worthy by the reader.

At the annual March Meeting it was unanimously voted, in acting on the article inserted in the warning for the purpose, "that all the town officers serve the town without fee or reward the year ensuing." And that the town officers of that year may have full credit for their patriotism, though sadly destined, it would seem, to perish with the year that brought it into existence, we subjoin the whole list:

Town Clerk—David Wing, Jr., Esq.

Selectmen—Jacob Davis, Esq., Capt. Barnabas Doty, Mr. Joseph Woodworth, Lieut. Andrew Nealey and Capt. Isaac Putnam.

Constable and Collector of Taxes—James Hawkins.

Listers—David Wing, Jr., Esq., Lieut. Andrew Nealey, Messrs. Ziba Woodworth, Joseph Woodworth and Joseph Wing.

Grand Juryman—Iram Nye.

Leather Sealer—Ziba Woodworth.

Pound Keeper—Maj. Pearley Davis.

Tithing Man—Joshua Wiggins.

Haywards—Maj. Pearley Davis, John Cutler, Daniel Woodworth, Lemuel McKnight, Benjamin Nash and Mark Nelson.

Fence Viewers—James Hawkins, Truman West and Joseph Woodworth.

Surveyors of Highways—Thomas Davis, Jona. Cutler, Hezekiah Davis, Caleb Bennett, Lemuel Brooks, John Templeton and Andrew Nealey.

Sealer of Weights and Measures—Capt. Barnabas Doty.

Auditor to Settle Accounts with the Treasurer—David Wing, Jr.

In the warning of this meeting, also, we find the evidence of the first movement made in town for public provision for the preaching of the Gospel. Among the articles inserted in that warning for the action of the meeting we find the following, the last one in the list proposing any new action:

"8th. To see if the town will take any measures as a town for the purpose of having preaching in said town the ensuing year."

This was the first movement of the kind ever made in town, though the article does not appear to have been acted on at all in the meeting of that year, nor does the subject appear to have been again agitated until nearly five years afterwards.

Two special Town Meetings were called in the fall of this year; one on the annual Freemen's Meeting, September 1st, to act on the question of petitioning the Legislature to be annexed to the County of Chittenden, and on the acceptance of the report of the committee for leasing the public lands; and the other meeting on the 5th of October, to take measures to fix on a spot for the location of the public buildings of the town.

At the first of these meetings it was voted unanimously "that our Representative, in our behalf, petition the Legislature, at the next session thereof, that Montpelier be annexed to the County of Chittenden." And the committee for leasing the public lands reported in part that having given public notice for bids, &c., they had leased

Lot No. 46, 1st Div. for Support of the Gospel, to John Holmes, for 2s 1d per acre;

Lot No. 67, 1st Div. of Town School Right, to James Hawkins, for 1s 6d per acre;

Lot No. 28, 2nd Div. of Town School Right, to Justus Lumbard, for 1s 5d per acre;

Lot No. 62, 2nd Div. for Support of the Gospel, to Hiram Peck, for 1s 11d per acre;

Lot No. 41, 2nd Div. for Minister Settlement, to Nathaniel Peck, for 1s 5d per acre.

The report of the committee was accepted, the leases established, and the committee continued in power.

At the October meeting there was appointed a committee for the purpse of locating the contemplated public buildings, consisting of David Wing, Jr. Pearley Davis, Jacob Davis, Isaac Putnam and Nathaniel Peck, who reported in one hour, indicating two spots "from which the town were to choose one for a Centre," and recommended that the decision be deferred to the next annual March Meeting, which was accordingly done.

At the annual March Meeting in 1796, the town, in acting on the subject of the two locations reported by the committee the previous fall, decided by vote "that the Centre of the town, or place for building public town buildings, be on Major (Pearley) Davis' land, not far from his barn, he turning out four acres of land for a common, at such place as a committee from said town shall see fit, two acres of which he to obligate himself to turn out gratis—the other two acres to be exchanged for two acres from the westerly part of Lot No. 40, now owned by Colonel Davis, which he offers to present to the town for said purpose, the town to clear off for Major Davis said two acres, likewise to clear two acres in lieu of the two acres given by him." And Colo. Jacob Davis, David Wing, Jr., Capt. Elnathan Pope,

Nathl. Peck and Capt. Barnabas Doty were appointed a committee "to stick the stake where the public buildings shall be erected, to fix bounds for a common, and to take deeds and give obligations according to the tenor and effect of the before mentioned vote of said town."

This contemplated Town House, however, was never built; for, after agitating the subject from time to time, for the next thirty years, without definitely settling on the manner of defraying the expense of erecting the building, the town finally, in 1828, made arrangements with the proprietors of the Methodist Meeting House, which had been built in the meantime on or near the spot designed for the Town House, for holding therein, for a stipulated annual payment, all town meetings thereafter.

At a special Town Meeting, held in the September and adjourned to the October of this year, all the six School Districts of the town were thoroughly remodeled, and their territorial limits clearly defined by designating the number of the Lots and the Divisions of land of which each District was thereafter to be composed.

Another special meeting was held in the December of this year to nominate a Justice of the Peace, and receive the report of the committee to lay out the Common, &c. At this meeting the town nominated Joseph Wing for Justice of Peace, and instructed their Representative to procure his election.

In the transactions of the annual March Meeting of 1797 we observe nothing out of the ordinary routine of town business. At the Freemen's Meeting of this year, however, a change was made of town Representative, and David Wing, Jr., was duly elected; while at the same meeting he had the additional honor of receiving from his townsmen their full vote for State Treasurer. Mr. Wing was the second Representative of Montpelier, and received four elections, but not quite in the four successive years, his first election being in 1797, his second in 1798, his third in 1800, and his fourth in 1802; while Pearley Davis, the third Representative of the town, was elected in the intermediate years of 1799 and 1801.

The years 1796 and 1797 were marked in the history of Montpelier by the action of the Legislature by which the town was made a component of the new County of Caledonia. That County was incorporated in November, 1792; but it does not appear that all the towns composing it were definitely decided on, nor that the County was fully organized, till the fall and winter of 1796 and 1797, when Montpelier was included within its boundaries, and one of her citizens, David Wing, Jr., was elected one of the Judges of its County Court—which office he appears to have held uninterruptedly through the remaining nine years of his life, notwithstanding his promotion to the office of Secretary of State in 1803, and his continuance therein for the last three years of that period. Though the town had previously petitioned to be set off to Chittenden County, this change appears to have been readily acquiesced in, the honor of having a Judge in so new a town possibly having something to do with the acquiescence at that time.

Nothing very noticeable appears among the proceedings of any of the Town Meetings of 1798, except the increased vote thrown for State Officers, which, at the Freemen's Meeting of this year, was for Tichenor, the Governor then elected, 47 votes. The town accounts were this year, for the first time, reckoned in dollars and cents, instead of pounds, &c.

In the year 1799, the School Districts were again remodeled at the March Meeting. And at the Freemen's Meeting the vote for Governor had increased to 67.

At a Town Meeting, called for the purpose, and held January 16th, 1800, the subject of providing for the preaching of the Gospel, after having been left undisturbed since the spring of 1795, was again agitated; and this time, it would appear, with an earnest purpose, since at this meeting it was

" *Voted* to choose a committee of three; and chose Arthur Daggett, Pearley Davis and Jerahmel B. Wheeler, for the purpose of employing a teacher of religion and morality. And also

" *Voted* that the town will indemnify the committee for such expense as they shall be at in procuring a preacher to preach in Montpelier."

And at the annual March Meeting, held a few weeks after, provision was made for the distribution of the rents of the Gospel lands, and carrying into effect the vote above mentioned, in the following manner:

" *Voted* That the money now received, or which may be received, as rent for land leased, belonging to the Right granted by charter for the Social Worship of God, be divided among the different Sects or Persuasions of people in Montpelier, according to the number of male polls over the age of twenty-one years in each society; and that the said money be appropriated for the uses intended by charter. And,

" *Voted*, That the said money, arising as aforesaid, should be paid over to the committee appointed the 16th of January last, to procure a preacher in Montpelier. And that all persons not wishing to have their share ot said money laid out as aforesaid, but dissenting in sentiment from the majority in said town, by leaving their names and sentiment with the Town Clerk, by the first day of May next, will be entitled to their proportion of said monies, to be expended under the direction of such persons as the different Secretaries may appoint. And all persons not leaving their names as aforesaid will be considered of the sentiment of the majority, and their proportion of said money laid out accordingly."

A vote forbidding hogs to run at large between the 1st of April and the 15th of November, was, for the first time, passed at the March Meeting of this year. At this meeting, also, Joseph Wing and Jerahmel B. Wheeler were nominated as Justices of the Peace, Wing having been the first and Wheeler the second Justice of the peace ever receiving appointment to that office on the formal nomination of the town, though it is very evident that Colonel Jacob Davis had been appointed one before or in the year the town was organized, and David Wing, Jr., soon after.

Two new Burial Grounds were, in the year 1801, by vote of the town, purchased, prepared and opened for use,—one in the neighborhood of Theophilus Clark, in the east part of the town; and the other on the Davis Pitch, on the swell twenty or thirty rods west of the falls of the North Branch, within the present bounds of Montpelier village. The latter was used as the Village Burying Ground till 1813, when the new one on the west bank of the Branch, a short distance below the falls, was opened and kept in use for the next forty years.

In 1802 an arrangement was established with the towns of Barre and Berlin for building a new bridge across the Winooski, between the Jacob Davis, Jr., farm and the Goodnow farm, on the road to Barre,—the subject of proportioning the expense having been submitted to Jona. Fisk, Cornelius Lynde and Seth Putnam, a committee from disinterested towns, who made the report (which was accepted by all concerned) that "the expense be divided into nine parts: that the town of Barre pay four parts, Montpelier three, and Berlin two. A similar arrangement appears to have been entered into with the town of Berlin for building and maintaining the bridge across the river where the old Arch Bridge now stands, at Montpelier village, at an early day—probably before the organization of the town. And these arrangements and proportionate responsibilities have, we believe, been maintained to the present day.

A new and methodical form for making the General List was this year, for the first time, drafted by David Wing, Jr., presented at one of the town meetings, and adopted.

At the March Meeting in 1803, David Wing, Jr., in consequence of a movement started probably by himself and Colonel

Davis for the purpose, was appointed the agent of the town to procure from the Legislature an act authorizing the Governor and Council to issue a new and corrected Charter of the Township of Montpelier.

At the Freemen's Meeting of this year Joseph Woodworth was chosen Representative, being the fourth individual chosen to that office in town. And the highest vote thrown for State officers was 71.

At the March Meeting of 1804, Pearley Davis, for committee appointed to act as agents, in conjunction with those of Barre and Berlin, to provide for building a new bridge across the river at the Jacob Davis, Jr , farm, on the road to Barre, reported that they had contracted with Joseph Palmer to build said bridge and warrant it to stand two years, for the sum of $270,50—the part of which devolving on Montpelier to pay being $90,83, which, the work being completed, they had settled by a town note. This report was accepted.

David Wing, Jr., who was appointed to procure the new Charter, also made his report, (which was accepted,) as follows:

"That he had found it necessary, in order to have the titles to lands in said town secure, to petition the Legislature for relief— who had passed an act authorizing the Governor to issue a new Charter of said town, which Charter he had procured and recorded."

Having thus somewhat minutely given the municipal history of Montpelier during the first twelve years of its existence as an organized town, noted all that was new and peculiar in its public proceedings, and shown the action on which most of the town institions of the present time were reared, we will now bring this long, to many perhaps dry, but necessary chapter to a close, to resume the specific subject, from time to time, as far as need be, in connection with other events, and in a form which to the general reader will probably be more interesting.

CHAPTER VI.

CLEARING OF THE FOREST LANDS.—PERSEVERING INDUSTRY OF THE SETTLERS, THEIR ECONOMY, THRIFT, INDEPENDENCE AND GENERAL CHARACTER.

WE have elsewhere said, and here substantially repeat, that few of the dwellers of populous towns, few indeed of the tillers only of the subdued and time-mellowed soils of the old States, have any adequate conception of the immense amount of hard labor required to clear off the primitive forest and prepare the land for the first crop; and fewer of them still any just appreciation of the degree of resolution, energy and endurance necessary to ensure continued perseverance in first clearing off, and then by second and third clearings in fully subduing one piece after another, until a farm of respectable size is at length thus redeemed from the wilderness. So herculean, indeed, is the task of clearing up a new farm that the best part of a man's life, and all the strength of his manhood are generally exhausted in that truly great achievement. It is no wonder, therefore, that so few of the pioneer settlers of a new country ever become the permanent residents and owners of the lands they first purchased and began to clear; that so many have grown faint while their resolutely self-imposed tasks were yet only half, or less than half accomplished, and left to the fresh hands of a later immigration the work of carrying out their designs, and finally enjoying the ripened fruits of their labors. In not half the towns in this State, probably, have a majority of the first settlers of a town become its permanent residents; while a far less proportion have succeeded in retaining for themselves and their descendants the farms which they first began to improve.

But to such a state of things no town in the State has presented in her example a more notable exception than the town of Montpelier. Among the whole list of the twenty-seven freemen who joined in its organization we find but one or two who did not become not only the permanent residents of the town, but the permanent owners of the farms they first purchased and improved for their homes. And in looking, now, over that ever to be honored roll of men, then all farmers, consisting of the Wheelers, the Davises, the Templetons, the Putnams, the Stevenses, the Cumminses, &c., and then glancing over the town, we can scarcely find one of the original homesteads of all those thus settling which is not still in the possession of some one of their descendants. This fact alone speaks volumes in praise of the original inhabitants of the town. It speaks in such praise, because it presupposes and proves the existence, in them, of that invaluable combination of traits of character which can alone ensure full success in building up an abidingly thrifty town, and a well ordered and respectable community—the resolution and physical endurance necessary for subduing the forests, the frugality and economy in living required for retaining and increasing the amount of their hard earnings, and the foresight and general capacity for business indispensable for the successful management of their acquisitions.

That the first inhabitants of Montpelier were generally men of great physical powers, resolution and stability of purpose, and that they applied their energies of body and mind to the best effect, in clearing up and improving their township, may be well enough seen in the pictures we have already drawn of the first years of the settlement, but more certainly so in the noble results of their exertions, which, after a period of twenty years, stood developed in their individual thrift, in their aggregate wealth and pecuniary independence.

But those results were not brought about by hard labor alone. Strict frugality in living lent its scarcely less important aid in the work. Nature has but few wants; and these settlers and their families seem to have been well content to put up with her real requirements. The ambition for display in dress, equippage and costly buildings was a forbidden, and an almost unknown passion among them. And all expectations of making property without work, or of living on credit, were ideas which were still more scouted. They dressed comfortably but very plainly, wearing, for the twelve or fifteen years of the settlement at least, scarcely anything but what was the product of their own looms and spinning wheels. With these implements, so necessary for the times, nearly every household was supplied. The girls spun, and the mothers wove, from their own wool, the flannels to be dressed or pressed for their best winter wear, and from their own flax the neat linen checks for their gowns and aprons for summer. Then the females of that day made their health, their husbands' or fathers' wealth, and established enduring habits of industry for themselves, as they were passing along in their daily routine of household employments. And who does not see how much better it would in reality be for the health, constitutions and habits of the females of the present day, if they were compelled to resort to the same way of clothing themselves and their families. In an interview we had the pleasure of having, in

1848, with the justly celebrated Lydia H. Sigourney, she, in commenting on the habits of American females as effecting their healths and constitutions, very seriously remarked that, among all the changes and revolutions in domestic habits and customs in modern times, she thought, so far as the welfare of her own sex was concerned, no one was to be more regretted than that which led to the disuse of the old-fashioned family spinning wheel, which, in drawing out and running up the thread, requiring a constant march backward and forward, while the arms were alternately lifted in the operation and that of turning the wheel, brought all the muscles into play, and made just the exercise necessary for the best development of the human system. We believe there is much force in that gifted lady's remark. And though we could hardly wish for a counter revolution to place us back to the olden times for that one object, yet we would earnestly insist that our females, in dispensing with their spinning wheels, should adopt some adequate substitute, such as active kitchen work within doors, and gardening, walking, riding and such like exercise, without. Patriotism among the men is accounted a virture and a glory ; but is its exercise all to be confined to the rougher sex ? Will not the gentler sex be ambitious to appropriate some of that virtue and glory to themselves ? And wherein can they better exercise it than in contracting habits which will ensure them vigorous health and good constitutions ? For do they not know that the physical constitutions of succeeding generations will greatly, if not mainly, depend on the constitutions they are now making for themselves ? And if they do not appreciate the force of this remark, and want a more tangible proof of its correctness, let them look upon the large and brawny forms of the old first settlers, and then upon the diminished sizes of the succeeding or second generation, and then follow the comparison among the still more dwarfed forms of the third, fourth and fifth generations. Why, in point of size, we have dwindled to a nation of Frenchmen already ; and at the present rate of diminution, a pass will in a few generations be reached when Guliver's fable of the Liliputians will be realized in our own descendants.

But to return to the subject on hand. Foreign manufactured goods were scarcely used at all for clothing during the first dozen years of the settlement. The wives who came into town with their husbands might have brought with them, perhaps, their calico gowns ; and it was known that "Marm Davis," as that pattern of housewives, the help-meet of Colonel Davis, was called, had brought with her a silk gown—the one, it is believed, in which she was married ; but it is not known that there were any others. The first silk dress that was ever purchased and brought into Montpelier for one of its lady residents was one obtained for the wife of Judge David Wing, and was first worn by her at a meeting late in 1803.

"I well remember when that first silk gown made its appearance," recently said an aged lady cotemporary of the favored possessor of the rare garment, to us while making enquiries about such matters. "It was at a meeting held in one of Colonel Davis' new barns. Hannah, that is Mrs. Wing, came in with it on, and made quite a sensation among us, but being so good a woman, and putting on no airs about it, we did not go to envying her. We thought it extravagant, to be sure; but as her husband had just been elected Secretary of State, and might wish to take her abroad with him, we concluded at length that the purchase might be perhaps, after all, quite a pardonable act."

Ribbons and laces were not worn nor possessed by the women; and the wearing of bonnets, which are thought to require trimmings made of such materials, was scarcely more frequent. Instead of bonnets, they generally wore, for head dress when going abroad, the more substantial, but no less neat and tasteful, small fur hats which were then already being manufactured in several of the older towns in the State. And it was not till a merchant had established himself in town that any innovation was made in these simple kinds of female attire. Then, for the first time, calico gowns became common—the best qualities of which cost seventy-five cents per yard, but of so strong and substantial a fabric that one of them would outwear two, or even three of most of those of the present day.

The men dressed as plain or plainer. Tow cloth for summer, and striped undressed woolens for winter, were the standing materials of their ordinary apparel. For public occasions, however, most of them managed to obtain one dress each made of homespun, woolen, colored and dressed cloth, which, as *they* used them, were generally good for their life times. The first "*go-to-meeting*" dresses of the boys were also, of course, domestic manufacture, and generally of fustian. A new fustian coat was a great thing in the eyes of a boy of fourteen in those days. But as their days of gallantry approached, their ambition sometimes soared to a new India cotton shirt, which then cost sixty-two cents per yard, though now not a fourth of that amount. The men wore fur caps or felt hats for every day use, but some of them fur hats on public occasions; and a few of the wealthier class, especially if they became what was called public characters, bought themselves beaver hats, which stood in about the same relation among the outfits of the men as did silk gowns among those of the women, such hats at that time costing thirty dollars each. But this was not so very bad economy as might be supposed, after all, since one of the clear beaver hats of that day would not only wear through the life-time of the owner, but the life-time of such of his sons as had the luck to inherit it.

The ordinary articles of family food were corn and wheat bread, potatoes, peas, beans and garden vegetables, pork, fish and wild game. Sweet-cake, as it was called, was rarely made; and pastry was almost wholly unknown. Indeed, we have been unable to learn that a pie of any kind was ever seen on a table in town till nearly a dozen years after it was first settled. About that time, however, one of the elder daughters of Colonel Davis, on noticing some fine pumpkins that were brought to the house during the harvesting, conceived the ambitious idea of making a mess of pumpkin pies, and obtaining at last the reluctant consent of her mother to let her make the experiment, she made a batch which *took to a charm* with the whole family and the several visitors invited to partake of the novel repast. After this, pumpkin pies became a staple of the tea table on all extra occasions.

Laboring men who, in felling the forest, logging, or boiling salts, as the first state of making potashes and pearls was called, often went considerable distances from their homes to work, generally took their dinners along with them into the woods, leaving the women to take care of the cattle and everything requiring attention about home. These dinners generally consisted of baked or stewed pork and beans, and not unfrequently of only bread and raw salt pork. Colonel Davis always used to recommend to his laborers to eat their pork raw or without any kind of cooking, contending that it was more healthy when eaten in that way than in any other. Some of the new hands that had been hired in by the Colonel at last, however, rebelled against the practice. Among the latter was Lemuel Brooks, the afterwards well-known Captain Brooks, who assured his fellow laborers, one day after they had been making their dinners on raw pork, that he was determined to set his wits to work and see if he could not, by the next noon, get up a more christianlike dinner. Accordingly he came on the next morning with gun and amunition, and just before noon stepped off into the neighboring thickets and shot two or three brace of patridges, which, in their chosen localities, were as plenty as hens about a farm house. And having speedily plucked and dressed the birds, he suspended them by the legs over a fire struck and built for the purpose, with a thick slice of pork made to hang directly above each, so that the salt gravey should drip upon or into them, and moisten and season them while cooking. As soon as he had thus prepared his meal, he hallooed to the men, and, in his usual jovial and humorous manner, bid them come in and partake of his "new invented dinner of *parched patridges.*" And *parched patridges* thenceforward became a favorite meal among the woodmen of the settlement.

The out-door work, at the period of which we have been speaking, was by no means all performed by the male inhabitants. Wives and daughters considered it no disparagement to go out to work in the fields, or even into the forest whenever the occasion required it at their hands. They boiled salts and made maple sugar at times in the woods, and often, in busy seasons, worked with their husbands, fathers or brothers, in making hay, harvesting grain, husking corn and digging potatoes in the field. The wives and daughters of the rich and poor alike cheerfully engaged in all these out-door employments, when the work, for want of the necessary male help or other circumstances, seemed to invite their assistance. Even Colonel Davis, whose family was regarded as standing in the first position in society, could be seen leading his bevy of beautiful daughters into his fields to pull flax.

But frugality in modes of dress, the supplies of the table, and other domestic arrangements for saving expenses and living within their means, did not constitute the whole of their system of economy. Their provident forecast taught them the evils of debt. For they felt that under the depressing influence of that sort of slavery, they could never enjoy that feeling of proud independence which they carefully cherished, and which constituted the best part of their happiness. They rightly appreciated, also, the bad moral tendencies of that evil, than which scarcely nothing more silently and surely tends, with its numberless temptations, to do what we otherwise would not do, to debase our best feelings and convictions as men, and undermine our best civic virtues as freemen. Our first settlers, therefore, carefully avoided it, making their calculations far ahead so to live, so to purchase, and so to enlarge their plans of improvement, as to keep out of debt, and often foregoing the most tempting of bargains rather than increase it.

Of this praisworthy system a good illustration may be seen in the example of the late William Marsh, the orphan son of the first settler of Waterbury—who, as mentioned in a former chapter, was drowned in the Winooski near Richmond. One day in the summer of, we think, 1790, as Colonel Davis was hoeing potatoes in the then mellow and wonderfully productive strip of meadow lying along the river, and now occupied by the buildings and gardens on the southerly side of Barre or Hubbard Street, a hardy, resolute looking boy of fourteen approached him and made known his wish to obtain a place to live and work till he was one-and-twenty. After scanning and examining the lad closely a few minutes, the Colonel made a bargain with him on the spot, conditioned, as usual, for his faithfulness and good behavior, and at once took him into the family, with whom he lived till he was of age, when he received from his employer the then rather generous sum of forty pounds for his services. With that forty pounds he immediately purchased, at four dollars per acre, twenty-five acres of land, which made the nucleus of his subsequent extensive homestead on the Worcester Branch, about a mile above Montpelier village. With the balance of his outfit, about eight pounds, added to his earnings the part of the summer he was left at liberty, he purchased a yoke of oxen and a cow, which, to his great uneasiness, left him, at the end of the year, about two pounds in debt. But as it was his first, so he resolved it should be his last debt. With this determination, he settled down upon his land, and living up to the rule he had thus established for himself, he would purchase no addition to his land till he had acquired the means of paying for it; but as soon as he had acquired such means he laid them out, as far as they would go, in purchasing an additional and adjoining piece of land. And so he continued, as he passed along in life and throve in his circumstances, to purchase, as his means warranted and opportunity presented, piece after piece of adjoining land, till his title deeds became eleven in number, and he at length found himself the possessor of a farm of three hundred acres, all lying in an unbroken body.

An equally instructive example may be seen in the life of Mr. Elisha Cummins, who now, at the unusual age of about ninety-three, is living at his ease, with handsome sums out at interest, and without owing a single dollar to any man in the world, on the well-conditioned and valuable homestead on which he began nearly seventy years ago. He made the purchase of the excellent lot of wild land which now constitutes his farm, as he informed us during a late visit at his house, in the year 1791, having first ascertained that he could pay for it in a job of felling and cutting up the timber on a tract of land in the eastern part of the town. The job was to fell and cut for logging, and perhaps help log off, the forest on forty acres of wild land. This it took him two years to accomplish; but when it *was* finally accomplished, he had the satisfaction of knowing that he had then a good lot of land of his own from which to make a farm, and that it was then fully paid for. He then commenced making an opening on his purchase, and building a log house for himself and prospective family; and since that time, he said, though he had raised a numerous family of sons and daughters, and assisted them to settle on farms around him, he had never been one hundred and fifty dollars in debt in all he owed at any period of his life.

To enable the reader to estimate the cost of living and the profits of farming, as well as to appreciate the frugality of of settlers, it will be well to note a few of the prevailing prices of labor, stock and other products of the day, as well as those of the few necessary articles which the settlers were compelled to import for their use and consumption in living, or in pursuing their ordinary avocations.

PRICES OF LABOR, STOCK, EXPORTED AND IMPORTED ARTICLES.

The wages of the best class of laborers were $9,00 per month, and 42 to 50 cents for casual days work.

The common price of wheat was 67 cents per bushel.
" " Indian corn, 50 " "
" " oats, 25 " "
" " potatoes, 25 " "
" " best yoke of oxen, $40 00
" " best horses, 50 00
" " best cows, 25 00
" " salts of lye, $4 to $5 per cwt.
" " pork, in dressed hogs, 4 to 6 "
" " beef, averaging 4 "

Of articles imported, the prices, fifty per cent. of which at least was clear profit, were:

For rock salt, $3 per bushel—commo, $2 50.
loaf sugar, 42 cts. per pound—brown, 17 to 20 cts.
common W. I. molasses, $1 17 per gallon.
green tea, $2 00 per pound—poorest Bohea, 50 cts. per lb.
nutmegs, 12 cts. each; ginger, 34 cts. per lb.; pepper, 75.
iron shovels, $1 50 each.
broad-cloth, $8 to $10 per yd.; W. I. cotton cloth, 62 cts.; calico, 50 to 75 cts.
W. I. rum, $2 per gallon.
dry salt fish, 11 cts. per pound.

And yet, with these extremely low prices for their products, and enormously high ones for their imported necessaries, the settlers, such was their industry and frugality, steadily progressed along the way to independence and wealth. But though the openings in the forest, rapidly increasing in extent and number, the more and more highly cultivated fields, the better and better filled barns, and the constantly multiplying stock of the

11

barn-yards, made their yearly progress in thrift clearly obvious to all, yet the ratio of that progress can be accurately estimated only from the financial statistics of the town. And for this purpose we subjoin the several Grand Lists of the town from its organization for the next succeeding fifteen years, or to and including 1806, all taken yearly and on the same plan.

GRAND LISTS OF MONTPELIER FROM 1792 TO 1806, INCLUSIVE.

For 1792 the Town	Grand List	was	$2,141 67
1793	"	"	3,075 00
1794	"	"	4,531 67
1795	"	"	5,705 83
1796	"	"	7,660 00
1797	"	"	9,794 18
1798	"	"	10,963 93
1799	"	"	14,538 75
1800	"	"	15,390 93
1801	"	"	16,979 77
1802	"	"	17,437 13
1803	"	"	18,126 99
1804	"	"	19,310 91
1805	"	"	22,920 55
1806	"	"	25,883 80

The increase of the population of the town, in the meanwhile, will be seen by the different enumerations of the U. S. Census, the whole of which, as we may not find a more convenient place for them, we will also here insert.

CENSUS OF MONTPELIER AT EACH OF THE SEVEN ENUMERATIONS.

By the 1st	enumeration in	1791,	the population was	113
2d	"	1800,	"	890
3d	"	1810,	"	1,877
4th	"	1820,	"	2,308
5th	"	1830,	"	2,985
6th	"	1840,	"	3,725
7th	"	1850,	Montpelier, 2,310; East M., 1,448 — united,	3,758

By these statistics the reader can make his calculations of the ratio of the increase of the property of the town, together with the ratio of the increase of its population, and also the ratio of the relative increase of each and both.

Thus lived and thus throve the early settlers of Montpelier; and thus, by so living, they not only established for themselves and their posterity habits and examples which insured the virtues indispensible for a well ordered community, but laid deep and safe the foundations of a town which now finds few rivals in stability of character, individual wealth and general prosperity.

And did these first settlers, in their simplicity of life, undergo any hardships and privations which were felt by them to be such? No. To them, with their dispositions, and with their robust health and strength, labor was alike their ambition and delight. All the substantials of life they had in abundance, and the want of its superfluities never cost them a single sigh.

And did they lose or forego any of the happiness which falls to the ordinary lot of humanity to enjoy? Again, no. In the first place, high health is but another name for happiness; and this, in its best development, they almost universally acquired through their constant exercise out of doors, and the well known invigorating effects of the more oxygenous atmosphere of new countries. "Why, sir," once said an old settler to us,—"why, the forest lands, among which we were generally at work, smelt so pure and sweet that we seemed to drink in health at every breath. And we *were* wonderfully healthy and strong. Rarely was any one ailing, and the doctors found mighty poor picking." And this animal happiness, these bounding pulses of health gave double zest to all the enjoyments of the young, in their wrestling and shooting matches, their husking and dancing frolics; and of the old in their more quiet social gatherings; and all seeming fully to realize in their lives the beautiful lines of the poet—

"Their best companions, innocence and health,
And their best riches, ignorance of wealth.
Then happy they who crown, in shades like these,
A youth of labor with an age of ease."

CHAPTER VII.

FIRST MILITARY COMPANY, TOWN LIBRARY, HEALTHINESS OF THE TOWN—DEATHS AND BIRTHS UP TO 1800.—FIRST SCHOOLS, MERCHANTS, MECHANICS AND PROFESSIONAL MEN.

WHILE thus far endeavoring to give, in the order of their occurrence, all the leading events and incidents connected with the settlement and growth of the town previous to 1800, we have omitted, for want of a convenient place for them, several things transpiring at different times, which have too important a bearing on its history to be omitted, and which we will now proceed to supply to bring our account up to that period.

During the winter of 1794, as near as we can now ascertain, a Military Company, consisting of seventy-two young or middle-aged men, including several soldiers of the Revolutionary War, then but recently brought to a close, was duly organized by the choice of officers, of whom Pearley Davis was the Captain. This office, however, Davis must have relinquished within six or eight months, in consequence of his promotion to that of Major in the regiment forming or formed of the companies of this and the neighboring towns; since at the March Meeting of that year we find him for the first time designated as Captain Davis, while at a Town Meeting in the following September we find his name written Major Davis. Captain Davis' successors in this office are believed to have been Barnabas Doty, Thomas McCloud and Isaac Putnam; while Davis himself passed rapidly along in the line of military promotion till he reached the office of General.

During the year 1794, also, a Library Association was organized, the books procured, and a Circulating Library established at the Centre of the town, probably in the house of Pearley Davis. Among the rules and regulations of this association there was one which, as showing the views of the leading settlers of that period, all of whom were members, is worthy of observation—and that was the entire exclusion of all works of fiction and all religious books. Works of fiction they doubtless excluded on account of their supposed tendency to engender a morbid imagination and undermine those practical virtues on which the permanent progress and prosperity of a new country must ever mainly depend. And in regard to the prevailing novels of that day—consisting of the works of Smollet and Fielding, and that still worse class of sickly, sentimental love stories and overstrained pictures of life then in vogue—the founders of that library doubtless judged wisely, and did well in excluding them. Religious books could not have been excluded by them from any want of reverence for religion, for there were no infidels among them, and we find them not only encouraging transient ministers to come and preach among them, but early making a move for the introduction of permanent preaching. Their object must have been the avoidance of sectarian discords, and the preservation, as long as possible, of social harmony among the people; and knowing that a large proportion of religious books were of a controversial character, and favored one sect or another, they thought it the wiser course, probably, with such an object in view, to exclude the whole of them. Their Library, therefore, containing about two hundred volumes, was made up of history, travels, biography, and works of a scientific, philosophic or moral character. These books were freely and constantly circulated, for a long period of years, through every part of the town. And who is there that can fully estimate the influence and ultimate beneficial effects of that general reading, on that and the succeeding generations of the inhabitants of the town, in creating a taste for reading, spreading information among all, and forming their intellectual characters? It has been written, published, and allowed to stand undisputed nearly twenty years, in a work read and known of all in this State, in relation to the inhabitants of the old town of Montpelier, especially the agricultural portion of their community, that they have ever been distinguished for a taste for reading, and a more than ordinary share of general intelligence. And if this be so, who need doubt the instrumentality to which it is to be mainly attributed?

The early settlers of Montpelier, as we have already intimated in the preceding chapter, enjoyed a degree of health which appears to have been almost unprecedented in the experience of any country. And their exemption from mortality, from the commencement of the settlement to the year 1800, comprising a period of twelve years and eight months, was certainly a very extraordinary one. The deaths were so few in number, indeed, during that period, that one can all but count two-thirds of them on his ten fingers by going over once. And as we doubt whether we can more acceptably occupy the little space required for the purpose, we will give the list entire, with the names of each, their ages as far as may be, the diseases or casualties by which they died, and the dates of their deaths, all appended.

For the first four years and seven months after the commencement of the settlement not a single death occurred, from any cause whatever, in any part of the town; and the list begins with the melancholly casualty which we have before described as occurring on the night of the first Thanksgiving and first ball held in Montpelier. We proceed, then, with the list, as follows:—

1791, Dec. 3—Theophilus Wilson Brooks, of drowning in the Winooski, aged 26 years.

1792—No deaths in town.

1793—No deaths in town.

1794, Nov. 4—Betsy Cate, child of Enoch Cate, of quinsy or croup, aged 8 months.

1795, Jan. 12—Debby Daphne, child of David Wing, Jr., of lung fever, aged 1 year.

" February—Twin infants of Allen Carpenter, of fits, aged 3 weeks.

" April or May—Luther Wheeler, son of J. B. Wheeler, of quinsy, aged 4 years.

1796—No deaths in town.

1797, March—Samuel Edwards, of consumption, first adult dying a natural death, aged 26 years.

" in summer— —— Caswell, step-daughter of B. Nash, from the fall of a tree, aged about 6 years.

" in summer—A child of Frank West, of disease unknown, aged about 1 year.

1798, Feb. 2—Infant child of Joseph Wing, aged 1 day.

" March 8—Lucy, child of Edmund Doty, from wound by scissors over the eye, aged 1 year six months.

" March 12—Anson, son of Thomas Davis, of fever, aged 2 years 5 months.

" in fall—A young man named Thaddeus White, on East Hill, of fever, age unknown.

" Dec. 14—A child of Robert Gifford, up the Branch, disease unknown, aged 4 months.

1799, May—S. Hamblin, disease unknown, aged, but age unknown.

" in summer—Hannah Parker, of consumption, aged about 20.

Thus it appears by the foregoing, which we have taken great pains to make a full and correct list, that only sixteen deaths occurred during the whole before named period of nearly thirteen years, being less than one and a fourth death a year on the average. The population of the town in 1791 was 113, in 1800 890; and could we average the population among the years, it would probably stand at about 400 through the whole time, which would give the rate of little more than one yearly death out of that number of inhabitants. It has been assumed, from the statistics of thorough and repeated registrations, made both in Europe and America, that one yearly death in every fifty inhabitants "may be fixed upon as a healthy and natural standard" at the present day. From these statistics it is seen that, in the rural districts of England, and also of the States of Massachusetts and Rhode Island in New England, the yearly deaths average not far from one in sixty of the inhabitants, the greater mortality in the cities (one in forty) reducing the general average, in the whole of the countries just named, to one in fifty. By the late registrations for 1857 and 1858 in Vermont, which is doubtless the most healthy state in the Union, the number of yearly deaths, after making reasonable deductions for deficiencies in returns, cannot be placed at a smaller rate than one yearly death out of seventy of its inhabitants. But by our calculations of the deaths in Montpelier, during the period for which they have been made, we make out but a little more than one yearly death out of four hundred of the inhabitants, a rate of mortality so unprecedentedly low as fully to justify us in calling it, as we did at the outset, a truly extraordinary one. And when we take into the consideration that of the sixteen deaths we have enumerated but five were adults,—that but four of those died of disease, and that the other eleven were infants or small children, and that but nine of that number died of disease,—the degree of health enjoyed by these early settlers is made to appear still more striking.

One reason of this remarkable exemption from mortality is, doubtless, to be found in the fact that nearly all the immigrants were persons in the prime of life and in the enjoyment of robust health when they came, few others being willing to encounter the supposed hardships of a new country. Other reasons may be looked for in the superior healthiness of *all* new countries, in our northern climes at least, and in their greater immunity from the destructive vices. But allowing the fullest force to all these reasons, such health as we have seen in this setttlement is, we apprehend, rarely experienced in any country, new or old; and as that health, as all the statistics of other towns yet published will show, has never ceased to compare with that of the most favored places, we may justly claim that the location of our town is at least one of the very healthiest in the State.*

The whole number of births in town during the period of which we have been speaking we make out to have been one hundred and thirty, which, calling that period thirteen years, would make an average of ten birhs a year. By the two late registrations of births and deaths in this State, to which we have already alluded, we find the whole number of births to have been a small fraction less than double the number of deaths; and two births to one death is as favorable a result as we may ever expect to see exhibited by the statistics of any State or County, at the present day. But in the case of the early settlers of this town we see the excess of births over deaths to have been seven fold, thus furnishing another test of the extreme healthiness of the settlement, and at the same time indubitable proof of as ex-

* The residents of Montpelier, at least, need only cast their minds back on the past to see the confirmation of our statement in the instances of longevity which, at any given period since the commencement of the present century, have been exhibited among the inhabitants of the town. A few years ago there were more than a dozen old men bordering on ninety, such as John Taplin, Aaron Grisworld and others. Last year old Mr. Levi Humphrey and Nath'l Clark, of the band of the first settlers, left us. And even now quite a number of the same hardy band are found lingering among us, at the extreme age of ninety and over, such as Elisha Cummins, Thomas Davis, Jonathan Shepard and the venerable Captain Nathan Jewett. The latter, the son-in-law of the once widely known Gov. Elisha Paine, from whom our present Hon. Elisha Paine Jewett took his name, is now ninety-four years old, probably the oldest man in Washington County.

treme fruitfulness in the incomparably most precious of its productions.

OF THE BIRTHS,

The first one that occurred in town was that of Clarisa Davis, youngest daughter of Col. Jacob Davis, who was born September 22, 1789, and who still survives, as the respected consort of the Hon. George Worthington, of Montpelier. The second one was that of James Dodge, the son of Solomon Dodge, who was born April 5th, 1790, and who still survives, in Montpelier or in the borders of Calais. The third was John Hawkins. son of James Hawkins, who was born March 25th, 1791, and removed from town with his father to Upper Canada soon after the year 1800. And the fourth was Mary Templeton, daughter of the first John Templeton, who was born May 3d, 1791, married Stephen Brown, then of Montpelier, and died somewhere about 1820.

OF THE MARRIAGES,

The first that occurred in town was that of Jacob Davis, Jr., of Montpelier, and Caty Taplin of Berlin, the ceremony being performed by her father, John Taplin, Esq., on the 3d of October, 1791. The second was that of David Wing, Jr., and Hannah Davis, second Daughter of Colonel Jacob Davis, which took place, before the same Justice, November 25, 1792. And the third marriage of a Montpelier settler was that of Clark Stevens with Huldah Foster of Rochester, Mass., where the ceremony was performed, Dec. 30, 1792. All these parties have long since passed away, existing now only in their numerous respectable descendants, and the good memories they have left with the public behind them.

OF THE COMMON SCHOOLS,

The first one ever opened in town was in a log school house, on the river near the Middlesex line, and taught by Jacob Davis, Jr., the scholars coming from Col. Davis' and some other families living nearest him, and from Middlesex and Dog River in Berlin. This was the only school in the town and vicinity for about two years. But during the winter of 1791–2 David Wing, Jr., taught a school in the new frame house of Col. Davis. A year or two after a frame house was built on the road to the mills on the Branch Falls, located near the spot now occupied by the old burying ground. The school in this house was taught by Abel Knapp, afterwards Judge Knapp of Berlin; and then by a college student who somehow found his way to this settlement. In a few years this school house was burned, when another was erected near where the Methodist Chapel now stands. To this school the pupils came the distance of many miles towards the centre of the town. But in 1794 the town was divided into six school districts, and so great was the increase of inhabitants that schools were thenceforward established in all of them.

OF THE MERCHANTS.

The first, who made pretensions to sell goods of any kind in town, was Dr. Frye, so called, though not a practicing physician, who imported and kept for sale, during the two or three years next succeeding 1791, a few heavy articles such as salt, rum, nails, and the few others deemed indispensable in the settlement. He kept his store, if such it could be called, in his own house—the third frame one built in town, situated on the west side of the then new road leading to Berlin, and within a few rods of the bridge over the river, built about that time, on the site of the present old arch bridge. This house is yet standing next the old paper mill, as one of the two only architectural relics of those times, still remaining, as it does, and though nearly seventy years old, in a state of very tolerable preservation. But Frye, who, even at that day, was hardly deemed a merchant, soon yielded his occupation to Col. Joseph Hutchins, who, in the year 1794, opened a far better assortment of goods, in a small house and store room built for the purpose, next north of the Frye house, and then standing on the site now occupied by the barn and stables attached to the old Shepard Tavern, now the Farmers' Hotel. In 1796, Col. Hutchins gave up his store to his two sons, Joseph and William Hutchins, Joseph continuing to manage or own the store ten or twelve years or to his death ; while William soon built the tavern house above named, and occupied it till his death, which occurred not many years from that of his brother. In June 1799, Timothy Hubbard and Wyllys I. Cadwell opened a store in the north west front room of the large old house now occupied by Wm. W. Cadwell, Esq., which had been built by James Hawkins, many years before, and now makes up the other of the two old houses above mentioned. This new firm went into a more extended variety than any of their predecessors, including a comparatively fair assortment of dry goods. In 1802, Hubbard and Cadwell dissolved partnership, leaving Cadwell to build the old store adjoining, and continue to trade therein till his death in 1824. In 1802, Col. David Robbins, who had, for a year or two, been trading on a small scale in the east part of the town, in a house situated near the old Quaker Meeting House, formed a partnership with Isaac Freeman and opened a store in the village, standing on the Branch near the Union House. In 1803, Langdon and Forbes opened their store ;

while, during the same year, Timothy Hubbard entered into a mercantile partnership with the then Hon. David Wing, when the two at once opened a store and continued the trade until Wing's death in 1806.

OF THE TAVERNS.

The first one was built in 1793 by Col. Davis, a large and commodious structure for the times, placed on the south east bank of the Branch, over which, by that time, the Colonel had extended his clearing all along the stream from the site then chosen for the building, to the mouth of the Branch. This was the original Union House, which was burnt in 1834, re-built and again burnt December, 1859. This was not only the first tavern of the town, but the first ever opened in the County as now constituted. It was kept several of the first years by David Wing, who then moved on to the farm where he died, now occupied by his grandson, David Wing, and by Henry Nutt, the farm having been divided between the first David Wing's two oldest sons, Columbus and Sydney Wing. The second tavern built and opened was by William Hutchins, not far from 1800, as we have already sufficiently noticed under the head of "the Merchants."

OF THE MECHANICS.

The first Carpenter, Mill Wright and Bridge Builder was Larned Lamb, the afterwards well known Colonel Lamb, who was noted for his towering form, for his military tastes, ready wit and lashing satire; and who, after having been many years a Colonel in the militia, received a Captain's commission from the Government of the United States in the War of 1812, and subsequently went west and died in St. Louis in 1828. Colonel Lamb built the new frame house of Colonel Davis, also his new tavern house, or the first Union House, as before mentioned. He likewise framed the first State House, and with Palmer, the old Waterbury Bridge Builder, he built also the first bridge over the river to Berlin, together with many other bridges by himself, and large buildings in this and the neighboring towns. The other Carpenters of the town, at that early day, were Luther Moseley, Esq., and a few others who had been in the employ of Colonel Lamb. And these were followed soon by the more ingenious and finished workmen, Elisha Town and Sylvanus Baldwin.

The first Blacksmith in town was James Hawkins, who, previous to 1790, bought the farm lying between the old Howard place and Henry Nutt's farm. Here, after having finished off the house, the frame of which was the first one raised in Montpelier, he erected a Blacksmith's Shop, and carried on the business to a limited extent, in connection with house-building jobs, for some years. But Jonathan Shepard was the first man who built a Blacksmith's shop and put it in operation in Montpelier village. He, at a little later period, erected a Blacksmith's shop somewhere in the public corner at the head of State Street, as near as he can now point out, no road then being opened across the Branch from the old Cadwell house ; and here, through a hired journeyman Blacksmith, he carried on the business till, some years after, he sold out his shop and custom to James Hawkins, buying the farm of the latter and turning in therefor, with the shop and other payments, the first Morgan horse ever known in Vermont or elsewhere.*

The first Clothier in town was David Tolman, who established a shop for cloth dressing, &c., adjoining the Davis Mills on the Branch, in about 1796, having moved from Greensboro' or vicinity.

The first Hatter was Erastus Watrous, Esq., who, having emigrated from Connecticut in May, 1799, with his young brother-in-law, George Worthington, as an apprentice to the trade, established his shop, in the first instance, in a part of the building occupied by Clothier Tolman.

The first Brick Maker was Paul Knapp, who opened a brick yard at the foot of the hill back of the old Cadwell house, at an early day enough, it is believed, to have made the brick for the chimnies of Colonel Davis' new house.

OF THE PROFESSIONAL MEN.

The first Physician was Dr. Spaulding Pierce, who established himself in Montpelier village at a very early period of the settlement—as early perhaps as 1790. The next was Dr. Philip Vincent, who settled in the east part of the town, as early as 1793. The third was Dr. Edward Lamb, who settled in the village in about 1797. Drs. Jacob P. Vargeson and Stephen Peabody, the former in the village and the latter in the east part of the town, settled and practiced a few years before and after 1800. While, during the whole intervening time, Mrs. Pearley Davis was often sought in preference to them all, in cases especially of dislocated bones, contracted sinews and injured limbs of long standing, whose cure had baffled others.

* The statement of Mr. Shepard, who is still alive, has been always uniformly and confidently made as follows :—He had purchased, at the great price for those days of about $200, a young stallion horse, of a Woodstock man, who had the animal of one Justin Morgan of that section, the latter having reared him from a colt. Mr. S. further vouches for his personal knowledge of the fact that Justin Morgan owned the mare that brought this colt—that the mare was so great a traveller that Morgan, who had a relative in Canada whom he often visited, used to make the journey, which was seventy miles, in a single day ; and that, on one of these visits, this colt was sired by a common Canadian stallion. And that it was from this colt, growing up and being kept in Randolph and other places, that the whole race of the noted Vermont Morgan horses originated.

The first Lawyer was Charles Bulkley, who came into town from Connecticut in about 1797, lived at first in the Frye house in Montpelier village, but in a few years moved across the river into the borders of Berlin, having built the one story brick house still standing near the bank of the river, about a dozen rods above the Arch Bridge. He was made a Judge of the County Court in 1813, and died in 1836, a wealthy and much respected citizen, leaving the bulk of his property for benevolent or religious purposes. The second Lawyer was Cyrus Ware, who also settled in the village in 1799, represented the town in the Legislature in the years 1805, 1807, 1808 and 1809, and in 1808 was made a Judge of Caledonia County Court. And the third Lawyer was Samuel Prentiss, who settled in the village in 1803, and subsequently became the distinguished Jurist and U. S. Senator whose history belongs not only to the town, but to the State and nation at large.

The first Ministers of the Gospel who officiated in the settlement during the period of which we have been treating, and even up to 1805, were mostly transient preachers, or missionaries, as the settlers were accustomed to call them. The good and willing Uncle Ziba, to be sure, being a sort of a spontaneous Free Will Baptist preacher, was ever ready to preach or pray among his fellow settlers of the town, when a more regular minister could not be obtained for the occasion.* And the devoted Rev. James Hobart, the first, and long the permanent Minister of Berlin, was also always equally prompt to come, pay or no pay, to officiate at funerals, or to give volunteer sermons on the invitation of the settlers. But, as we said, most of the preaching came from the Missionaries, consisting of Methodists, Baptists and Universalists, all of whom, for aught that now appears, were alike well accepted—for whatever the doctrine might be, it was preaching, and that seemed to have sufficed with a people too seldom served to be very particular. Even this class of Preachers, however, did not very often make their appearance in the settlement until the town, as such, began to agitate in earnest the question of devoting the rents of the Gospel Lands for the procurement and support of preaching; when, by a singular coincidence, their visits suddenly became quite frequent.

In the summer of 1799 there was got up a great public meeting for a doctrinal debate between the ministers of two of the rival persuasions of which we have been speaking. The champions on the occasion were the Rev. Mr. Mitchel, of some other

* Ziba Woodworth, the first Town Clerk of Montpelier, the crippled survivor of the massacre of Fort Griswold, and the ardent, eccentric man, christian and politician, was universally known by the appellation of *Uncle Ziba.*

part of the State, on the part of the Methodists, and the Rev. Mr. Farewell, of Barre, on the part of the Universalists. The spot chosen for the meeting was in the then open meadow near the east bank of the Branch, twelve or fifteen rods south of the new tavern, or first Union House, a little back of the present Lyman store building and opposite the Brick Church. And here, in the open air and among the still standing stumps, and on the exuberantly growing grass, a platform for the speakers was made, by placing side by side long tables brought out from the tavern; when, one at a time, the ecclesiastic gladiators mounted the rostrum and proceeded with the appointed encounter. It had been mutually arranged between the speakers that neither should occupy but fifteen minutes at a time, or before yielding the stand to his antagonist, each doubtless feeling conscious of his ability to give the other in that time as much as he could digest and answer in the like succeeding interval. And thus, alternately speaking and retiring and preparing for the renewed onset, they hotly continued the contest hour after hour, till their intellectual ammunition and the patience of the audience were alike exhausted, when the meeting broke up—both of the speakers claiming the victory in argument, but leaving their hearers, in fact, far more distracted in religious sentiments than they had ever been before.

And to the divided state of doctrinal opinions among the people, which from that time grew more decided and apparent, was, in a great measure, attributable, perhaps, the fact that they did not agree, till more than five years after this memorable disputation, to appropriate any of the public monies for any stated preaching of the Gospel.

In taking a final retrospect of this important period of the first dozen years of the settlement of the town of Montpelier, and while noting the rapid and steady progress of its improvements during that time, and in glancing over the names of the hardy, resolute and enterprising little band, who were most instrumental in effecting what had been so clearly accomplished in giving a start towards building up a permanently prosperous town and community, we cannot but perceive the controlling agency exercised by two men among them, to whom the town should forever hold itself especially indebted for the foundations of its subsequent growth and importance. Those two men were Colonel Jacob Davis and the Honorable David Wing—the former, by his indomitable energy and far reaching sagacity, begining and driving forward the work of settlement, shaping its course for its *future* as well as present interests, and giving it an impetus which might, even under any ordinary agencies, insure its onward movement through many generations to come—

and the latter, by his great intelligence, correct tastes and elevated public spirit, moulding all its municipal polity, systematizing its form of business, and ever using all his influence for measures to insure its intellectual and moral improvement, thus establishing precedents in town business, and securing legislative enactments in its behalf, the effects and advantages of which have continued to be felt to the present day.

But in justice to others, it should be added that these two men were ever well seconded and sustained in their exertions for the welfare of the people and the prosperity of the town, by all the principal settlers, among whom, the most conspicuous in action, might be named the energetic and public spirited Pearley Davis; the pure minded and intellectual Clark Stevens; the intelligent and judicious Jerahmel B. and Benjamin I. Wheeler; the frank, genial and active Lemuel Brooks; the ardent Ziba, and the sensible Joseph Woodworth; the noble Isaac Putnam, together with Joseph and Josiah Wing, Simon, John and Elisha Cummins, Thomas Brooks, Capt. Thomas West, William Marsh, Nathaniel and Hezekiah Davis, Nathaniel Clark, Theophilus Clark and his brother, the Pecks, the Dodges and the Templetons—all of whom, as the representatives of the town in the Legislature, Justices of the Peace, or as different town officers, acted more or less important parts in the public affairs of the settlement.

CHAPTER VIII.

GROWTH OF THE VILLAGE. — EDUCATIONAL INTERESTS. — EPIDEMICS. — ECCLESIASTICAL AFFAIRS. — NEWSPAPERS. — THE TOWN MADE THE SEAT OF GOVERNMENT. — TOWN EMBRACED IN THE NEW COUNTY AND MADE THE SHIRE.

By the year 1800, the Lower Pitch of Colonel Davis, embracing the meadows on the lower half mile of the Little North Branch, and nearly another half mile on the Winooski, then and for years afterwards universally called *The Hollow*, had become a clustered settlement containing a score or two of houses and as many hundred inhabitants. It then could boast of its two stores, two taverns, two lawyers, and the usual assortment of mechanics,—all combining to dignify it with the name of Village, and make it, as the nearly exclusive seat of trade, litigation and mechanic work, a general resort and a place of much comparative importance with all the surrounding country. And, as thenceforward a large and yearly increasing share of the public transactions, secret or social movements calculated to exercise influences on the community at large, and the consequent important or interesting events, connected with the history of the town, had their origin here, the Village must now be allowed to occupy a proportionate share of our attention.

EDUCATIONAL INTERESTS.

The year 1800 was marked by the movement which resulted in the founding, and the eventual funding of the present Washington County Grammar School. On the 7th of November of that year, the "*Trustees of Montpelier Academy*" were incorporated, the act of incorporation being procured by the Honorable David Wing, then the town representative in the Legislature. The Trustees thus incorporated were Col. Jacob Davis, Charles Bulkley, David Wing, Jr., Jerahmel B. Wheeler and Thomas West, Jr. And in pursuance of the laudable and spirited design here involved, a building, 44 by 36 feet on the ground, and two stories high, affording space above and below not only for two large school rooms but apartments for a teacher and his family, was, within the next year or two, erected and finished off for immediate use, by money raised from the subscriptions of the citizens of the town.

The first preceptor employed in this Academy, was a Mr. James Whorter, a temporary teacher, or one, at least, who could not have remained over one year. His successors were James Dean, Joseph Sill, Benton Pixley, Ira Hill, Thomas Heald, Justus W. French, Seneca White, Heman Rood, John Stevens, Jonathan C. Southmayd, J. B. Eastman, A. A. Wood, A. G. Pease, Calvin Pease, J. H. Morse, M. Colburn, Geo. N. Clark, Davis Strong, Horace Herrick, J. E. Goodrich, Charles Kent, C. R. Ballard, and the present preceptor of 1859 and 1860, Dr. M. M. Marsh.

Of these, James Dean became Professor of Mathematics in the Vermont University, and Calvin Pease and Geo. N. Clark became Professors also, at a later period, in the same institution, and Mr. Pease finally its President. Several others besides those above named have, at intervals, been employed for one or two terms, but not as permanent teachers. And of those enumerated, far the greatest proportion taught but one or two years. Those who continued longest Preceptors were Calvin Pease, who taught four years, and Jonathan C. Southmayd, who taught twelve years. And these two last named were also among the very best instructors to be found in any country. To Jonathan C. Southmayd especially, from his long stay and his peculiar combination of fine qualities, both as a teacher and a man, not only the educational interests of the town, but its social, moral and general intellectual improvement were deeply indebted.

During the October session of the Legislature, 1813, on the petition of its Trustees, an act was passed changing the Corporation to a County Institution, under the name of *The Trustees of Washington County Grammar School*, and appropriating the rents of the Grammar School Lands lying within the County to its exclusive use.

The old Academy was burned in 1822, and the present old brick one built in 1823, at a cost of $1600, about $800 of which was also raised by subscription. The present brick edifice for the Academy and Union School was built in 1858–9, at an expense of $19,000, and has no superior in the State.

During the years 1800–1–2 the Common School districts of the town, then consisting of ten in number, received a final remodeling, destined to stand, in the shape then established, for the next twenty years. An enumeration of the scholars in all the several districts was also made in 1802, and the whole number found to be about four hundred. The common schools of that and the succeeding period of twenty or thirty years were, notwithstanding the absence of all general State school systems, by no means of an inferior character. The common English branches of education, such as Reading, Spelling, Writing, Arithmetic, Grammar and Geography, were generally well and thoroughly taught. The modern text books, simplifying most of these sciencies for the more ready comprehension of the pupil, and prepared with questions for more rapid progress in study, may have indeed ensured greater acquisitions in a given time; but it may yet remain a question whether the benefits of the greater acquirement under the newer systems are not mostly or quite counterbalanced by the less mental discipline.

EPIDEMICS.

Endemics we have none. From first to last no diseases have made their appearance in town which could be discovered to be peculiar to the place, or to have been generated by any standing local causes. Of Epidemics, Montpelier has had its share, but still a light share compared, as we believe, with a majority of the towns in the State, only four deserving the name having occurred from the first settlement of the town to the present day.

The first of these was the *Dysentery*, which fatally prevailed throughout the town, in common with most other towns in Vermont, during the summer and fall of 1802. The victims of this epidemic, in Montpelier, were Mrs. Sophia Watrous, wife of Erastus Watrous, Esq.; Erastus Hubbard, a younger brother of Timothy Hubbard; John Wiggins, another young man; and a considerable number of children.

The second of these epidemics was the *Typhus Fever*, which prevailed in town to a considerable extent in the summer season of 1806, and proved fatal to Montpelier's favorite and most honored citizen, David Wing, Jr., then Secretary of State. Luther Mosely, Esq., another valued citizen, also fell a victim to the same disease, together with a young man by the name of Cutler, a girl by the name of Goodale, and several others.

The third epidemic visiting the town was that fearful disease known by the name of *Spotted Fever*, which, to the general alarm of the inhabitants, suddenly made its appearance in the village in the winter of 1811. The first victim was Sibyl Brown, a bright and beautiful daughter of Amasa Brown, of the age of nine years, who, on Saturday, January 2d, was in school,—on the evening of that day sliding with her mates on the ice,—and the next morning a corpse. The wife of Aaron Griswold, and the first wife of Jonathan Shepard were next, and as suddenly destroyed by this terrible epidemic, which struck and swept over the village, to which it was mostly confined, like the blast of the simoon, and was gone. There were over seventy cases in this village, and, strange to tell, but three deaths of the disease, which, at the same time, was nearly decimating the then four hundred inhabitants of Moretown, and sweeping off sixty or seventy of the two thousand inhabitants of Woodstock. The chief remedy relied on here, was the prompt use of the hot bath, made of a hasty decoction of hemlock boughs; and the pine board bathing vessel, made in the shape of a coffin, was daily seen, during the height of the disease, in the streets, borne on the shoulders of men, rapidly moving from house to house, to serve in turn the multiplying victims. So stange and unexpected were the attacks, and so sudden and terrible were often the fatal terminations of the disease, that it was likened to the Plague of the Old World. Some of its types, indeed, so closely resembled the Plague, as well to justify men in deeming them one and the same disorder. A bright red spot, attended with acute pain in some instances, appeared in one of the limbs of the unwarned victim, and, like the old Plague spot, spread, struck to the vitals and caused his death in a few hours. In other instances, a sort of congestion of the blood, or silent paralysis of all the functions of life, stole unawares over the system of the patient, his pulse faltered and nearly stopped, even before he dreamed of the approach of the insiduous destroyer. The late worthy Dr. James Spalding once told us, that he was the student of an eminent physician, in Alstead, N. H., when the epidemic visited that place, that he frequently went the rounds with his instructor in his visits to his patients, and that on one of these occasions they made a friendly call on a family in supposed good health, when the master of the house congratulated himself on the prospect that he and his young family were about to escape the disease which had been cutting down so many others. Something, however, in the appearance of one or two of the apparently healthy group of children present attracting the attention of the old Doctor, he fell to examining their pulses, when in two of them he found the pulse so feeble as to be scarcely perceptible; but keeping his apprehensions to himself, he made some general prescriptions for *all* the children and left, hoping his fears would not be realized. Within three days both of those children were buried in one grave. The Physicians who had charge of these cases were Dr. Lamb, Dr. N. B. Spalding, Dr. Woodbury, and Dr. Lewis of Moretown. Volumes have been written on the causes of this and similar epidemics, and yet to this day the subject is involved in clouds of mystery. We have long believed that the causes of this and other like epidemics are to be looked for in the occasional disturbed condition of the electric fluid, that universal agent of the air, the earth and the water, which is now known to be intimately connected with all the organizations of the vegetable and animal creations, and its presence indispensable to the growth and health of both. We will suppose, then, a sudden cessation of the natural pervasion of this quickening and all-important fluid, in given localities, and ask what would be the probable consequences on the human system, where its effects would be most likely to be visible? What more probable than, in the results manifested in the epidemics which we have had under consideration, this disturbance, or suspension of the fluid, intensifying, or modifying and giving character to the disease in proportion to the degree in which it may happen to exist.

The fourth epidemic in town followed soon after the last, and in some instances, assumed some of its peculiar types. This occurred in the winter of 1813, and was here generally called the *Typhus Fever*, though it partook more of the characteristics of Peripneumony, or Lung Fever, being the same disease which first broke out, the fall before, among the U. S. troops at Burlington, and by the following mid-winter had become a destructive epidemic in nearly every town in the State, carrying off, according to the statistics of Dr. Gallup, more than six thousand persons, or one to every forty of its whole population. In this whole town, during the year 1813, the number of deaths—most of which were of this disease—was seventy-eight, among which were those of Capt. N. Doty, R. Wakefield, C. Hamblin and others, in the prime of life. This great number of deaths in one year was, beyond all comparison, greater than ever occurred before, or has ever occurred since, it is believed, in proportion to the population, which was then about two thousand; while the average number of deaths in town per year, about that period, was, as near as can now be ascertained, but a little over twenty, and of course but little more than one death in one hundred. In the village, according to records left by the Rev. Chester Wright, the average number of deaths for the five years preceding 1813 was but four per year, which must have been considerably less than one to one hundred yearly. This seems to be confirmed by another record left by Mr. Wright, of the number of deaths occurring each year in the village for the fourteen years succeeding 1816, by which it appears that the average number of deaths in the village, during that whole period, was but ten yearly, while the population during the last named period increased from nearly one thousand in 1816 to nearly two thousand in 1830; so that the rate of mortality during the whole nineteen years, of which we have given the approximate statistics, was, with the exception of 1814, always greatly less than one to every one hundred inhabitants: all going to confirm what we have before stated respecting the peculiar healthiness of the location of our town, and especially of our village, from the earliest times to the present day.

PREACHING OF THE GOSPEL, &c.

The first stated preaching in town was by the Reverend Clark Brown, who came from Brimfield, Mass., where he had been previously settled and dismissed. He was hired in 1805, in accordance with a vote of the town, to preach one year for a stipulated salary, amounting to about five dollars a Sunday for every Sunday through the year, with what he could pick up in perquisites from marriages and extra sermons. But he did not officiate in that capacity, it would appear, much more than half the period for which he had been hired; for, owing to the little faith felt in his piety on the part of some, disagreement with some of his doctrines, which favored Unitarianism, on the part of others, and the little interest felt on the subject on the part of more, probably, his audiencies so dwindled away by the end of six months that he thought to arouse them by preaching them a pointed sermon on their neglect of religious duty. This however only made the matter the worse for him; for the offence thus given, together with the already existing causes of disaffection, led his employees to meet and decide to pay him up for his whole year, but to wholly dispense with his further services as a preacher. Brown was a man of good education, some literary taste and quite respectable talents, but not much of a man, nor probably much of a christian. So, at least, must have thought his employers, since they would have no more of his preaching, though they could have had it, the next six months at least, for what they had already paid him, for he continued to remain in town; and the next year, 1806, started a weekly journal—the first newspaper ever published in town—called the *Vermont Precursor*, published it one year and sold out to Samuel Goss, who rechristened it the *Vermont Watchman*, and made it the foundation of the prominent political journal which has ever since gone by that name. Brown afterwards went west and died; but his wife, the better man of the two, pushed on further west with her children, till she reached Oregon at last, opened a school, which finally grew into the first college of that country, under Sydney Marsh, President.

For the next year or two after the dismissal of Mr. Brown there was no stated preaching in town. Sometime in 1807, however, a preacher by the name of Hovey was employed, but left the same year.

In 1808, on the 12th of April, eighty-three of the leading citizens of the village organized themselves into a religious society, under the name of the "*First Congregational Society in Montpelier*," for the maintenance of regular preaching. And in the July following a Congregational Church was organized, consisting of Amasa Brown and wife, Sylvanus Baldwin, Andrew Dodge, H. Estabrooks, Samuel Goss, Timothy Hatch and wife, Joseph Howes and wife, Solomon Lewis and wife, Mrs. B. Burbank, Lydia Davis, Polly Baker, Rebecca Persons and Sarah Wiggins. About the same time the Rev. Chester Wright was employed as a stated preacher, and continued acceptably to act as such until August 16, 1809, when he was ordained and permanently settled as pastor of the church and society, at a salary of $350 for the first year, $375 for the second, and $400 per year thereafter, with the use of a parsonage. From this time Mr. Wright continued the able and devoted preacher and pastor of his people until the close of the year 1830, when, for causes involving not one single stain on his character as a preacher, as a christian or as a man, he was dismissed. The next succeeding settled minister was the Rev. Samuel Hopkins, ordained October

26, 1831, and dismissed April 29, 1835. The next was Rev. Buel W. Smith, ordained August 25, 1836, and dismissed July 15, 1840; the next Rev. John Gridley, installed December 15, 1841, and dismissed December 9, 1846; and the next, and last to the present writing, the Rev. Wm. H. Lord, ordained September 21, 1847. The number admitted into the church during all this time were:—under Mr. Wright four hundred and twenty-eight; under Mr. Hopkins forty-eight; under temporary preachers, one hundred and thirty-seven; under Mr. Smith, eighty-two; under Mr. Gridley, forty-six; and under Mr. Lord, two hundred: who, with the seventeen original members, make the aggregate of nine hundred and fifty-eight.

In the year 1835 a new church, called the *Free Church*, was formed, mostly from seceders from the old church, a meeting house built, and the Rev. Sherman Kellogg settled. But this society kept up its organization but about four years, when the members either returned to the old church or united with the Methodists.

The present brick meeting house of the Congregationalists was built by the society in 1820, under the contract and superintendence of Deacon Sylvanus Baldwin, at a cost of about $8000.

A Methodist Church or Class, was formed in town even as early as 1795, and continued to hold meetings in different places, under the occasional preaching supplied from the adjoining Circuits. In the years 1825–6, a meeting house was built at Montpelier Centre. In 1828, the Montpelier Society was set off to the Barre Circuit and preachers from that Circuit thenceforward regularly were supplied to this Society, which held its meetings, for a considerable period, alternately in the Centre Meeting House and the Old State House in the village. But in 1837 the Methodist Chapel was erected in the village and the meetings no longer alternated, but the Society mostly then worshiped in the Chapel, the Centre Meeting House being left for the occupation of transient preachers. The Rev. J. G. Dow was the first preacher appointed to this station, though the Rev. Mr. Sneething had been sent here previous to the transfer of the Society to the Barre District. Since then the succeeding preachers, embracing a long list of faithful and laborious christian ministers, have generally been changed once in two years.

The Friends, or Quakers as they are generally called, organized themselves into a Society for meetings in 1803, and soon built a meeting house in the east part of the town, at which, though few in number, they have ever since continued to meet for worship. Of this Society the late worthy Clark Stevens was, up to the time of his death a few years ago, the leading and most unfluential member.

The Universalists have had three Societies in town,—one formed in the village in 1831; one at the Center, previously formed; and one at the East village, formed subsequently, but much the largest of the three, and proprietors of the respectable meeting house they there soon erected for their use.

The Episcopal Church was organized in this village in 1842, and the present neat church edifice erected. The Rev. George B. Manser was the first Rector, who was succeeded in a few years by Rev. Frederick W. Shelton, who officiated one or two years, and was succeeded in turn by the Rev. Edward F. Putnam, who remained till a few months before his death in 1854; when Mr. Shelton was again engaged and settled, and remains the Rector at the present time. This Society, though smaller than the Congregationalist, is yet respectable in numbers, and embraces a large proportion of our best and most influential citizens.

There was a *Freewill Baptist Church* organized in town in 1830, and the Rev. Ziba Young was, about 1840, for one year or more, its pastor. This arose perhaps from the seed planted by Uncle Ziba Woodworth. But as the followers were too few and limited in means to support preaching for any considerable time, the Society did not long keep up any living organization.

Having thus, at considerable length, given the ecclesiastical history of the town, we will now turn to other subjects.

NEWSPAPERS AND OTHER SERIALS.

As we have already incidentally mentioned, *The Vermont Precursor* was the first weekly journal ever published in Montpelier; and, as it has also been stated, this paper, by transfer from its publisher, Clark Brown, to Samuel Goss, was, in 1807, merged in the *Vermont Watchman*. In October, 1810, the *Watchman* was again transferred to Ezekiel P. Walton and Mark Goss, and by them published until the year 1816, when it became the sole property of Mr. Walton, and was published by him, or by him and his sons, under the name of the *Vermont Watchman and State Journal*, till 1853. It then became the sole property of Eliakim Persons Walton, who still continues the editor and proprietor.

In addition to the *Watchman*, the Waltons, father and son successively, have published, every year since 1817, the now well known and valuable statistical serial and calendar entitled *Walton's Vermont Register and Farmers' Almanac*, which, from the mass of information it furnishes and its general accuracy, has assumed a sort of official character, and, among business men, become an almost indispensible work in every part of the State.

The numbers published have been for many years steadily increasing till the present time, when twelve thousand copies are annually printed and sold.

The Freeman's Press, of Democratic, in contradistinction to Federal politics, which were then those of the *Watchman*, was established in 1812 or 1813, by Derrick Sibley, who was soon joined by Sereno Wright in the publication, which was continued by the two till about the close of the war of 1812, when it was discontinued.

In 1826, George W. Hill, by the aid of his brother, the noted Isaac Hill of New Hampshire, established the *Vermont Patriot*, and continued to publish the same about a dozen years, when he sold to Wm. Clark, who, in about two years, sold to J. T. Marston, Esq., who, after carrying it on about a half-dozen years, sold out in turn to Eastman & Danforth, and the latter going out of the firm in 1851, it has ever since continued to be published under the sole management of Charles G. Eastman, the present editor and proprietor.

The State Journal, an Anti-Masonic paper, was commenced here in 1830, by Knapp & Jewett, and continued by them till 1836, when the establishment became merged in the *Vermont Watchman*.

The Voice of Freedom was commenced here by C. L. Knapp, and continued until 1842, when it passed into the hands of the Anti-Slavery Society, and finally led to the establishment of

The Green Mountain Freeman, in 1843, by Joseph Poland, who continued the publication of the same, as the organ of the Liberty and Freesoil parties, till 1849, when he sold out to Jacob Scott and D. P. Thompson, the latter of whom after one year assumed the proprietorship of the paper, published it till 1856, and then sold it to S. S. Boyce, the present proprietor.

The Universalist Watchman, first published at Woodstock and then, we think, at Lebanon, N. H., was removed to Montpelier in about the year 1836, and its publication continued by the Rev. Eli Ballou, who after some years changed the name to the *Christian Repository*, under which it is still published by Ballou, Loveland & Co.

The Green Mountain Emporium, a religious monthly, was commenced here in 1838, by J. M. Stearns, published about one year, and removed to Middlebury.

The Temperance Star was commenced here in 1841, under the auspices of the State Temperance Society and the editorial care of George B. Manser, published about two years, and gave place to another Temperance and Moral Reform paper, entitled *The Reformed Drunkard*, and published by F. A. McDowell.

This also, after taking the name of *Reformer*, was in a year or two discontinued.

THE TOWN MADE THE SEAT OF GOVERNMENT.

The year 1805 was made to constitute an important era in the history of Montpelier. During the October session of the Legislature of that year, holden at Danville, the following act was passed :—

"AN ACT ESTABLISHING THE PERMANENT SEAT OF THE LEGISLATURE AT MONTPELIER.

"SEC. 1. *It is hereby enacted by the General Assembly of the State of Vermont*, That Elijah Paine, Ezra Butler and James Whitelaw be, and they are hereby appointed a committee to fix upon a place, in the town of Montpelier, for the erection of buildings for the accommodation of the Legislature of this State, and to prepare a plan for such buildings.

"SEC. 2. *And it is hereby further enacted*, That if the town of Montpelier, or other individual persons, shall, before the 1st day of September, which will be A. D. 1808, erect such buildings on the place designated by the aforesaid committee, to their acceptance, and shall compensate said committee for their services, and also convey to the State of Vermont the property of said buildings and the land whereon they shall stand, and lodge the deed of conveyance duly executed, in the Secretary of State's office; then and in that case said buildings shall become the permanent seat of the Legislature for holding all their sessions.

"SEC. 3. *Provided nevertheless, and it is hereby further enacted*, That if any further Legislature shall cease to hold their sessions in said town of Montpelier, those persons who shall erect said buildings, and convey the property of the same, and of the land aforesaid, shall be entitled to receive from the Treasury of this State the full value of the same, as it shall be then fairly appraised.

"Passed November 7, 1808.

"A true copy,

"Attest, DAVID WING, JUN., Secretary."

In pursuance of this act, the committee therein designated fixed upon, as the location of the State House, almost precssely the place which Colonel Davis, in his far-sighted calculations, had years before prophetically pointed out in his meadow as the site of the future Capitol of the State. The exact place thus fixed on by the committee was about twelve rods north-east of State Street, and just about the same distance west of the back end of the Pavilion Hotel, which brought it within a few rods of the hill as then shaped, and mostly within the State House yard as now laid out. On this spot, the necessary funds being raised by citizens of Montpelier and vicinity by individual subscription, and the necessary land given and deeded by Thomas Davis, a State building of wood, fifty by seventy feet on the ground, thirty-six feet high to the roof, septangular shaped in front, but square on the sides and rear end, was, during the years 1806 and 1807, erected and finished for the occupancy of the Legislature for their October session 1808.

The act locating the seat of government here was not obtained without some struggle among the rival towns contending for the honor and the advantage. The Hon. Cyrus Ware was the Representative of Montpelier that year, while the Hon. David Wing, Jr., was Secretary of State, and of course in attendance on the Legislature. And these two, one by his shrewd management, and the other by the exercise of his great and justly acquired influence, appear to have presented the merits of their case with such good advantage as to have secured an easy victory. Some attempts, indeed, were made at the two succeeding sessions of 1806 and 1807, held at Middlebury and Woodstock, to effect a change of the location; but they were unsuccessful. And the Legislature, for the first time, assembled in their new State House in Montpelier for the October session of 1808.

On the 8th of November, 1832, the old State House having been found inconvenient, and dilapidated at that, the Legislature, after another struggle among the contesting towns, passed a second act re-establishing the seat of government at Montpelier, on the condition that the inhabitants of the place, by the first day of January following, pay into the Treasury of the State the sum of $15,000—one half to be paid in one year, and the other half in two years from the passage of said act. And the citizens of Montpelier having given acceptable bonds for the fulfillment of the condition, and having further paid $3000 for suitable grounds round the location again selected, by Samuel C. Crafts, Allen Wardner and George T. Hodges, the committee appointed for the purpose, Ammi B. Young was appointed Architect and Lebbeus Egerton Superintendent of the building of the new State House, and the work put in train early the following spring. To obtain a sure foundation, a high, rocky spur of the hill, about a dozen rods north-west of the old site, was, by the advice of the Architect, blasted down, and at an expense of about $10,000, till a level area was obtained broad enough to receive the walls of the whole buildings, which became thus founded on a continuous solid rock. And the granite structure then arising thereon, the particular description of which has been too widely spread before the public to need repetition here, was sufficiently completed to be used by the Legislature at their October session, 1836, at a cost, then and subsequently incurred about the grounds, of $132,077 23 in the whole. This neat and durable edifice, whose plan and construction reflected great credit on the Architect, stood till the 5th of January, 1857, when it accidentally took fire, and all but its bare walls was destroyed.

At a special session of the Legislature, called for the purpose, and assembled on the 18th of February, 1857, an appropriation, after a third keen contest among rival claimants for the location, of $40,000 was voted for the rebuilding of the State House on the old site in Montpelier: " *Provided* the inhabitants of Montpelier, or any individuals, shall, before the rising of this Legislature, give good and sufficient security to the Treasurer of this State to pay into the Treasury of the State a sum equal to the whole cost of the work mentioned in the first section of this act—one half of said sum to be paid in one year, and the remainder in two years from the passage of this act, or on the completion of the work."

In compliance with the conditions of this act, a bond was executed on the 27th day of February, 1857, and before the session closed, by E. P. Jewett, G. W. Collamer and Erastus Hubbard, in the penal sum of $100,000, conditioned as provided by the act. And the Governor thereupon appointed Dr. Thomas E. Powers Superintendent of the building or rebuilding of the house, and George P. Marsh of Burlington, Norman Williams of Woodstock, and John Porter of Hartford, Commissioners to draw plans and decide whether the House should be wholly rebuilt or the old walls taken as a part. The Commissioners decided not only to rebuild wholly, but to enlarge and improve the structure by lengthening both the main building and the wings, and adopting new plans for the dome and internal arrangements. And all this being settled, the work was vigorously prosecuted during the working seasons of 1857, 1858 and 1859, so that it was sufficiently finished for the occupancy of the Legislature at their October session for 1859. The Legislature for 1858 having failed to make any further appropriation, the work was carried forward, during the spring and summer of 1859, on funds advanced by the citizens of Montpelier, who, however, were thenceforward relieved from further expenditures by an appropriation by the Legislature of 1859 of $34,000, to pay for the furniture of the House already purchased, and liquidate sundry outstanding debts arising in the course of the construction. And how far the money furnished by the citizens of Montpelier for the prosecution of the work will be refunded by the State is a question which, at the present writing, (January, 1860,) remains undecided.

MONTPELIER MADE THE SHIRE TOWN OF A NEW COUNTY.

On the first of November, 1810, the Legislature incorporated a new County, taken from the south-easterly part of Chittenden, the south-westerly part of Caledonia, and the north-westerly part of Orange Counties. To this new County, after some controversy among the interested members of the different political parties, the Legislature, in which the Democrats that year predominated, gave the name of Jefferson. This name, in the session of 1814, when the Federals had again obtained the ascendency, was altered to that of Washington, the name which it has ever since borne,—the Democrats, who the next year recovered their power, showing the better wisdom by acquiescing in the change, instead of following the example of their predecessors and opponents. The new County was organized Dec. 1, 1811, the Legislature of the preceding October having elected the Court and County Officers, consisting of Ezra Butler, Chief Judge, and Salvin Collins and Bradford Kinne, Assistants ; John Peck, Sheriff; Timothy Merrill, State's Attorney; and David Harrington, Judge of Probate. When the County was thus organized, George Rich was appointed County Clerk, and Joshua Y. Vail Register of Probate. The above named members of the Court all held their offices two years, when Charles Bulkley was elected Chief Judge, in place of Ezra Butler; Seth Putnam Assistant, in place of Salvin Collins; Chapin Keith Sheriff, instead of John Peck; Nicholas Baylies State's Attorney instead of Timothy Merrill; and Abel Knapp Judge of Probate, instead of David Harrington.

The Court held its sessions in the Council Chamber in the first State House until the year 1818, when a new wooden Court House was erected on the west side of the State House grounds, in a line with the State House. And this Court House continued to be used as such till the year 1843, when a new, but rather cheap and unsatisfactory brick Court House was erected, a little back from the corner where the present one stands ; but it caught fire and was burned during the November term of the Court of the same year. And in the summer of 1844 the present commodious brick Court House was erected, at a cost of about $14,000. To the last the citizens subscribed a handsome sum, to make the building what they believed it should be, but what the tax raised by the County for the purpose would be, they thought, insufficient to make it.

The first Court House was built by money raised from a County tax; but for the jail, the County was indebted to the liberality of the citizens of Montpelier. In the first place, the old Jail House, which was the former dwelling-house of Colonel Davis, was given to the County outright by his son, Thomas Davis, and the jail or dungeon placed within it, which was constructed of common, heavy stone, covered with broad, long, flat rocks, was built by private subscription. The County, however, at its own expense, rebuilt the Jail of granite in 1832, under the supervision of Captain Timothy Hubbard; and about the same time generously gave back one-half the Jail House to Thomas Davis, who, in the interim, had become a man of reduced circumstances. And still further to show their good faith in the return gift of 1842, the County, on erecting the present fine brick and granite Jail House and Jail in 1857, fully paid Mr. Davis for his half of the house.

CHAPTER IX.

INCREASE OF THE VILLAGE IMMEDIATELY SUBSEQUENT TO THE LOCATION OF THE STATE HOUSE. — OPENING OF STATE STREET. — CELEBRATION OF THE FOURTH OF JULY. — FIRST ELECTION DAY. — GREAT WAR MEETING OF 1812.

Montpelier, the village favored with the location of the State House, and which thus received a new impulse, began to move on apace in the increase of its population and the importance of its improvements. The building of the State House, of itself, brought quite an addition to the number of its inhabitants, and the influx of those who now came here to settle in consequence of the place being made the Capital, and in the prospect of its becoming one of the most important towns in the state, together with the necessity they created of new dwellings, stores and workshops, added, and for years still continued to add, still far more to its population, and proportionally to increase its thrift and business activity. New streets were now opened, new bridges over the streams built, and new houses, stores and other buildings everywhere erected. Well does the writer of these pages remember the appearance of the village the first time he entered it, which was on the fourth of July, 1807. State street had then been surveyed, but not opened. There had been before one bridge across the Branch, and that was at the Union House; but even that had been carried away, we think, by the flood of the previous spring. At all events, no bridge was there then. The men and women rode through the stream on horses, or in carts and wagons, and we boys rolled up our trowsers over our knees and waded across, not one in ten of us being cumbered with either stockings or shoes. The point of attraction was the new State House grounds, and our way led along the old road down the river, under the hill, where the back street now extends from the Union House to the Catholic Church. All on our left, after passing the Colonel Davis establishment, and one or two small houses on the bank to the east of it, was a smooth, broad, well-tilled meadow, covered with waving green corn. Two lines of stakes running east and west could be traced through the midst of the meadow.

"What in the world are all those stakes for, setting up so straight and curious, all in a row there?" asked one of the older, out of town boys. "Those stakes? Why they are to show where we are to have a new handsome street from the new State House right across the Branch, with a fine, elegant new bridge," replied a village boy, pricking up with pride at the thought.

"A street!" rejoined the other, "well, I wonder where they expect to find houses to put upon it? It appears to me you village folks are trying to grow grand all at once. When you get the new State House up I expect we shan't be able to touch you with a rod pole."

This natural little bout of words among the boys of that time, showed two things better than a page of elucidation;—first, the extent of the important changes and improvements in contemplation for the village, and second the starting points of the simultaneous growth of that village pride and country jealousy, which, probably, are ever in a greater or less degree to be found, wherever villages exist, to crow and affect superiority, and country towns to build up and sustain them.

When we reached the place where the then novelty of our national jubilee was to be celebrated, we found the exercises of the day were to be performed on the ground-work of the new State House, the foundation walls of which were all up, the sills and flooring timbers framed together, and roughly floored over, and the plates and some other of the heavy upper timbers ranged round the borders of this ground frame-work. Near the centre of the area thus formed, was erected a broad platform, on which was placed a table and several chairs for the orator of the day and those who assisted in the usual services; while around it, on the borders of the whole area, were erected bushes or rather small trees, freshly cut and brought from the adjoining woods on the hill, to serve for shade for the speaker and the audience. The oratar was Paul Dean, a Universalist minister, who resided in Boston, but who about that time, preached for some small period, in different parts of Montpelier.

This was the first general public celebration of the Fourth of July ever held in Montpelier. A small village celebration was however, held the preceding summer in a booth, built in the meadow near the Davis' Mills on the Branch, and Dr. Edward Lamb, wrote and delivered the oration. A few weeks after the above described celebration of the Fourth of July, 1807, the frame of the State House was raised and a large force of workmen put in requisition to cover the building and hasten on the work towards completion. During that summer also, the foundation and brick work of the present Pavilion House, were built by Thomas Davis, who finished it previous to the session of the Legislature the next year, and, as he was the first owner, so he was the first landlord of that ever since well known hotel. In the fall of the same year State Street was opened and worked through its whole length, as now located, and a good bridge built over the Branch. Early the next Spring the work on the State House was resumed and prosecuted with the utmost vigor. This work was done under the supervision of a building committee, of whom the leading member was the late Captain Ebenezer Morse, who, being a carpenter by trade, personally superintended the whole work. A head carpenter by the name of Timothy Pickering, with the hands under him, finished the outside of the building; but Sylvanus Baldwin was the head workman of all the interior work, having with him, however, an efficient assistant in Sylvester Churchill, a carpenter by trade, but now Inspector General of the United States Army.

During this, and the next year, several buildings for dwelling-houses and shops were erected on State Street, on the part west of the Branch, and still more on the part on the east side, and on Main Street, among the latter of which, were the stores and dwellings thrown up for the occupancy of four new merchants or firms—U. H. Orvis, Dunbar & Bradford, C. W. Houghton and Josiah Parks. These, in the two succeeding years, were followed by as many more, together with various mechanical establishments in different parts of the village.

By the terms of the act, locating the seat of government at Montpelier, the State House was to be completed by the first of

September, 1808. It was done ; and great were the preparations made among the villagers, and great the anticipations raised among them and through all the surrounding community, in view of the advent of the new and important day of " *Election.*" Streets were cleared of lumber and rubbish, side-walks prepared of plank or gravel, houses painted, new suits of clothes purchased, and everything made to assume the sprucest appearance. A fine artillery company uniformed throughout with plumed Bonaparte hats and the dress of field officers in all except the epaulette on the privates, was organized from among the first citizens of this and the neighboring towns, to serve as the Governor's Guard, and be in especial attendance on Election days. Of this company Isaac Putnam, a man nearly six-feet-six high, weighing over two hundred pounds, well proportiened, and as noble in soul as in body, had the honor of being chosen the first captain, and no one of those present now living can fail to recall his fine and commanding military appearance on those occasions as he stood up between his soldiers and the encircling crowd, like Saul among the people. An iron six-pounder field piece had been procured ; and a thrill of excitement ran through the excited hearts of all the boys of the community at the news, that when the election of State officers was declared on Election day, " a cannon, a great cannon, was to be fired in Montpelier Hollow !"

The eventful day at length came, and with it two-thirds of the population of all the neighboring country, fifteen or twenty miles around, came pouring into the village. But instead of attempting any further general description of the then entire novelties of the day and their effect on the multitude, we will, at the risk of the imputation of losing our dignity as a historian, again have recourse to the reminiscences of our boyhood. We were, of course, there on that day among the throngs of excited boys, congregated from all quarters, to witness the various sights and performances expected on that important occasion. A showy procession had been formed in the fore part of the day, led by the military in all the marching pomp of flying colors and rattling drums, and followed by the State officers, members of the Legislature and a concourse of citizens, and the Election Sermon had been preached by the Reverend Sylvanus Haynes, Pastor of the Baptist Church of Middletown. The House of Representatives had been organized by the election of Dudley Chase, Esq., of Randolph, Speaker ; and a Canvassing Committee appointed still earlier in the day and put to work in counting the votes for State officers. And as the hour of sunset approached, and as there had been for some hours no public demonstrations to be witnessed, a great proportion of the crowd was scattered all over the village. We and a lot of other boys were standing in the street somewhere against our present Court House, when, sudden as the bursting of a thunder clap, the whole village shook with the explosion of the cannon on the State House common. We all instantly ran at the top of our speed for the spot. When we had got about half way there, we met a gang of other boys from one of the back towns, who, taken by surprise and siezed with panic at the stunning shock, were fleeing for their lives in the opposite direction; but gaining a little assurance from seeing us rushing toward the scene of their fright, one, braver than the rest, stopped short, boldly faced about and exclaimed "Hoo! I an't a n'attom afraid!" and all now joining in the race, we were, in another minute, within a few rods of the smoking gun, which had been discharged on the announcement of the election of Isaac Tichenor as Governor. The next moment our attention was attracted by the voice of Israel P. Dana, sheriff of the county, standing on the upper terrace of the State House, and loudly proclaiming—"Hear ye! hear ye! hear ye! the Honorable Paul Brigham has been elected Lieutenant Governor, in and over the State of Vermont, by the suffrages of the freemen. God save the people!" Then another discharge of the piece saluted our recoiling ears and sent its sharp echoes from side to side between the encircling hills. Then came the announcement of the election of Benjamin Swan as Treasurer, followed by a third gun; then the last announcement of the election of Councillors, followed by a fourth gun; and then, without further official announcements, the salute of guns was continued till one for each of the States had been fired.

Such were the performances on the first Election day in Montpelier, and such the interest and excitement they created among the multitude.

As there were but three hotels in the village at that time, including the large new brick one just completed by Thomas Davis, and even these not much more than half as large as they afterwards became, a very large proportion of the members of the Legislature boarded in private families, all the best houses being opened for their accommodation. Only about two dollars per week was generally charged for board, though no pains nor expense was spared to furnish the best of tables. But this low rate of board was not disproportional when compared with other prices. The pay of the members was then, we think, but one dollar per day, the old first fee bill having then not been altered. And yet it is very doubtful whether the members did not then generally carry home more money with them, at the end of the session, than they do now with just double the amount of pay. The pay of the officers of the House and employees of the Legislature were on the same low and economical scale. And it is a matter of great interest and curiosity to compare the various expenses of the Legislature of that time with those of the present day. The first constable of the town was made ex-officio *Door-Keeper*, who for his dollar per day, did all the waiting upon the State officers and members, and, with one man, styled the *Overseer*, who was allowed not over five dollars per session, attended to the heating, lighting and sweeping of the State House, providing everything, and performing everything, then required to be done about the Legislature, the whole expense of which, over the daily pay of the Door Keeper, and the pittance allowed such *Overseer* for time actually spent, not being generally over thirty dollars per session; while at the present day, we find, in place of these, a salaried *Sergeant-at-Arms*, with his twelve or fifteen sub-officers and assistants, each receiving two dollars per day, and all going to make up a contingent expense for each Legislature amounting to more thousands of dollars than it then amounted to hundreds. The debentures and contingent expenses of the Legislature of 1808 were, in round numbers, twelve thousand dollars; in 1858, thirty-six thousand dollars, a very large proportion of which is made up from the excess of contingent expenses.

While relating events and incidents connected with, and illustrative of the history of the town, we will describe another village scene which occurred a few years later. It was in February, 1812, a few months before the declaration of our last war with Great Britain. Party spirit, which had been almost unknown in town for the first twenty years of its settlement, had for the last few years been creeping in to disturb the political, and even social harmony that had so happily prevailed among them. And by this time, all had taken firm or decided stands in favor, or against the war in contemplation by our National Government; the Democrats feeling our nation to have been grossly insulted and injured by Great Britain, warmly advocating the war; and the Federalist, professing to believe a war wholly unnecessary, as bitterly opposing and denouncing it. The Democrats were now in the ascendency in the State, and largely so in the county; and the latter, as the same bitter contest was going on in Congress, and the administration were appealing to the nation to be sustained in their war measures, considered it important and right that some great and general demonstration of their principles and sympathies with the general government, should be made at the capital of the State. And accordingly a day was appointed for such a meeting at the State House in

Montpelier, and notice of the appointment industriously circulated through every part of the surrounding country.

We have seen some rather piping political times since that period, but none, which, for intense excitement and party animosity, could at all compare with those that were everywhere exhibited on the approach of the war of 1812. Though but a boy at the time, we can now easily recall many a demonstration of party feeling in towns and neighborhoods, which we now find it difficult to make appear as a reality. There was an old man named Joseph Goodenow, one of the first settlers of Berlin, and the progenitor of the families of that name, still mostly residing on the original homestead, lying in the North-east part of the town, on the Winooski, two or three miles above Montpelier village. The old gentleman, who lived in the same neighborhood with us, was a flaming Democrat and war man. He used to go on foot to the village, very often, to hear the war news, and learn the machinations of the Tories, as he always called the Federalists. When going to the village, he was always seen walking slowly, and with two stick canes. When returning, after having got his irascible feelings kindled up by what he had heard of the Tories at the seat of news, he was generally seen walking fast and with only one cane. And once when he had been particularly excited by some important piece of war news and a personal altercation with some of the village Tories whom he had found discussing it in the streets, he was seen leaning towards home as fast as a man walking on a wager and with no cane at all.

But to return to the great war meeting. Like most other boys, we were for drums, guns, &c., and of course for the war, anyhow, and we resolved to attend: so when the day arrived, we mustered out a few boys of the neighborhood, and with them proceeded on foot, to the scene of action. As we neared the village we found every road almost literally black with the throngs of men and boys on foot, on horse back, in cutters and thickly packed double sleighs, all pouring into town and hurrying forward to the place of the appointed meeting. On reaching the State House, we found the doors just being thrown open; and, standing amidst the waiting and impatient crowd, we were borne on, in the mighty rush through the principal entrance, which was then instantly made, till we were forced up close to the broad plank platform, that had been erected over the clerk's desk for the accommodation of the opposing speakers; for it was understood, that even here, the Federalists would appear in force, to prevent the passage of any resolves going to encourage the threatened declaration of war by Congress. We now unexpectedly found ourself not only in the midst of the Democratic managers of the proceedings, but in the best possible position for hearing and seeing everything that transpired. The war party, who however were found far to outnumber their opponents, ranged themselves on the west side, and over all the front part of the representative's hall, leaving for the other party, about one-third of the room, next the south-east corner, where they defiantly took their stand, in spite of the angry and threatening looks and glances of the overpowering crowd of the exasperated friends of the administration, by whom they were on everyside now completely hedged in. At this stage of affairs, one of the numerous Democratic Committee was dispatched to invite the Reverend Chester Wright, the settled minister of the village, to open the meeting with prayer. But the messenger shortly returned and, with excited looks, announced that Mr. Wright, on account of conscientious scruples about the war, as he inferred, declined to accept the invitation. A low burst of indignation at once followed the announcement, from those who gathered at once about the messenger, while he was making it. And the next moment, the calls of "*Uncle Ziba!*" "UNCLE ZIBA!!" rose from twenty voices around, when instantly a leading committee man hastily mounted the platform and cried aloud—

"Is the Reverend Ziba Woodworth present in this audience? If so, he is respectfully invited to come forward on to the platform, and open this meeting with prayer."

Mr. Woodworth, who, as before intimated, was as ardent a Democrat as he was a Christian, and who, from his wounds at Fort Griswold, had a stiffened and crooked leg, which seemed always to become stiffer and straighter in moments of excitement, now came rapidly stumping through the crowd to the indicated stand; when, hastily drawing a chair before him, he quickly dropped down on one knee, and, throwing out the whole of the other leg with a jerk, straighter than ever before, instantly raised his sharp, ringing, and peculiarly emotional voice, in the invited invocation. After an unnsually brief introductory address to the throne of mercy, he was hurried by his feelings at once into the political spirit of the meeting, and poured forth a torrent of blessings on our rulers for their far-seeing wisdom and noble patriotism in so fearlessly taking their stand in resisting the aggressions of British tyranny. He then turned to "the enemies of the war, and the enemies of our blessed-blessed country," and began to ask God's pity on their blindness, and his forgiveness of their treasonable dereliction of patriotic duty, and still more treasonable opposition to the wise measures of our God-appointed rulers, in language which indirectly involved the rebuke of some scathing satire. At this stage of the prayer, one of our village Democrats, who was a wicked wag as well as a hot politician, and who was standing at the end of the platform within reach of the heated speaker, reached over and sharply punching his extended leg, in a low, eager, half-whispered tone, exclaimed—

"That is right! Give it to 'em—give it to 'em, Uncle Ziba!"

And Uncle Ziba did "give it to 'em," on that occasion in a manner and with a severity, which was perhaps never paralleled by anything ever heard purporting to come in the shape of a prayer.

The leading speakers of the two parties, now took their seats with their several party backers on the opposite ends of the platform. On the one side sat the small-sized, keen-eyed, ready-witted and really talented James Fisk of Barre, who was then the member of Congress for this district, and who had now come on to act as the champion speaker for the Democrats, at this meeting. On the other hand, as the champion of the Federalists, sat the large-sized, stern-looking, and ever cool and self-assured Nicholas Baylies, Esq., who had not long before settled and became one of the leading lawyers in the village, and who now appeared here with his satchel of documents, newspapers and constitutional law books, to give unflinching battle to the "fierce democracy," and everything their leaders should bring forward in favor of war measures.

A long string of resolutions, approving the course which was then being pursued by the Administration, and warmly recommending a declaration of war against Great Britain for the injuries and aggressions therein enumerated, was read and moved by one of the leading Administration men; whereupon Mr. Fisk rose and advocated the passage of the resolutions, in a long, pointed and zealous speech, which was interrupted, every few minutes, by his keenly sympathizing party adherents, in uproarous bursts of applause. Then came the turn of Mr. Baylies, who, nothing daunted by the significant opposing demonstrations around him, rose and commenced his argument for demolishing the positions of the rival speaker; and having effected his object, to his own satisfaction, he proceeded to a general onslaught upon President Madison and his legal advisers at Washington. He had gone but a short way in this part of his speech, however, before old Matthew Wallace of Berlin, a tall, resolute, intelligent Irish immigrant, who was then to this side the mountain what his countryman, Matthew Lyon, had previously been on the other side, leaped suddenly to his feet, and, in a voice that rang through the crowded room, exclaimed,—

"Can't stand that! Can't stand that, Mr. Chairman! Anything in reason, but, by heavens, sir," he added with flashing eye and brandished fist, "I shan't sit here to listen to outright treason!"

This rather brought the speaker to a stand; but after wisely qualifying his remarks, and promising more moderation in future, he was permitted to go on with his speech to the conclusion. After this, Mr. Fisk replied, and some others on the same side; when Mr. Baylies, plucky to the last, rose to close the discussion, and proceeded on to do so, till the coughing, hissing and whistling of the impatient audience drove him from the stand.

The resolutions were then again read; and the question of their adoption being put, they were passed with one tremendous acclamation, and the meeting broke up with a round of hurrahs for Madison and the war, that made the old State House shake and tremble from mudsill to reach-pole.

Such was this great and notable war meeting in Montpelier in 1812, a faint description of which we have here introduced, both because its occurrence properly demanded a place in the history of the town, and because it may be well for our young readers to know that as high as they may think party spirit runs at this day, it no more compares with the party feeling of that day than a zephyr compares with a tornado.*

*Since writing the above account of this noted war-meeting of 1812, in which we attempted only to describe what we, then a boy spectator, heard and witnessed, there have come to our knowledge several curious historical facts connected with the meeting, which may interest the political reader at least to know; and which, at any rate, it may not be amiss to add to our description.

All the leading politicians and most active members of the Federal party, of Montpelier and vicinity, had organized themselves into one of those political associations known at the time as the *Washingtonian Societies*, the more effectively to oppose the National Administration, and thwart its then contemplated measure of a declaration of war against Great Britain. And the leaders of this society in this section having seen the exertions the Democrats, who were in a majority in this County, were making to get up a large meeting to sustain and encourage the Administration, laid a scheme to control the meeting, and thus prevent any expression in favor of the war from going forth from this place. But it would seem they were destined to be caught in their own trap. Although the Democrats, at the opening of the meeting in the forenoon, happened to be in force enough to elect one of their party, the Hon. Ezra Butler, Chairman, yet scarcely was this effected before the Washingtonians entered the hall in a body, and so completely outnumbered the Democrats that not a single vote looking to the support of the Administration could be carried. Whereupon a scene of confusion ensued—both parties for a while claiming a majority vote; while the disappointed Chairman, hardly willing to trust his own senses, was heard shouting, in his usual slow, deep toned and peculiarly emphatic manner,—"*Silence* in the house—I say SILENCE!" But so warm and decided were his feelings and sentiments in favor of war measures that he could not be brought to declare any vote tending to contravene the object of his party in the meeting. And after once or twice attempting to evade declarations of votes, on account of his doubting which of the yea and nay responses was in majority, he was soon pressed so hard by the out-clamoring Federalists that he resigned his post, and left the chair empty. The Federalists then, with exulting acclamations, instantly elected the Hon. Charles Bulkley—one of the most high toned Federalists and decided opposers of the war in the whole country—Chairman of the meeting. But their triumph was of short duration. By this time the Democrats from abroad came pouring into the village, and before the Federalists were able to

CHAPTER X.

INVENTIONS. — IMPROVEMENTS. — NOVEL ENTERPRISES. — VERMONT MUTUAL FIRE INSURANCE COMPANY. — BANK OF MONTPELIER.

Between 1810 and 1830, there were undertaken a number of enterprises in Montpelier, which were of so novel and peculiar a character, and which so well bespeak the inventive genius, mechanical skill and adventurous energy of many of its individual citizens of the period, as richly to deserve a place in its history.

In 1810, Napoleon Bonaparte published to the world the offer of a reward of a million of francs to any one who should invent and exhibit to the approval of the commissioners to whom it was to be submitted, at his capital, a machine which should prove successful in spinning flax in the manner of spinning silk and cotton by water power. As soon as this magnificent offer became known in Montpelier, Mr. Elisha Town a most ingenious inventive Cabinet Maker, who had been doing a small business in that line, in the place, since about 1804, on the suggestion and with the encouragement of Sylvanus Baldwin, who was then erecting a factory to spin cotton where Langdon's mill now stands on the Montpelier side of the river, and who was one of the most scientific mechanics of those times in this section, immediately set his brains to work to achieve the great desideratum; and for the next eighteen months, day and night, waking and dreaming, was Mr. Town's brains engrossed with the important project. Rough model after model was got up, and experiment after experiment made on each, and each successively cast aside as they were found to be failures; yet nothing discouraged he persistently returned to the work of getting up new ones in full confidence in his ability eventually to accomplish the object.

pass a single vote expressive of their views, the hall was filled with the excited, war breathing friends of the Administration, who, being now an overwhelming majority, took everything into their own hands, commenced proceedings *de novo*, and proceeded and ended as above named in our description of the meeting. Esquire Bulkley, as he was universally called, did not, however, follow the example of his predecessor by resigning, but, from some pique or policy, retained the chair to the end; but was compelled to see his name, in the published proceedings, signed to the war resolutions which were finally so triumphantly passed—as much to his chagrin and that of his party, probably, as to the sly exultation of the victorious Democrats, who thus not only carried their war resolutions, but had the wicked pleasure of seeing one of the most influential opposers of the war made to give them the sanction of his name.

A few years ago the old yellow house, which stood in the place of Timothy Cross' present residence, and which was the dwelling of Sylvanus Baldwin, the consulting friend to whom Mr. Town was in the habit of coming to report progress, show parts of his experimental machinery and take advice—the old yellow house was torn down; when, in the garret, were found sundry curious specimens of parts of this machine, made in the different stages of its perfection, and of so singular a construction as to become a great puzzle to all attempting to conjecture the object of their manufacture, till Mr. Town's connection with the former owner of the house, in the construction of his flax-spinning machine, was recalled. One of these specimens is still preserved by Mr. Cross as a curiosity. It is a delicate steel spring confined to a corresponding slat of iron, opening and shutting like tweezers, which is understood to have been one of a row of the same kind, fixed in the feeder of the machine to sieze the harl of the flax and conduct it to the spindle, the great difficulty consisting in making the spindles take, and draw out the flax as they do the more adhesive fibres of cotton.

After an unremitting perseverence of a year and a half, however, Mr. Town, believing he had mastered every difficulty, and obtaining the pecuniary assistance of his friend Sylvanus Baldwin and Josiah Parks of Montpelier, and David Harrington of Middlesex, who thereby became sharers in the profits or loss of the enterprise, constructed a handsome model, a miniature machine operative by hand-power, and, in company with those gentlemen proceeded with it to Boston, to find a passage to France. Soon after arriving in Boston, where they exhibited the machine, the company sold out one quarter of their right in the invention to some gentlemen there who became confident of its success, for a sum of money sufficient to defray the expense of taking it to Europe, and divide between seven and eight hundred dollars apiece among the shareholders. Mr. Baldwin and Mr. Parks then sailed with the machine to France. But when they arrived in Paris Napoleon was absent on his great expedition to Russia, and had just reached that dizzy pinnacle of his fortunes at Moscow, from which he was soon to be hurled, never more to rise again sufficient to carry out those great plans which he had laid for the improvement of his empire. The commissioners appointed to decide on the flax spinners presented for the reward were either with him, or so much engrossed with the momentous events on which the destinies of their country were turning, that they could not be got together; and Mr. Baldwin and Mr. Parks took the machine to England. Here they sold out the whole right of the company for constructing machines in that country, for quite a large sum, but payable in merchandize, consisting mostly or wholly of nails. By that time a war had sprung up between England and the United States, and there was a difficulty in getting the nails home in the most direct manner. They therefore sent them to the West Indies, to be reshipped in some American bottom and brought to one of our ports. But the ship taking them was lost or captured, and nothing consequently ever realized, either from rewards or sales arising from the invention in Europe.

Mr. Sylvanus Baldwin, however, taking with him his brother, the present Honorable Daniel Baldwin, then working for him, went to Boston the next summer after his fruitless voyage to Europe, and commenced building a flax spinner on the old model. While Mr. Sylvanus Baldwin was there engaged on the work, he received, from Mr. Samuel Salisbury, Jr., of that city, the offer of $6000, for his right in the machine, which was about one quarter of the number of shares into which the stock had been divided. But contrary to the advice of his younger brother, he declined to accept the offer, on the ground mostly, that if the machine was to be a success, he should have an altogether greater sum, and if not, he should not like to reflect that he had taken so large a sum from a man who failed to receive any benefit from the outlay.

Mr. Sylvanus Baldwin thenceforward continued to prosecute his labors on the machine till it was nearly completed, when peace between the United States and Great Britain taking place, and with it and the dethronement of Bonaparte, the particular demand for such a machine ceasing, both in this country and France, the project was abandoned, and Mr. Baldwin, returned to Montpelier, having never received, probably, half enough to compensate him for his time and expenses. What became of this machine is now not certainly known. We recollect, however, to have once seen it stated in some public journal that it was taken to Pittsburgh, Pa., and to some extent put in operation, but not with sufficient success, probably, to warrant the continuance of the experiment. That the machine would spin very fair thread, when the flax was properly prepared, was demonstrated; but there were several little difficulties which had not been fully overcome, and which prevented the machine from being worked profitably. Had half the ingenuity and expense been laid out on it which has been devoted, through a half century of successive improvements, to cotton spinning in bringing it to its present state of perfection, it would now probably be in successful operation, both in this country and Europe.

Before dismissing this subject we cannot forbear a passing

tribute to the genius of Mr. Elisha Town, the chief inventor of the machine, the history of which we have been giving. Montpelier never produced, and it is doubtful whether the whole state ever produced, a man of a more truly inventive mind. But his book knowledge of mechanics and previous mechanical inventions, was quite limited; and he was known to have studied out principles and spent much time in building machines for their application to inventions, which, though perfectly original in him, were found, at last, to have been long before made and put in operation by others. And although he was continually getting up something new, yet we now find his name coupled with no invention of much importance, except what may attach to his flax spinning machine. Like most men of inventive genius, he was through life emphatically poor, but was ever esteemed, up to the time of his death a few years ago, a most inoffensive and worthy citizen.

The old Arch Bridge extending across the Winooski to Berlin, just above the falls, as it was the first structure of the kind ever attempted in town, if not in the whole State, and as it was a triumphant success, certainly deserves, with its Architect, a passing notice in the history of Montpelier. It was built in the summer of 1826, by Sylvanus Baldwin and Winslow & Owen, the latter being partners in house building, and the former, as we have seen by his connection with the building of the first State House and the construction of the flax spinning machine, a general mechanic of skill and information, for the times, in the practice and theory of the various applications of mechanical science. In the construction of this bridge, Mr. Baldwin was the sole projector and chief engineer. Several bridges, built on the old plan—with tressels set in the middle of the river, and two sets of string pieces—had been built at this place and swept away by the floods; and it now, therefore, became a desideratum to have a bridge here which should reach across the river with a single span. Mr. Baldwin, feeling confident of his ability to accomplish this object, undertook the job with Winslow & Owen, for the insufficient sum of $1800, which had been voted for the purpose by the towns of Montpelier and Berlin. In due time the structure, at the close of a hard day's work, was pronounced finished; while it was further announced that the next morning, after breakfast, the slight tressel supporter in the middle of the stream, on which the bridge appeared to rest, would be knocked away, when it would be seen whether the fabric would stand, or, as had been often predicted, come down with a crash into the river. At the appointed hour the next morning, many curious citizens were seen wending their way to the spot, and among the rest the quaint and witty old Judge Ware, who, on being asked where he was going, replied that he "was going to see what a splash Deacon Baldwin's new fangled bridge would make when it tumbled into the mill-pond." When they reached the bridge they saw the supporting tressel-work still standing in the middle of the river, and for a while stood expectantly awaiting the action of the workmen which was to afford them the expected spectacle. After listening to their predictions with a knowing smile, and enjoying their manifestations of doubt and boding expectation awhile, Mr. Baldwin invited them down to the edge of the water under one end of the bridge, where a near and clear view could be obtained of all underneath; when, to their surprise, they saw that the top-most piece of the blocking, laid on the plate of the tressel to shore up the bridge while building, had already been removed. Mr. Baldwin had slyly been there alone, an hour or two before, and knocked out eight or ten inches of the upper part of the blocking, and the bridge was now hanging, by that distance, perfectly clear of all support from beneath, not having settled an inch on the removal of its apparent supports. And from that day to this, now going on thirty-four years, this noble and workman-like structure has neither given way or settled, but stands as firm and safe, to all appearance as it did when it was finished and opened for travel.

This was the monument which Mr. Baldwin, while conferring a great public benefit, reared for himself in Montpelier. And few have left a prouder memorial. But these visible proofs of the genius and general character of Sylvanus Baldwin are not the only things which should cause his memory to be cherished by the citizens of this town. He was the first chosen Deacon of the Congregational Church in Montpelier, and ever acted well his part in sustaining the religious and moral interest of our village community; while his amiable disposition, unvarying urbanity, liberality in all benevolent movements, and all objects on foot for social advancement, made him highly esteemed at home, and respected wherever he was known abroad. He removed to the West soon after building this Arch Bridge, and died near Columbus, Ohio, about ten years ago.

During the summer of 1827 was started the novel and since somewhat widely noted enterprise of boring for salt water in Montpelier. The origin of this enterprise is traceable to the following circumstances:

Salt, about that time, which was before the day of cheap transportation by railroads or canals, was from three to four dollars per bushel; and reflecting men among our citizens were very naturally casting about in mind for the means of lessening this great tax on our inland community for the supply of this indispensable article. They were aware of the existence of salt springs, opening at the surface, in Western New York, not over two hundred and fifty miles distant in a direct line from Montpelier, and the open mineral springs, in which salt is a considerable component, at Saratoga, only about one hundred miles distant. And they had further learned that in Ohio and Pennsylvania, just about as far west of the surface salt springs of Western New York as Montpelier is to the east of it, salt water had almost always, by sinking wells, or boring down by machinery to different depths, been abundantly obtained. And to add to the probability that salt water might also exist at no unapproachable depth beneath the surface here, the fact was called to mind that there was reputed to have been a salt lick spring about two miles above Montpelier, on the borders of the farm of Daniel Thompson, in Berlin. And as a better authority than the writer of these pages, who could testify to the old tradition about this spring being once a salt lick, and could also vouch to the brackish taste of its waters at the present time, an old hunter, by the name of Thomas Gaylord, had been consulted and found ready to declare that while hunting in the locality, before any settlements were begun in this section, his attention was attracted to this spring by the well beaten moose and deer paths which he traced to it, and that on approaching it he found the hard earth and mud all around it beat and poached up by the feet of these animals as thoroughly as the ground by the feet of cattle round a spring in a cow pasture. The geological formations of the place were also examined, by the aid of the best treatises on the subject then extant, when it was ascertained that most of the salt beds, or the springs coming from them, thus far discovered, had been found located in secondary lime stone formations, often alternating with sand stone, and generally in the vicinity of extensive clay beds, and sometimes in the neighborhood of primitive granite ranges. And here in Montpelier, all along the borders of the hills south of the Branch and east of the river, extended the required clay beds; and just over the river on the west appeared abundance of the secondary lime stone; while in sight, a few miles distant, towered ridges of the primitive granite. Thus all the indications seemed to combine to show the probable existence of salt, or salt water, somewhere beneath us.

While these enquiries and speculations were going on, the Hon. Daniel Baldwin, of this village, received a letter from a friend, of the name of Jesse C. Smith, formerly of this place, who had seen people successfully engaged in boring for salt water near Pittsburgh, Pa., and who suggested the probability that salt might also be found by boring at Montpelier; whereupon Mr. Baldwin, with the concurrence of a few spirited individuals, wrote on to his friend to send on some competent person to make an examination of the indications of subterranean salt water at this place. And in pursuance of this request, a Mr. Patrick Finley, who had bored several of these salt spring wells in Ohio, in due time made his appearance, went into a careful investigation, and reported that the geological formations and other indications of salt, were much the same here as in Ohio and Pennsylvania, where salt water had been obtained, and that he thought circumstances warranted the attempt of boring for it at Montpelier.

On this, Mr. Baldwin set to work in getting up a company for the purpose; and he soon succeeded in obtaining one of about sixty subscribers, who organized, employed Mr. Finley, assisted him in getting up the requisite water power machinery, and set him to boring down through the rock with steel drills and spruce pole shafting, at a spot still to be found on the east bank of the river, about equi-distant from the old paper-mill and the abutment of the Arch Bridge.

By the journal kept by Mr. Finley, and now lying before us, we find he got all his machinery (which was very simple, consisting mostly of a contrivance for alternately lifting and letting fall the shafted drill by means of a water-wheel,) in operation, and commenced boring on the 8th day of August, 1827. And from that time the work was prosecuted, with occasional respites and interruptions, caused in extricating drills or shafts becoming fast in the operation, until the 4th day of January, 1830, a period of two years and nearly five months. For the first two years the boring was conducted principally by Mr. Finley, and afterwards, a large proportion of it at least, by Thomas Davis and his son, Norman Davis. At the date last named, the drill, or some of the shafts, by loose stones or some other means, become wedged in so tightly that no power could be applied sufficient to draw them out; and the work consequently had to be abandoned.

The whole depth obtained, at this time, as appears by the footings found on the journal, was *eight hundred and fifty feet*, and all the way, except an occasional interstice shown by the sudden sinking of the drill a few inches, through continuous solid rock.

It had been the intention of the company to prosecute the experiment until the depth of one thousand feet had been reached; and but for the accident, which brought the work to its final stand, this would doubtless have been done, in despite of the fruitless expense already incurred, which was thirty-five dollars on each of the sixty shares of the stock, making a total outlay of $2,100 00.

This expense appears to have been cheerfully paid by the shareholders, and was not probably by most of them ever regretted. For many of them were actuated by scientific objects, deeming the expense well incurred with the view of ascertaining, even if nothing else was gained, the rock formations and mineral substances existing in the earth beneath us here at Montpelier. And in this, at least, they were fully gratified. Every time the drill was withdrawn for cleaning out the well, or drill hole, the sediment was drawn out, the kind of rock of which it was composed ascertained, and the result entered on the journal. These cleanings were made about twice a week, and the journal furnishes, therefore, a pretty correct knowledge of the kind of rock to be found every ten feet, or oftener, all the way down to the bottom of the perforation.

By these records it appears that the rock formations, for the first seventy feet, consisted of a hard or soft slate, the hard slate sometimes running into impure lime, with an occasional seam of white flint or quartz. Then came a layer of ten feet of sand stone, then forty-one feet of soft slate, then another ten feet of sand stone. From one hundred to two hundred feet the formation consisted of alternating layers of slate and lime, with two seams of sand stone occurring in the distance. From two hundred to three hundred feet, the formation become almost wholly blue lime. Then was found three feet of flint and lime intermingled, and then a layer of five feet of white sand stone. From this depth to the bottom of the well were found alternating layers of lime and slate, the slate soon running into lime, and the lime more and more predominating, with no other rock through the whole distance to vary the formation.

At the depth of four hundred feet, we think—for there being no record of the circumstance, we can only speak from recollections founded on what we heard stated in our frequent visits to the works—the drill suddenly broke into a cavity of the depth of five or six inches, and in a few moments a copious stream of water gushed out over the top of the drill hole. One or two small springs had been encountered before, and one or two afterwards, but the latter not sufficient to vary very perceptibly the volume of water here found, or to modify its taste or quality. This water was not pure soft water, though it seems difficult to decide what renders it otherwise. It appears to be of a septic or corrupting quality, not very dissimilar in taste to the water of springs impregnated with bog iron ore and rotten wood. We boiled down a few quarts of it to half a gill, but with no other result than to show that it contained no salts of any kind, which could be detected by evaporation. The dirt and rubbish lying over the mouth of this perforation was last summer removed under the direction of our enterprising citizen, James R. Langdon, about two hundred feet of the old shafting of the drill drawn out, and a lead pipe inserted, from which may now be seen running the same old spring in a volume of about an inch in diameter, which would probably be twice as large, but for the obstruction of the shaft still remaining wedged in below.

Such is the history of the attempt of boring for salt at Montpelier, which has often been lightly treated by the unreflecting, but which has ever been regarded by the reflecting and scientific, with much interest, and with a disposition to honor the chief projector and his associates in the laudable undertaking; for it has given them a correct knowledge of the rock formations to a great depth of this central part of Vermont, which otherwise had never been obtained; and as to the main object, it is by no means a settled thing, that, had the intended, or a greater depth, been attained, salt water could not have been found. The formation was becoming, at the lower portion of the perforation, one of continuous hard lime stone, which is known to be full of cavities and often of very extensive fissures, through which the salt water, even admitting no salt to be indigenous to the locality, might have found its way from its great central fountains in western New York.

During the years 1827 and 1828 was also started and established an association, which was destined to result in the most extended and important institution in the State. This was the VERMONT MUTUAL FIRE INSURANCE COMPANY. The company was incorporated by the Legislature in October or November, 1827, and organized in March, 1828. James H. Langdon was chairman of the meeting of organization, and D. P. Thompson Secretary. A board of Directors was then chosen, and the Hon. Daniel Baldwin was chosen the first President of the company, and Joshua Y. Vail, Esq., the first permanent Secretary. But Mr. Baldwin declining, the Hon. Chapin Keith of Barre, was chosen in his place, and held the office about one year. Hon. Israel P. Dana of Danville, was next chosen the President, and held the office till 1838. The Hon. John Spalding was then chosen President and held the office till 1841, when the Hon. Daniel Baldwin was chosen; and, this time accepting, he has continuously filled the office of President from that time to the present, a period of almost twenty years. Mr. Vail continued to fill the office of Secretary of the company to January 1850, when Charles Dewey was chosen in his place, and has continued to hold the office ever since. The Treasurers were changed often during the first fourteen years of the existence of the company; but in 1842 James T. Thurston was chosen to the office, and has ever since been continued the Treasurer of the company.

This institution became, even from the first, under the regulations then adopted, a safe and a measurably prosperous one, but after the accession of Mr. Baldwin to the Presidency, it seemed at once to start ahead upon a new career of prosperity; and under his able financial and prudential management, together with that of the efficient Treasurer and Secretary, soon after elected, it has continued to grow steadily and rapidly, till the number of policies issued now stand at 93,416, the amount of capital, or premium notes now in force, $1,596,492 41, and the amount insured and now at risk, $20,622,809; thus making it, when the capital is compared with the risks, probably the safest and best grounded Fire Insurance Company in the United States.

The old Bank of Montpelier, about this time, or rather the year before, in October 1826, was incorporated with a capital of $50,000, and went into operation in 1827, under the Presidency of Hon. Elijah Paine, who was succeeded by James H. Langdon, Timothy Hubbard and John Spalding; Thomas Reed, C. R. Cleaves and George Howes having been the Cashiers. It was rechartered with a capital of $75,000 in 1840, and the charter extended in 1853.

CHAPTER XI.

CONCLUDING VIEW OF THE VILLAGE FOR THE PERIOD FROM 1800 TO 1830.—STATE OF MORALS AND THEIR REFORMATION.—TRADE, ITS IRREGULARITIES AND REFORMATION. — THE MONEY MAKING PERIOD OF THE VILLAGE, ETC.

HAVING thus, in the three or four preceding chapters, noted the principal events, the starting of new and peculiar enterprises and the establishment of new institutions, marking the history of the town, during what may properly enough be called its second period, extending from 1800 to 1830, we will now return for a cursory view of the condition of its society in the interim, its moral progress and reforms, and the progress and reforms of its trade and manufactures.

A village is like a school of children and youth. When the school is small, it is an easy task to preserve order and good behavior. The few who may be viciously inclined are, as in a family circle, immediately confronted by an equal or greater number of those of an opposite character, by whom they are restrained from exposing their secret propensities, either in their own acts or in tempting the few others at hand of the intermediate class, whose facile characters might otherwise render them obnoxious to bad influences; so that the voice of authority is scarcely needed to restrain the free inclinations of the generally well disposed little group, in preserving order and ensuring good and virtuous conduct. But when that school is swelled into large numbers, the viciously inclined, measurably freed from the immediate restraining presence of the good, and finding more of the like evil propensities to countenance them, and more of the facile, whom they can covertly draw into their train, still further to strengthen and give them courage in misconduct, this school-house community soon becomes filled with confusion and projects of mischief or vice, which demand a strong reforming hand to bring it into the condition required for its own good, and to prevent it, indeed, from falling into a state of utter disorder and ruin.

And so it was of the village—not the whole town—of Montpelier, during the forepart of the period now under consideration.

As the village increased in numbers, and the prospect became more and more certain, that it would become one of the largest and most important places in the State, it was constantly receiving large accessions, not only from mechanics and tradesmen, who were willing to get their living by honest industry, but from quite as many, perhaps, who came to make their living out of others, by the unscrupulous exercise of such means as should be found best calculated to effect the object. Among these, to be sure, were many who were not vicious in their habits, and who adopted unscrupulous means only to accomplish their objects of ambition, in the acquisition of wealth or to reach positions were they could lord it over others; but among them, also, were many who came to make enough only to indulge depraved appetites and seduce enough others to make them the victims of their designs, or the companions of their vices—the one being necessary to support them in their courses, and the other to keep them in countenance and prevent them from being singled out for particular marks of reproach by the virtuous part of community.

And from the natural operation of all these agencies, it was not long before the industrious and orderly first settlers and founders of the town, found their village in a rapid process of moral deterioration. The taverns became common and constant resorts, inviting to idleness, money spending, and all sorts of dissipation. Rum drinking rapidly increased, bringing along with it the usual train of street broils, acrimonious quarrels and keen litigations. Gambling was a common practice; libertinism found but too many victims in the unsophisticated, unsuspecting and therefore unguarded female community. All these stained the records of week days, while the sabbaths were generally desecrated by horse racing, match shooting, street games, holly day amusements, visiting and pleasure parties.

It needed a moral Hercules to meet and grapple with these social deformities, which were so nearly threatening both the temporal and eternal welfare of this strangely blinded or strangely thoughtless village community. And a moral and religious Hercules was at length found in the Reverend Chester Wright.

A movement in the right direction, however, had previously been made by a small band of the more religious and moral men of the village and town, who met, and by resolution associated themselves together, under mutual pledges to take all due and reasonable measures for the observance of the Sabbath, and for getting up religious meetings on that day, and, whether preaching was to be obtained or not, to see that some kind of religious exercises were performed, and that their influence should be exerted to secure the attendance of their families and friends.

And in the winter of 1808 Mr. Wright was invited to spend a short period here in preaching, which being prolonged, there was formed, in connection with his ministrations, in the following July, a regular Congregational Church, that in the first instance consisted of seventeen members, but which during the year was increased by the addition of a dozen more. Mr. Wright, who in the meantime had received a call by this church and society to become their permanent preacher, was ordained according to the ecclesiastical usages of the denomination, on the 16th of August 1809, to be the regular pastor of their church and people.

From this time the church and congregation steadily increased; religious revivals occurred at comparatively brief intervals; attention to religion and religious institutions became predominant in the public mind; the arm of vice became more and more paralyzed, her votaries more and more abashed and scattered, open immoralities more and more unfrequent, until the village of Montpelier, redeemed and regenerated through the blest instrumentalities of the affectionate and untiring labors of the devoted, self-sacrificing and high-souled Father Wright, at length took its stand among the most moral and orderly communities in the State.

While the moral delinquencies and inequalities of which we have spoken were in progress, the condition and character of trade and traffic were fast becoming such as justly to incur, according to their relative importance, an almost equal reprobation and to demand an almost equal reformation. The profits of trade on all imported articles had been in the first place enormous. An average of nearly one hundred per cent. clear profit was probably realized on the sales of all imported goods by the merchants, for the first ten years after stores were opened in the village. Such profits, it is true, were gradually lessened by the competition created by incoming traders, who, to gain their share of custom and distance their rivals, would put their wares at a lower figure, and thus compel the old traders, if they would retain their customers, to come down also. But what the buyers gained in price was too often lost by the tricks and unfair dealings of the sellers. The latter in their avidity to make up for loss of profits and monopolize custom, would sell by no general or established rule, and abide by no established prices. They traded, to use the cant phrase of the times, as they "*could light o' chaps.*" An intelligent and influential man might perhaps purchase at comparatively reasonable prices; but the next uninformed or poor man would be made to make up, by the prices demanded, what, through motives of policy, had been conceded to the former. Boys and girls could not be sent to trade with the merchants without the liability of being cheated. Needy men, who could not command the money, or were depending on their yet ungrown produce to pay for their goods, would be wheedled into purchases at enormous prices, and under promise of lenity of payment; and within a month, perhaps, a sheriff would be sent after them to attach their crops. Sheriffs and constables, indeed, in the employ of the different competing firms, with their pockets full of writs and executions, were always on the alert, and, at particular seasons of the year, might be seen, thickly as the Arabs of the desert, scouring the hills to be first in for the plunder, or, "for want thereof," to drag the victims to jail on executions.

But while the character of trade was thus reaching its worst pass, a man was growing up in the village whose good fortune and praise it was to be the chief instrument in reforming its abuses and irregularities. That man was James H. Langdon. As soon as he had set up trade for himself, which was about the year 1807, he established for his store the one price system; and while he determined that he would sell his goods as low as any others, he also determined that the poor man and stranger should fare as well in their purchases as the best of customers. He also at once wholly repudiated the cruel and outrageous system of suing and grabbing which had been so commonly practiced by the merchants in the place. He further soon reduced trade, in all its bearings and principles, to a better, and, for the purchaser, a far safer system than had ever before here prevailed. And in this he was efficiently aided by the intelligent, discriminating, and upright John Barnard, who was for many years his book keeper and chief clerk, and who eventually became his partner. The books of the establishment were consequently always found correct, the prices charged exactly corresponding with the prices agreed on at the time of the purchase. All this the people were not long in discovering. To their surprise and gratification, they soon found that they could send a boy or girl, or any indifferent person, to the store, and obtain as good bargains as could have been obtained had they been present to make them for themselves. And when they came to settle, everything on the books was found as it should be, and no reasonable man ever went away dissatisfied. The fruits flowing from the adoption of, and steady adherence to such a system, at such a crisis, were, before long, made on all sides, abundantly manifest. Custom from all classes poured in to Mr. Langdon, as custom never poured in to any merchant in this part of the country before. Men saw that he was conferring, by his course, a public benefit, and preferred to trade with him, not only for their own safety and advantage, but to reward him for the benefaction thus conferred on community. Nor was this the only effect and public advantage, arising from Mr. Langdon's commendable system and general fair dealing. All other merchants and traders soon found that they could not much longer secure confidence and patronage, without adopting the same course of fair and liberal dealing, and the same regular system. And the result was, that in a few years, the character of trade underwent a revolution, and the mercantile profession became thereafter essentially reformed and elevated.

And in looking back on events, agencies and public results, developed during this period, in matters connected with the most important interests of our people, morals and trade, we cannot help regarding Chester Wright and James H. Langdon to have been, in their respective spheres of action, and through the various enduring influences they exerted while living, and their examples have to this time continued to exert since their death, the best benefactors the town of Montpelier has been so fortunate as ever to number in the long list of its worthy or distinguished citizens.

The period of which we have been treating might have been properly termed the transition state of society, alike in moral, mercantile and social relations. The first crude, unassimilated elements, had all the while been gradually arranging themselves and settling down into fixed and permanent conditions. And during the last half dozen years of that period, the process had been in a great measure completed. We have seen how the moral and religious character of the village had been reformed and put on a new and respectable footing. We have seen also how the character of trade had been reformed, systematized and brought under the government of more legitimate and honorable principles. Let us now glance at a few of the most important of the results of the progress made under these improvements, as they stood developed at the end of that period, in the year 1830.

The Congregational Church had become large, active and influential, four hundred and twenty-eight members having been admitted under the ministrations of Mr. Wright, a large majority of whom were then resident, living, laboring members. A Methodist Church, respectable in numbers, and earnest workers in the duties of their profession, had also become firmly established and was disseminating its good influences. Sabbath Schools, under the auspices of both these churches, had been formed, embracing the greater part of the children and youth of the village, and were regularly and generally well attended. Societies for religious and benevolent purposes, had been established and were effectually prosecuting the objects of their formation. The animal enjoyments, boisterous or vicious amusements of the former times, had given place to more quiet, virtuous and rational recreations; and the refined and intellectual were now prevailing over the rough and sensual, in the general tone of society. A Village Library of several hundred well selected volumes had been established in 1814; and a Lyceum, with another and still more choice library, had been started in 1827, and were now in successful operation, affording alike instruction and entertainment to all classes of the people, continually softening the asperities and monopolizing selfishness of the businesslike character of the place, and diffusing beneficent and elevating influences, not only through our village community, but to a good extent, over all the surrounding communities of the county and state.

And while all that goes to make up good and enlightened society had been so favorably progressing, trade and all kinds of legitimate business had been making an equal or greater progress and increase. There were now, besides the several smaller and less permanent ones, eight extensive, well established mercantile firms or individual establishments for retail of dry goods and groceries, whose annual sales amounted to from twenty to fifty thousand dollars apiece, making an aggregate of sales, with those of the smaller concerns in the place, of the probable amount of two hundred and fifty thousand dollars a year alone. This was on the sales only of articles imported; and if to this were added the amount of the sales of produce and other articles exported, that sum would have doubtless been swelled to nearly a half million of dollars. This was the golden period for trade in Montpelier. Railroads had not then been built, to revolutionize trade, and form direct communication between the cities and the larger farmers and the small stores or leading posts scattered over the neighboring country. Montpelier then commanded nearly all the trade for a distance of about twenty miles in extent in every direction around, and a good proportion of it for nearly double that distance. The profits were still large, trade was not then overdone by competition, and the amount of it for such an interior village was immense. And it was during that period that the present fine capital of the village was mainly acquired. James H. Langdon alone, within a space of twenty years, rolled up a fortune of about one hundred and twenty thousand dollars, and certainly no fortune was ever more fairly acquired.

But the class of stores we have named by no means embraced all the business establishments of the place. One or more book and stationery stores and drug stores, for the last twenty years, were always maintained, shoe-stores, tin and iron ware stores, hatting factories and stores, and grocery establishments, had long been in operation to make out the full variety of trade and business generally to be found in the largest class of interior villages.

An extensive tannery had been established as early as 1806 by Silas Cobb, who was succeeded after a few years, by Elijah Witherell, who carried on the business for a much longer period, on the same ground latterly occupied by the more extensive tannery of Keith & Peck. A cotton factory in 1810 had been fitted up in the old Oil Mill built by Larned Lamb five years before, on the Montpelier side of the river falls, though it was destroyed by fire near the close of the year 1813. A Paper Mill had been previously built on the same falls and kept in operation by the elder Silas Burbank, till 1818; when that also was burned, with Richardson's Clothing Works, but before many years rebuilt and carried on a long time by Goss & Cobb, who sold out to E. P. Walton & Sons. A Woolen Factory had been built about 1820, by Araunah Waterman and Seth Persons, on the North Branch Falls, and kept in successful operation by them until that likewise was unfortunately destroyed by fire, in March 1826. Clothiers, Wheelwrights, Cabinet-Ware, Blacksmiths, Painters, Goldsmiths, and all other Mechanics' shops, needed to meet the wants of the people, might have then been found, in short, still further to swell the business and increase the growth and prosperity of this stirring and ambitious village.

There were at this time six or seven different lines of daily, tri-weekly, or semi-weekly stages coming into this place. The stage on the great thoroughfare from Boston to Burlington and Montreal, drawn by four, and often six superb horses, and every way finely equipped, run by that justly noted stage contractor and hotel keeper, Mahlon Cottrill, (whose horses and stage equipments were doubtless the finest ever known in New England,) arrived, heavily loaded down with passengers, every day from Boston and Burlington, making, in fact, two arrivals of stages on the same day on this important line. A stage from Barton, and another from Danville, arrived here every other day; while stages from Johnson, Topsham, Chelsea and Waitsfield arrived at least twice a week. Most of these staid over night, and all long enough to dine their passengers. These stages consequently brought a large and constant influx of the more monied class of people, who tarried in the place at least long enough to leave considerable sums of money every week, not only with the hotel keepers, but with the merchants and traders, in the various purchases which necessity or fancy might prompt them to make while in the place. All this, with the continual arrivals and departures along all the principal roads of large baggage teams, coming in with produce or returning with heavy articles of merchandise, combined to make, when added to our usual business, very lively and prosperous times for the village of Montpelier—far more lively, and even, we had almost said, far more prosperous than they have ever been since the opening of the railroad, which she had so drained herself in aiding to put in operation.

CHAPTER XII.

NEW INSTITUTIONS ESTABLISHED BETWEEN 1830 AND 1860:—FOUNDERY, FACTORIES, BANKS, INSURANCE COMPANIES, TELEGRAPH AND EXPRESS OFFICES, FIRE DEPARTMENT, NEW CEMETERY, UNION SCHOOL.—OPENING OF RAILROADS, AND THEIR EFFECTS; AND THE DIVISION OF THE TOWN.

WE now come to the last period into which, for convenience of arrangement, we have divided this town history. And we will endeavor to take up in chronological order the principal new enterprises, improvements and public institutions which were carried out and established between 1830 and 1860, but which have been left undescribed, or have been only incidentally mentioned in the course of this work.

An extensive *Iron Foundery and Forge* was erected and put in operation, on the easterly side of the Branch Falls, in 1832, by Alfred Wainwright, then late from the Foundery firm of the Wainwright Brothers in Middlebury. A good and profitable business was done at the Foundery in this village by Mr. Alfred Wainwright for many years, and nearly up to the time of his death in 1852; when the establishment passed into other hands, and, in connection with a Machine Shop, has been continued under various new proprietors to the present time.

A large *Woolen Factory*, in a three story building, about eighty by forty feet, built for the purpose, was put in operation, also on the easterly side of the same falls, in 1837–8, by Horatio N. Baylies, who, alone or in company with C. W. Storrs, carried on here quite an extensive business in woolen manufactures, employing twenty or thirty hands; when the establishment passed into the hands of Mr. A. W. Wilder and son, and later into the hands of that son, Artemas W. Wilder, and an uncle in Massachusetts, by whom it was converted into the largest lumber manufacturing establishment ever existing in town, and still remains so under the management of the new firm of Wilder & Wheeler.

An extensive *Woolen Factory*, with all the accompaniments for carding wool, picking, dying, &c., was established, in 1839, by Maj. Nathaniel Davis, an early settler and relative of Col. Jacob Davis, on the falls on Kingsbury Branch at North Montpelier. The buildings were large and extensive, the chief one being three hundred feet long and three stories high. A large number of hands, male and female, were employed, and for some years an apparently prosperous business was done; when a gentleman from a neighboring town, of more pretensions and extravagance than fitness for the business, or integrity of character, bought himself into the company, and the consequence was its speedy failure, and the almost total ruin of the fine estate which Major Davis had been a life-time accumulating by his honest industry. After this, the establishment went into the hands of Judge William Martin, for creditors or himself, and somewhere about 1850 was purchased by the enterprising and business-like Walter Little, who soon put the establishment on a prosperous and productive footing, which, by his good management, he continued not only to sustain but yearly to improve, up to the time of his death in 1858; when the concern went into the hands of his son, by whom it is still conducted.

This important manufacturing establishment, together with the stores, post-office, common mills, and the shops of the various mechanics, that have been latterly springing up there, has made North Montpelier a thrifty little village of several hundred inhabitants, and the centre of quite a handsome amount of business. Long previous to the establishment of this factory, as we should perhaps have before stated, Major Davis, for many years, carried on an extensive business as a merchant at his residence in the vicinity of that village, and his store and house were, at one time, a fashionable resort for trade and visiting, for a large tract of the surrounding country, including even to a considerable extent, the great village of Montpelier. And we should have also stated that, at the falls of North Montpelier, Mr. Amasa Bancroft, one of the first settlers of the town, who died about 1817, established the first forge for working iron by trip-hammer ever erected within the town of Montpelier, or as far as we know, within the present limits of Washington county.

A very pretty and thriving little village has also, during the last thirty years, been springing up round the falls of the Winooski, at the place formerly known as *Daggett's Mills*, and latterly as the village of East Montpelier. Here, for many years, a Post Office has been established and continued, a store, tavern, and several mechanic shops have been sustained, which, with the mills of a longer standing, have made this place, likewise, one of considerable importance in the town.

At the place now known as *Wright's Mills*, on the falls of the North Branch, three miles above Montpelier village, which furnish the most safe and efficient water-power on that stream, and one of the most advantageous to be found on any stream in the county, another little village has latterly been springing into existence. These remarkable falls have thus far been improved only by the Machine Shop and Mills of Medad Wright, Esq. But capital is only wanting to make this a place of great business; for a supply of water might here be taken from the mill-pond in a flume or canal and safely extended down along the bank of the Branch, sufficient, in the greater part of the year, to accommodate a line of factories a quarter of a mile long, and drive ten times ten thousand spindles.

The *Vermont Bank*, the second institution of the kind established in Montpelier village, and therefore indicative of the increasing amount of business in this and the surrounding communities, was incorporated November 11, 1848, with a capital stock of $100,000, divisible into two thousand shares, and the subscriptions therefor to be opened within six months, under the directions of Daniel Baldwin, Julius Y. Dewey and Edward H. Prentiss of Montpelier, David P. Noyes of Morristown, John A. Page of Danville, George W. Collamer of Barre, and Roderick Richardson of Waitsfield. And the aforesaid commissioners having, in the early part of 1849, opened the subscription books and allotted the shares among the subscribers, according to the provisions of the act of incorporation, the Banking Company was organized by the choice of a Board of Directors, of whom Hezekiah H. Reed was appointed President. Mr. Reed's successors have been George W. Collamer and Roderick Richardson, both now for many years residents of Montpelier, and the latter being now the incumbent of the office in question; while John A. Page was from the first appointed the Cashier, and has been continued in the office uninterruptedly to the present time. This Bank has ever done a prosperous business, and has generally been able to boast of as clear a record as any bank in the State.

The State Bank was organized, at Montpelier, under the general banking law, April 3, 1858, with a capital of $100,000, and put in operation on the 5th day of the May following. Of this Bank James R. Langdon has thus far been the President, and is understood to be the principal owner of the stock. The redemption of the bills is well insured by deposits with the State Treasury, of Vermont six per cent bonds, mortgages and United States Treasury notes. But the circulation has not been permitted to be large, and it may not be intended for a permanent institution.

The National Life Insurance Company was incorporated November 13, 1848, with a capital, at first, of $100,000, but which, by an amendment of the act of incorporation, in 1849, was reduced to $50,000, and the company located at Montpelier. The company was organized in the winter of 1850, by the election of Hon. William C. Kittridge of Fairhaven, President, who held the office about one year, and was succeeded by Dr. Julius Y. Dewey of Montpelier, who has ever since been the President. The first regularly appointed Secretary, who, by the usages of such institutions is also made the Treasurer, was Roger S. Howard of Thetford, who resigning was the same year succeeded by James T. Thurston; and he, in turn resigning, was succeeded by George W. Reed, who has ever since held the office.

The number of policies which, to the present time, have been issued by this successful Company are 2,644, insuring lives on amounts from $500 to $10,000. The number of policies in force Jan. 1, 1860, was 1,150, insuring the amount of $1,754,296. The whole amount insured from first to last is $3,490,047. The whole capital and accumulations are $250,000.

The number of policies issued each year has, with the exception of 1858—following the commercial revulsions attending the close of 1857—gone on steadily increasing, and the institution promises to become one of still greater prosperity and importance.

The Vermont and Boston Telegraph Company was also incorporated at the October session of the Legislature in 1848, and a station established at Montpelier, in connexion with an *Express office of Cheney & Co.*, of Boston. The Telegraph and Express office was accordingly opened the next year in the Montpelier Railroad Depot; and the two enterprises have ever since been in successful operation, and doing an increasing business, under the direction of Mr. H. D. Hopkins, the Express Agent at this place.

The Farmers' Mutual Fire Insurance Company, located at Montpelier, was incorporated November 13th, 1849, and that day, November 14th, 1849, duly organized by the election of

Hon. Azel Spalding, President, and the Hon. Joseph Poland, Secretary, and Samuel Wells, Esq., Treasurer. Mr. Spalding held the office about three years, and was succeeded by William Howes, who removing from town in 1853, was succeeded by the Hon. George W. Bailey, of Middlesex, the present incumbent. There have been no changes thus far in the offices of Secretary and Treasurer, Mr. Poland and Mr. Wells having retained their respective offices, and had the chief management of the concerns of the company up to the present time.

The whole number of policies issued by the company is 26,340. The whole amount now at risk is, in round numbers, about $13,-000,000; the amount of premium notes now inforce is $568,807 27. Besides a gradual and healthy increase from the outset, the books of this company show an amount of insurance business for the past year of 1858, nearly double that of the previous one. They have therefore good reason for considering their Institution a success, the extent and safety of which is demonstrated by the statistics they are able to show, as above given.

The Green Mountain Mutual Health Association, located at Montpelier, was incorporated November, 1851, and was organized the following winter by the choice of F. F. Merrill, President, Seth Thompson, Secretary, and Dr. Oren Smith, then of Montpelier, later Professor in the Medical School at Burlington, and now of Chicago, the examining physician of the company. But it did not prove very successful, on account of the want of patronage among the healthy and honestly industrious, and the multiplicity of petty frauds practiced upon it by the dishonest unhealthy and lazy; and after it had been in operation a year or two the whole enterprise was abandoned.

The Fire Department. In 1814 the first Fire Company was organized in town, the sum of $380 raised by subscription among the citizens of the village for the purpose, and an engine and hose purchased. In 1835 another company was formed, and a second engine purchased. And in 1837 a third engine was purchased, with about eight hundred feet of hose; and a third company was organized to man it, with a hook and ladder company to act generally. About this time the whole Fire Department was reorganized, and placed under the direction of the Hon. Daniel Baldwin, who was appointed Chief Engineer. Mr. Baldwin acted in this capacity many years, and, at length resigning the responsible post, was succeeded by Carlos Bancroft, who in 1852 was succeeded by Captain Almon A. Mead, who has ever since been the efficient Chief Engineer of the Department. In January, 1860, two large Button engines were purchased, and companies organized to manage them.

The Fire Department of this village has been eminently successful, and has unquestionably already been instrumental in saving hundreds of thousands of dollars of property. And now, with its five engines, nearly two thousand feet of hose, ladders and all other needful equipments, and with its almost three hundred firemen to work and manage them, is probably the best and most efficient Fire Department in the State.

Green Mount Cemetery, lying on the northerly bank of the Winooski, about one mile below the center of Montpelier village, was established and prepared for use in the years 1854–5. The act establishing it, and vesting its superintendence and management, at the outset, in a Board of five Commissioners, was passed at the October session of the Legislature of 1854. The act was accepted by the town at their March Meeting in 1855, and $5000 placed at the disposal of the first Board of Commissioners, who, by the terms of the act, were made appointable by the town, and were now made to consist of Elisha P. Jewett, Hezekiah H. Reed, Charles Reed, James T. Thurston and George Langdon. During the spring and summer ensuing, the work of enclosing, laying out, grading and ornamenting the grounds, purchased of Isaiah Silver for the sum of $1,210, and consisting of about forty acres of land, was so vigorously prosecuted, under the directions of Mr. Daniel Brime of Roxbury, Mass., and Mr. Patrick Farrelly, the first and second engineers, both acting under the immediate supervision of the Commissioners, that the Cemetery was deemed sufficiently completed to open it for dedication and use on the 15th of September, 1855.

The origin of this beautifully located and singularly variegated Cemetery is to be found in the will of the late Calvin J. Keith, Esq., of Montpelier, who died on the 23d of September, 1853. Mr. Keith, a single man, who had acquired a handsome fortune in his profession of the law and settling estates at the South, had made his will, by which, with bequests of money, gold watches and other valuable keepsakes to his numerous circle of particular personal friends, and liberal sums for parsonages, the Sabbath School libraries of the churches of Montpelier and Barre, and for the library of the Washington County Grammar School, he bequeathed the sum of "One thousand dollars, to be expended in purchasing a suitable place for a burial ground in Montpelier, and in enclosing and planting trees in the same; and request that my executors and Constant W. Storrs be Trustees of the same, and lay out the ground into lots, and dispose of the same at reasonable prices, reserving a portion to be given gratuitously to the poor."

This bequest was executed in the manner above described, as

was also another appropriation made by the testator, in connection with his above named bequest, of $500 for a monument to himself, to be erected by his executors ; and accordingly a chaste and handsome monument now adorns the central and front part of the grounds, suitably inscribed to him personally on one face, and on the other designating him as the originator of the Cemetery.

The Cemetery was dedicated on the 15th day of September, 1855, by a set of exercises prepared for the occasion—all original, all prepared by citizens of Montpelier, and all of a high order of excellence. These were a chant written by Mr. H. D. Hopkins, and performed by the musical choir led by him ; reading of appropriate passages of Scripture by Rev. F. D. Hemenway, Minister of the Methodist Society ; prayer by Rev. W. H. Lord, Pastor of the Congregational Society ; address by Rev. F. W. Shelton, Rector of the Episcopal Church ; presentation of deeds by H. H. Reed, Esq. ; dedication by Rev. W. H. Lord ; and an original hymn by Charles G. Eastman, Esq., sung to the tune of Old Hundred. This hymn is so fine in conception, and so neat and beautiful in execution, that it cannot but make an acceptable close to our remarks on this subject.

"This fairest spot of hill and glade,
Where blooms the flower and waves the tree,
And silver streams delight the shade,
We consecrate, O Death, tc thee.

Here all the months the year may know
Shall watch this 'Eden of the Dead,'
To wreathe with flowers or crown with snow
The dreamless sleeper's narrow bed.

And when above its graves we kneel,
Resigning to the mouldering urn
The friends whose silent hearts shall feel
No balmy summer's glad return ;

Each marble shaft our hands may rear,
To mark where dust to dust is given,
Shall lift its chiselled column, here,
To point our tearful eyes to Heaven."

The new Union District School House and *Academy* building was commenced in the spring of 1858, and completed early in the summer of 1859, under the constant personal superintendance of the Hon. Roderick Richardson. The edifice is about one hundred feet long by forty-five, in the main body of the building; with a central projection in front setting out twelve feet in width, extending thirty-three feet in length, and rising to the same height as the rest of the structure. It is three stories high above the basement, which is of granite, while the whole superstructure is of brick, with cast iron window caps and other ornaments, the whole making an unusually handsome and imposing exterior. The two first occupied floors are divided each in to four more or less extensive school rooms, and the upper one is devoted to a large hall for general examinations or other public exercises, connected with the Union School or the Academy. The whole building, with its furnishing, cost nineteen thousand dollars.

While the building was in progress, the four common school districts, acting under powers granted by a general statute some years ago, for the purpose, united and organized one Union School District, with the object of establishing a graded and High School, to be kept in the new building, each district, however, retaining its old organization. And about the first of September, 1859, the new institution was put in operation in the the new school house, together with the Washington County Grammar School, the latter occupying distinct and separate apartments, and remaining, as heretofore, under distinct and independent teachers.

All the scholars of the village, numbering, with those coming in from abroad, about four hundred on an average, have thus far attended in the different graded departments, and in the Grammar School. There are now in employ eight different teachers in the whole establishment, two in the Grammar School and six in the Union School, all well qualified and competent for their respective posts, and combining to furnish, from the most primitive, to the highest and most classical studies, facilities for education scarcely exceeded by any schools, except the Colleges, in the whole of New England. Among the first movers of this great project was the late H. H. Reed, Esq., who left one thousand dollars for such a purpose; and, as in the case of the Cemetery, the impulse thus given was doubtless not a little instrumental in causing the work to be prosecuted to its final triumphant accomplishment.

The Vermont Central and other Railroads may now demand our consideration, so far as they have operated to affect and change the amount and character of the business of the town.

The Vermont Central Railroad was commenced in 1846 and opened for travel and freight, from Connecticut river to Burlington, in the latter part of the year 1849. The only other Railroad that can have much affected our business relations, is the Connecticut River and Passumpsic, which was opened two years afterwards.

Ten years before the Vermont Central Railroad was commenced, there was not probably one man in a thousand in the

State, who could have been brought to believe that a railroad could, or at least ever would, be constructed through this, the heart of the Green Mountains. And now it is difficult to tell how soon that object would have been accomplished, but for the long continued, untiring exertions and indomitable energy of one man, the late Governor Charles Paine. And even after the practicability of the object was demonstrated by surveys, the stock would never have been taken but for the great miscalculations which the railroad men of that day appear to have made respecting the vast expense required to build a railroad through such a mountainous country as this, and but for the almost equally great miscalculations of the expense continually required for the repairs and the running of the road after it was finished. On the calculations then presented, it appeared to be demonstrated that the stock would be a profitable investment; and it was therefore taken with the double object of benefiting the country and making money. But experience has shown that the calculations then made were strangely fallacious, and that the expense not only of construction, but of repairs of the road, machinery and running, were nearly double what had been estimated. The Central Road was no doubt built at a great disadvantage by borrowing money at high rates of interest and large sums as undoubtedly uselessly expended on pieces of the road partially wrought, found impracticable and abandoned. But all this does not account for the steady sinking of the price of stock till it resulted in a dead loss to the purchasers, so far as money was concerned, of all they had invested in the enterprise; for so it happened with the Rutland Railroad, and all other railroads built through such a rough country, and one furnishing comparatively so little travel and freight to sustain them and compensate for the vast outlays of their construction. The stocks of all such roads are now worthless. But though the railroad enterprise has here resulted in great individual loss to all who contributed their money towards it, yet the general benefits it has brought to the country at largely have been unquestionably important. Here, again, however, another great mistake appears to have been made in regard to the class of community most to be benefited by the opening of railroads. The inhabitants of the villages bordering the line of the road, supposing it would cause a large increase of the trade and business of their respective towns, taxed themselves to the utmost of their means, and often far beyond them, in contributing to the enterprise; while the farmers, seeing few or no prospective benefits from it in store for themselves, hung doubtfully back and took scarcely any stock, though, as the matter resulted they should have been the very ones to have taken the lead, and contribute the most liberally in the whole movement: for, if there is one thing more palpable than another in the business world, it is the fact, that the villages have built the railroads and the farmers have reapt all the great benefits.

Some kinds of trade, it is true, have been increased in Montpelier village, since the opening of the railroad. The purchases of produce for transportation by cars to the cities, consisting mostly of articles which before would not pay for transportation, such as potatoes, hemlock bark and other heavy products, have unquestionably greatly increased in amount, if not doubled.

One of the two stores which, for many years, have been established at the Railroad Depot in this village, has latterly done a business, in the sales of both exported and imported articles, of full fifty thousand dollars per year on an average, while the business of the other will average nearly forty thousand dollars. The opening of the railroad by affording facilities for the cheap importation of Western Wheat, has led to the establishment, through the business tact and energy of our enterprising citizen, James R. Langdon, of one of the most extensive sets of flouring mills to be found in New England. The sales of the flour, corn meal and feed of these mills, which have capacities for turning out three hundred barrels of flour per day, amount generally to very nearly or quite, a quarter of a million of dollars a year. The opening of the road also has led to the establishment of extensive lumber manufacturing establishments in Montpelier and vicinity, the largest of which are those of Wilder & Wheeler, in this town, and of Putnam & Whitney, on the North Branch, in Middlesex, whose mills are constantly exporting immense quantities of boards and other kinds of prepared lumber, which would never bear transportation before the opening of the railroad.

The retail trade of the village, however, as well as most kinds of mechanical business, has, we think, unquestionably been diminished. The trading establishments that have sprung up, and the Depots of Northfield and Waterbury, have mainly cut off important avenues of our trade in those two quarters; while the stores springing up at the various stations on the Passumpsic Railroad, have considerably clipped our trade in parts of Orange, Caledonia and Orleans counties. And the general result has been that out village trade and business has been greatly changed and revolutionized, but the amount done, counting that, and the greater part probably, which has more directly inured to the benefit of those out of the village, has undoubtedly been much larger since the advent of the Railroad era.

But, as before intimated, the class which have been by far the most benefited by the opening of the railroads are the agricultural portion of the community. In the first place, their farms, for many miles back on each side of the line of the railroad, have risen in value and marketable price far beyond all former precedent, those nearest having within the last ten years nearly doubled their values, and those more remote risen to proportional prices. The cheapness of transportation of their produce, making a great annual saving of money formerly lost in freightage, and the great rising of the prices of all products in the city markets, mainly through the effects probably of the influx of California gold, have made the period last mentioned a golden one for the farmers. They have gone on steadily advancing in thrift and wealth until they are now, as a body, the most forehanded and independent class of community. The nearly twenty thousand acres of land comprised within the present limits of East Montpelier, which a dozen years ago would not have commanded over fifteen dollars per acre, or in the whole the sum of $300,000, would now be valued at twenty-five dollars per acre, or in the whole the sum of half a million of dollars. And with the increase of the value of their farms, their stocks of cattle, horses and other domestic animals, their farming tools, their buildings, and especially their purses, have fully kept pace with the march of improvement. This state of things, indeed, seems to have almost entirely reversed the relative positions of the farmers and the villagers. Once the farmers, even of the better class, were content to have the prices of their products dictated by the merchant and tradesman; now they dictate their own prices. Once they were found humbly asking the merchant and trader for leniency in the payment of their debts, or at best, of the balances of trade that were generally found against them; now the debts and balances are found on the other side, and the farmer, to the petition of the trader, carelessly remarks—" Why yes, that balance may stand, and perhaps I can let you have a few hundred dollars more, but I shall expect about nine per cent." Once the farmer came into the village with his old work horse, plain harness and plainer sleigh or wagon; now he comes with his two hundred dollar horse, the best plated harness and the gayest and most costly sleigh or wagon, with corresponding equipments. Once the farmer's son's highest aspirations were to be a merchant, his daughter's to be the wife of a villager; now the son " don't know about going into the small business of measuring out tape," and the daughter looks clear over the head of the counter-jumper. In short the villagers have had their day, and the farmers are now having theirs.

We now come to an event which we would have gladly been spared the necessity of here recording. We mean the compulsory division—compulsory certainly so far as regarded nearly half the inhabitants of the whole town, and the portion who inhabited a vast preponderance of its territory—the compulsory division of the town by act of the Legislature of 1848.

Few will now deny, we suppose, that, with some complaints of the villagers in regard to a temporary inequality in the distribution of high-way taxes, and the standing inconvenience to which they were subjected in going up to the Center to attend Town Meeting—few will now deny that this division was effected by political considerations. But the particulars character of the appliances then used to accomplish the object are now, perhaps, of too little consequence to justify an attempt to describe or recall them. Let the remembrance of them pass away with the transient afflatus that blew them into such strangely successful action. The more tangible facts connected with the transaction are simply these:—The territory set off under the name of East Montpelier comprised more than four-fifths of the territory of the whole town; and the inhabitants occupying it comprised about two-fifths of the whole population, or fourteen hundred and forty-seven in East Montpelier to the twenty-three hundred and ten in Montpelier. There was a petition for the measure got up in the village, and, under the influence of various arguments, political and financial, signed by perhaps a majority of its legal voters, who, with a few exceptions, were of the same politics which largely predominated in the Legislature to whom it was addressed; while there was a remonstrance got up in the part proposed to be set off, signed by nearly the whole mass of the legal voters of all parties, together with a respectable minority of the legal voters of the village. No vote of the town was taken on the subject previous to the movement, and no public notice was given of applying for the proposed division; nor was the bill permitted by the petitioners to be so framed as to allow the voters of either division ever after to act on the question of adoption or rejection of the measure. And on this state of facts, the Legislature assumed the power and responsibility of passing the bill making an unconditional division of the town, and thus arbitrarily breaking up this old chartered corporation, in which the inhabitants therein embraced, and ever to be embraced, had been perpetually guarantied their franchises under one undivided municipality.

It is not necessary now to enquire how far this act, setting off the great body of the territory of the town in the face of the united remonstrance of its inhabitants, would be found constitutional, when tested in the Supreme Court of the United States. Suffice it to say that not another such an instance of the exercise of arbitrary power, in regard to town corporations and their chartered franchises, can be found to mark the legislation of Vermont; and but one other, as far as can be ascertained, in the whole confederacy of States, and that solitary instance was involved in a similar division of the town of Memphis, in the State of Mississippi.

The town from this era in its affairs became, of course, divided into two distinct, independent municipalities, and has so ever since remained. But as we commenced necessarily with an account of the whole of this noble township, and have had the gratification of rightfully treating it as such up to this late stage of our work, and as both its parts are still connected by the bonds of one common charter, we shall not now imitate the legislation we have been questioning, by breaking our history into two pieces, but pass on to the end as we begun, and as if no division had ever been effected.

CHAPTER XIII.

FIRES, FLOODS AND THEIR CASUALTIES, TOGETHER WITH FATAL CASUALTIES IN VILLAGE AND TOWN SINCE ITS SETTLEMENT.

Fires, &c.—The number of really disastrous fires, which have occured in Montpelier, either in the village or the town at large, has fortunately been small. Few villages of the size, indeed, have been more favored in that respect than ours. The first one that ever took place, it is believed, was in 1801, when the first frame school house, standing near the west end of the old burying grounds on the Branch, accidently caught fire and was consumed. For the next dozen years, we find no report of any destruction of property by fire. There might have occurred several small fires, during that period; but, if so, they were of so insignificant a character, comparatively, as to have passed out of remembrance. In the month of December, 1813, however, a fire occurred which involved a severe calamity, as it resulted in the entire destruction of the large two story cotton mill, that had been for some time, in successful operation, at the river falls, not far from the site now occupied by the old Paper Mill. In 1815 the dwelling house of Seth Parsons was burned, at a loss perhaps of $1,500.

December, 1818, a Paper Mill and Clothing works occupying the same ground on which stood the cotton factory, was burned, with a loss of about $4,000. In 1822, the blacksmith shop of Joseph Howes was burned. In 1822, the old Academy building was totally consumed by fire. In March 1826, occurred, considing the loss of life and the personal injuries it involved, the most calamitous fire, perhaps, ever experienced in Montpelier. The Woolen Factory and Grist Mill, on the falls of the North Branch, owned by Araunah Waterman and Seth Parsons, caught fire about day-break, and was totally consumed, causing a loss of many thousand dollars to the proprietors.

While the fire, which, when discovered, had gained too much headway to leave much hope of saving the factory, was raging in one part of the lower story, Mr. Waterman, Mr. Joel Mead, and Robert Patterson, a leading workman in the establishment, made their way to the upper story and fell to work to gather up and throw from one of the windows what cloths and stock they supposed they might have time to save. But the fire below spread with such unexpected rapidity, that before they were aware of any danger, the fire burst into the room, cutting off their retreat downwards by the stairs and even preventing access to the windows the least elevated from irregular ground beneath. At this crisis Mr. Waterman, closely followed by Mr. Mead, made a desperate rush through the smoke and flame for a window in the end of the building next the Branch, stove out the sash with the heel of his boot and threw himself half suffocated through the aperture to the rough and frozen ground or ice some thirty feet below. Mr. Mead followed in the perilous leap, and they were both taken up nearly senseless from the shock, terribly bruised and considerably burned in the face and hands. But none of their bones were broken and they both in a few weeks recovered. Nothing more was seen of the fated Patterson except his charred skeleton, which was found in the ruins after the fire subsided. For some reason he had decided not to follow Mr. Waterman and Mr. Mead in the only way of escape then left open to them, and the next minute probably perished in the smoke and fire which must then suddenly have enveloped him.

In May, 1827, a two story wooden building, standing on the site of the present Lyman building, and then owned and occupied by Wiggins & Seely as a store, was burned, causing a loss of probably not over two thousand dollars.

In April, 1828, a Paper Mill owned by Goss & Reed, of Montpelier, but situated at the falls on the Berlin side of the river, was burned, occasioning a loss of about four thousand dollars.

In 1834, the Oil Mill and Saw Mill, in the former of which was W. Sprague's Machine shop, standing also on the Berlin side of the river, but mostly owned and worked by Montpelier men, were both wholly burned.

In February, 1835, the first Union House, built by Colonel Davis, about forty-five years before, caught fire about midday, and was entirely consumed, occasioning a loss of probably about three thousand dollars, the furniture being mostly saved.

For the next seven years, the village appears to have enjoyed a happy exemption from all destructive fires, or fires indeed of any kind, except perhaps that of some worthless shantee, or such as caught and were extinguished before any but trifling damage was sustained.

But in 1842, the dwelling house of O. H. Smith, Esq., caught fire and the roof part of the building was destroyed

In 1843, the new brick Court House standing near the present one, was burned, but the records and files were mostly saved; and here was another and still larger exemption of the ravages of the devouring element.

In 1853, the dwelling house of Harry Richardson, near the Union House, was wholly destroyed by fire.

In 1854, the building of Ira Town, occupied by him as a Goldsmith's shop, and standing on the present site of A. A. Mead's shop, was burned in part, and the adjoining building of the Patriot Office considerably injured.

In 1854, also, the roof part of the upper story of Walton's Bookstore, was destroyed by fire, and but for the timely striking of a shower on the excessively dry roofs, that whole block of wooden buildings would probably have been destroyed.

In 1854 was burned a two story houe standing back of Masonic Hall.

In 1855 a barn belonging to Araunah Waterman, was burned.

January 6th, 1857, the State House, which was being warmed up on the eve of the septenary Constitutional Convention, caught fire from the furnace, and all but the empty granite walls, with their brick linings, was destroyed, and all the contents except the Library, which was got out, and the books and papers in the safe of the Secretary of State's office, a few articles of furniture and the portrait of Washington, was reduced to a heap of ruins. Within the same year also two small houses were burned near the brick yard and one near Keith's ledge.

In 1858 a new one story house of one Cookson, standing on

the road leading from the cooper's shop north, through the great pasture, was burned; and, in the beginning of the next year, another building erected by the same man, and on the same spot, was also burned down.

In December, 1859, the large three story brick and wood, second Union House, valued at about five thousand dollars, was entirely destroyed by fire with a portion of the furniture, making the loss several hundreds more.

By this list of fires, which is the most full and complete we have been able to obtain, and which certainly embraces every fire of any consequence that ever occurred in Montpelier village, we make the whole number to have been, from the first settlement of the town to 1860, but *twenty-four;* and the amount of property destroyed, except that of the State House, which was public property, according to an estimate we have made as we passed along, will clearly come within the sum of $50,000. Was ever a village of the size, in this respect, more signally favored?

In connection with the village fires, may be appropriately named the fatal casualty, which occurred from an explosion of gunpowder in the store of Erastus Hubbard, in the fall of 1849. It was on election day, and Mr. Hubbard, or his clerk, was weighing out a parcel of powder to some one of the promiscuous crowd in the store room, and around the door. Powder had doubtless been scattered on the floor, in filling the can from which the amount called for was being poured into the scales; and one or more persons were smoking cigars in the room, when suddenly a terrific explosion followed. Two men were so burned and fatally injured that they survived but a short time, and one or two others were sadly maimed. Mr. Hubbard's life, in consequence of the burns then received, was for months despaired of, but he finally recovered, though wearing the palpable marks of the accident to this day. The second floor of the building was hoisted by the force of the explosion about six inches from its place, and the store was set on fire, but the flames were soon extinguished with little additional damage.

Two fatal accidents from the use of gunpowder occurred, also, in blasting out the rock for the foundation of the second State House. Elisha Hutchinson, of Worcester, was struck down dead, near the Insurance office, by a stone thrown by a blast on the ledge about thirty rods distant; and John W. Culver, a mechanic of Montpelier, was, the same season, struck at the distance of twenty rods and killed, by a wooden roller placed over the mine to prevent the stones from flying; while a young man by the name of Tucker, from Calais, one of the workmen on the

State House foundation, was so injured by one of the blasts that he lost his eye-sight and his prospects were ruined for life.

The fires out of the village, and through the rest of the original township have been still fewer, and have involved the destruction of a less amount of property even in proportion to the population. The following is the fullest list we can obtain, and must comprise all the fires of much importance, and nearly or quite all of every kind that have ever occurred.

In August 1813, the barn of J. B. Wheeler, Esq., with most of his crop of new hay, being struck by lightning.

In the winter of 1816, a School House on East Hill, while the school was being kept by Shubael Wheeler.

In about 1820, the dwelling-house of Abijah Howard, about a mile from the village.

In 1824, the two story house of the late Hon. David Wing, on the present farm of Nutt and Wing. About the same period, a blacksmith shop, and also a small house at the Centre village.

In 1829, a dwelling-house of James Gould, in what is called the Gould neighborhood.

In 1840, the dwelling house of Simeon Nash on the road from East village to Plainfield.

In 1847, the two story hotel, known as the Merrill Williams tavern, at East village.

In 1848, the School House in the Wheeler district.

In 1849, the barn of John Gallison, with considerable hay and five horses and colts.

In 1849 also, the dwelling-house, barn and sheds of Charles Burnham.

In 1852, the Union store at East village. At about the same period, the old Hamblin house near the Centre village.

In 1854, the dwelling house of Orrin Slayton.

In 1854 also, three barns of Orlando F. Lewis.

In 1858, the School House in Henry Nutt's School District. Also the dwelling-house of Clark Templeton.

In 1859, the blacksmith shop of George Lewis, at East Village.

These make in the total nineteen in number and involved a destruction of property, according to the rough estimate we have made, of about $14,000.

Floods, &c. We have already mentioned, in one of the few first chapters of this work, that, two or three years before the first settlement of Montpelier, or somewhere about the year 1785, there was a very remarkable flood in the valley of the Winooski, in which the water in that river in this vicinity, rose many feet higher than that of any flood that has ever since occured. From incontestible indications, it appears that the water in that unprecedented rise of the Winooski, rose some three or four feet higher than the highest parts of State Street. This would have submerged nearly every acre of the whole of the present site of Montpelier Village, to depths varying from one to a dozen feet, from the rise of the hills on one side to that of the corresponding one on the other side. Should such another flood occur what destruction of property must ensue?

Floods filling the channels of the river and branch to the tops of their banks with overflows in all the lower places, were of almost yearly occurrence during the first twenty years after the settlement of the town. But the first one that fairly overflowed the banks and came into the streets to much extent, occurred, as far as we have been able to ascertain, in the summer of about 1810. The water at that time submerged all the lower parts of Main and State Streets, and in bursting over the western bank of the branch, just above State Street Bridge, tore out the earth near the bridge to an extent that rendered the street nearly impassible for wagons, and left, on the subsiding of the flood, a pond hole of water six or eight feet deep and twenty in diameter, on one side and extending to the border of the street. Into this hole one of the lawyers blundered on a dark night, sometimes afterwards, as we recollect from the circumstance that the wags of the village dubbed him for the time, *Walk-in-the-Water*, in allusion to the name of an Indian chief, who, about the same time, had in some way become known to the public.

In this hole, was subsequently drowned, from falling in during a dark evening, Carver Shurtleff, a little man with a big voice, noted for two things, his expertness in flax-dressing, and his propensity for trading in dogs.

On the 24th and 25th of March, 1826, there was, on the breaking up of the river, an unusually high spring flood, which swept away the old trussel bridge leading across the river to Berlin, and undermined and at length carried off the grist mill of James H. Langdon, on the Berlin side. This flood occurred in the night, and was entirely unexpected. Probably less than a dozen people witnessed it and can testify to the imminent peril in which many families were placed. As the ice broke up in the river above Langdon's mill, it formed a dam upon the piers of the bridge and the bridge itself, and almost the entire flow of the river was turned through what is now Barre Street and the lower part of Main Street, in a compact body like a wall or a large wave. My informant saw it coming near the Shepard tavern, was forced to run with all speed, and found no refuge until he reached the portico of the Union House. Fortunately this change in the course of the river lasted but for a few minutes, else many houses would have been undermined and swept off. The bridge gave way, and with it the dam, taking a part of one of the paper mills, and the river wall of Langdon's grist mill, and on the following day the grist mill fell into the stream.

On the 5th of September, 1828, occurred the first of what are usually called the two great floods, at Montpelier village. After nearly three days of almost continued rain, which grew more and more copious every day, and ended with an excessively heavy and prolonged shower on the night of the fourth, the water rose four or five feet higher than had been known since the town was settled. Nearly the whole village, including cellars, streets and ground floors, was inundated. Two bridges and a barn, on the north branch, were wholly swept away, and fences, wood-piles and lumber along the banks of the streams were very generally upset and carried down stream; while the damages to provisions and goods, in the cellars of stores and dwelling-houses, must have amounted to a large sum. The office of the writer of these pages was then in Langdon's great brick building at the corner. His boarding place was at W. W. Cadwell's on the opposite side of the street; and a pretty correct idea of the depth of the water may be had in the fact, which we distinctly remember, that at noon, when the water had attained its height, Mr. Cadwell came for us in a skiff, and running it into the entry way leading to the offices on the second floor took us in from the third stair, and rowing us across the street and into the front hall landed us on the fourth stair leading to the chambers of his own house, where the cooking for the family on that day could only be done.

The second, and still greater of these floods, took place on the 29th of July, 1830. The character of the preceding rains had been very similar to those of the other great flood; but the water rose full six inches higher, and ran over the window sills and into the lower rooms of several houses around the head of State street. The two lower bridges over the Branch were again swept away. The office building of Joshua Y. Vail, on State Street, was floated off and lodged in a low branching tree near the present Episcopal Church, from which it was afterwards lowered down and drawn back to its old stand. Two other small buildings standing near the bank of the Branch, were carried down stream and wholly broken up in the rapids below the village. Much damage in various ways was also occasioned by this great flood. But it was marked by the still greater calamity of the loss of life. Nathaniel Bancroft, of Calais, a middle aged farmer of considerable property, was unfortunately drowned. But, by way of showing the circumstances under which this melancholly casualty occurred, as well as demonstrating the depth and extent of the overflow of our streets, we will again beg leave to refer to personal remembrances. We then resided near the easterly end of Main Street, on the swell where Carlos Bancroft now lives. Towards noon, at the height of the water, we threw together a few plank in the edge of the water which came to the foot of that rise, about ten rods from the Loomis house, near the residence of Dr. Charles Clark, mounted our rude raft with a setting pole, and sailed through the entire length of Main Street to the end of the Arch Bridge over the river. When about midway on the voyage, Mr. Bancroft, with one or two others from the same quarter, who had come down to see the flood, rushed past us on the side walk, which was covered with less depth of water, all evidently much excited by the novelties of the scene, and, regardless of a wetting, making their way through the water as fast as possible towards the corner, where the greatest damage was expected to occur. As we were nearing the old Shepard tavern stand, a pile of wood at the north-easterly end of the barn, began to rise, tumble and float away in the strong, deep currant, which here made from the street through by the way of the barn towards the confluence of the branch and the river. At this juncture, the luckless Bancroft, who had by this time just reached a dry place before the barn door and stood eating a cracker, rushed down into the water with the idea of saving some of the wood; and not being aware how rapidly the ground fell off here, he was in a moment beyond his depth, and sunk to rise no more. When his body was recovered twenty or thirty minutes afterwards, his mouth was found full of half masticated cracker, and life was gone beyond all the arts of resuscitation. It is highly probable, indeed, that he was strangled at the outset, and, as others have been known to do under peculiar circumstances, died almost instantly.

There have been numerous partial overflows of the streets, at various times, filling up grocery and other cellars, and doing injuries to bridges, mills and other buildings, by sudden winter floods, and the consequent breaking up, and daming of the ice in the streams, within, and above and below the village. Among the best remembered of these winter floods, was one that suddenly occurred in February, 1825, in the middle of a night preceded by a remarkably warm and heavy rain. There was a ball at the Union House that night, and as John Pollard, of Barre, with his sisters and others, were returning from the ball, their team became completely imprisoned on a little knoll in a road about a mile above the village, by monstrous blocks of the disrupting ice of the river, which were being driven with amazing force into the road immediately above and below. The party escaped to the hills and the ladies waded through the snow, two feet deep, to a house half a mile distant, while the team was not extracted till the next morning. Another sudden breaking up of the ice occurred in January, 1840, in the evening, after an unusually warm and rainy afternoon. The ice, having broken up in the river above, was, under the impetus of the rising water and a strong south wind, driven through the whole length of the mill pond, three-fourths of a mile in about ten minutes. But it was suddenly brought to a stand at the narrowing of the channel at the arch bridge, when half the whole river was thrown over all the lower part of Barre street; and, for a short time, all the buildings on that part of the street were in imminent danger of being swept away. Before much damage was done, however, Mr. Langdon's mill dam was crushed down and forced away beneath the tremendous pressure of the ice above, when the river at once fell back into its ordinary channel.

Montpelier village ever has been, and ever must be, liable to damage from floods. And the clearing up of the country on the streams above will not lessen, but increase such liability. When the lands lying along the slopes of rivers are covered with forests, the earth, made porous by the roots of growing trees, the rotting timber, the beds of leaves and the mosses spread everywhere over the ground, take up, like a sponge, the falling water, which consequently is at first mostly retained, and will flow off into the streams with comparative slowness. But clear up these slopes and remove all these absorbents, and the water is almost at once thrown into the main stream, and goes rushing down towards the outlet, in a volume proportionate to the quality of water which has fallen. The valley of the North Branch, which lies in the form of a trough, is now being largely cleared of its forests, and when it shall be wholly cleared up, except the usual reserves of woodlots, he must be a bold philosopher who would guarantee our village against disasters from floods coming down on us in that direction. And the village will never be effectually guarded against such disasters, till they have built high, strong walls along each bank of this stream, and extended the width of the channel to at least one-third more than its present dimensions.

Most of the casualties that have occurred in Montpelier, involving a loss of life, have been, like those above mentioned, in deaths from drowning, though not the most of them at times of floods. In about 1824, Mr. Theron Lamphere, though an excellent swimmer, was drowned in the mill-pond, while attempting to swim over from Captain Hubbard's hay field, at the close of his day's work at night, to his home on the Berlin side, was drowned, probably, through the effects of a fit of cramp seizing and sinking him in the last part of the passage, as the next morning he was found dead, with his hand firmly clenched upon a root at the bottom of the river, within a few feet of the bank on the Berlin side.

During the early part of the winter of 1857—8, a Mr. Williams of Middlesex, who had become partially insane, and of wandering habits, threw himself through a break in the ice into the flume of Langdon's mill, and was drowned, though the fact was not known till the next spring, when his body was found in the flume. And about the same period or before, a man, not a resident of this town, drowned himself by forcing his way through a hole in the ice in the North Branch a mile or two above Montpelier village.

In August, 1859, a promising son of Charles Lyman, Esq., of this village, aged about twelve years, was unfortunately drowned at the mouth of Dog River, while bathing.

There have been two other fatal casualties in Montpelier village, which, though not caused by any of the various agencies of fire or water, may here as properly as elsewhere be mentioned.

Somewhere about the year 1828, a laborer, by the name of Mead, from Middlesex, was killed by the falling of a heavy body of earth or clay from the excavated bank, under which he was engaged in filling a cart a short distance in the rear of the house of W. W. Cadwell, Esq. About the year 1840, an Irishman was killed in a fight with one of his countrymen, which took place near the old Arch Bridge, in this village; and the homicide we believe was tried and sent to the State's Prison, but in a few years pardoned.

There have been, as far as we have been able to ascertain, from first to last, as many as four persons killed within the whole township of Montpelier, by the falling of trees. The first was, as mentioned in one account of the deaths in town previous to 1800, a little girl old enough to attend school, a step daughter of Benjamin Nash, in the east part of the town. She was approaching her father, wholly unnoticed and unknown to him, while he was cutting down a tree in the border of the woods near his house, when the tree fell in the direction in which she was unconsciously making her way, and killed her. The second was a young man of about twenty-one by the name of Chamberlain who was killed by the falling of a tree in a central part of of the town during the year 1801. And another of the name of Robinson, during that or the following year, was killed by the falling of a tree in the north part of the township. And, yet another, an idiotic man of the name of Charles Davis, we think, was killed by a tree of his own falling, while undertaking to get out of danger by running in the same direction in which the tree had started to fall. To this list, should, perhaps, be added the suicide of the wife of John Cutler, who hung herself in 1801, and Nancy Waugh who thus destroyed herself. At a later period, also, that of a stranger who, in the first years of the settlement, was drowned in attempting to wade through the Winooski, near the mouth of the river on his way to Montpelier, having probably mistaken the right place for fording.

And while on the subject of fatal casualties, it may not, perhaps, here be amiss to mention one or two of the most remarkable escapes from death, and acts of perilous daring, which occured in this town, and which were often the themes of fireside conversation for years after they happened.

In the summer of about the year 1790, Mr. Theophilus W. Brooks, of Montpelier, came very near experiencing the same melancholly fate that befel him on the memorable Thanksgiving night of the following year. He, in company of Thomas Davis, was passing along the steep rocky banks of the North Branch just above the Poor House about a mile above the village, where his feet slipping on the wet and slimy rocks, he was precipitated into a deep hole below, and being unable to swim, soon sunk to the bottom and lost all consciousness. Mr. Davis in the mean time hastily procured a long pole and thrusting it down to the drowning man, twisted it into his clothes, drew him up to the surface at the shore and soon succeeded in bringing him to life.

Not far from the year 1806, Mr. Charles Stevens, who lived on East Hill, made a horse-back journey to Massachusetts, passing down on his way from home over the high bridge across the Winooski about three-fourths of a mile below Daggett's Mills village. During his absence the bridge had been stripped of all the plank, preparatory to replanking or putting in some new string-pieces. While the bridge was in this dismantled condition—which condition was wholly unknown and unsuspected by Mr. Stevens—he reached home, on his return from his journey, at a late hour on an unusually dark night, totally unconscious that he had passed through any peril in passing over the river, which was only a mile or two from his house.

"Which way did you come?" asked his family.

"The way I went, of course."

"No, you couldn't, for the river is roaring high, and there is not a single plank on the bridge."

"Yes, I did come the same way and over the same bridge, and you can't beat me out of it."

Here was a complete issue, and neither party being in the least disposed to yield, they the next morning, in company with a neighbor, a Mr. Parker, repaired to the bridge, and to their amazement discovered, by the tracks on the ground and the calk marks of the animal's shoes on the timber, that the horse, after selecting the broadest hewn string-piece, had mounted it and passed so quietly and safely over it to the other side that the rider was not made aware, in the great darkness of the night, that he was undergoing the dangerous transit.

We have seen published, we think, later accounts of similar feats performed in the darkness of night by horses bearing their unconscious riders in safety over bridge timbers; but of the truth of such accounts there is much room to doubt, and it is not impossible that this one, which is as true as it was remarkable, and which soon passed into one of the wide spread traditions of the country, may have been the only original of all such reported stories.

About 1806, there moved into Montpelier village a man of the name of Parrot Blaisdell, who, while becoming a permanent resident and rearing a smart and respectable family here, exhibited perhaps more personal daring, and by his acts, caused his name to be coupled with more perilous adventures and hair-breadth escapes than any man of his day in this part of the country. Soon after moving here he became the driver and perhaps the proprietor of the principal stage team running from Windsor to Montpelier. On one of his return trips from Windsor, when the old trussel bridge across the river, where the present Arch Bridge stands, had been partially carried away by flood, or otherwise rendered impassable, Mr. Blaisdell, with his passengers, reached the river, which, as it was before the dam was built, he had forded with his team on the outward-bound trip, a short distance above the bridge at the head of the falls. He now, however, found the river much swolen by a recent rain, turbid, and of a strong, swift current; and he was warned not to attempt the dangerous passage. But he despised the asserted danger, and saying he was not to be frightened by a little flash-flood of dirty water, plunged his horses into the angry stream. But his horses soon lost their footing and the whole team was swept rapidly down towards the falls. He had the coolness and presence of mind, however, so to guide the horses as to bring up the carriage against the old trussels standing about midway the stream, when by an effort of his great strength he seized the trussel with one arm and a part of the carriage with the other, and kept the whole establishment on the brink of the falls till help arrived, ropes were fastened to the carriage, and carriage, horses and all were drawn safely ashore, with no other damage than what might have been occasioned by the drenching they received. But the greatest and most note-worthy feat ever performed by Mr. Blaisdell was achieved by him a year or two subsequent to the one just related; when, having changed his route, he was running his stage between Montpelier and Burlington. On one of his return trips from the last named place, with a full load of passangers, he came on to the top of *Rock Bridge*, or *Blaisdell's Rock*, as it was often afterwards called, about a mile south of Waterbury, on the Moretown side of the Winooski—it being the difficult and dangerous pass over or along which Thomas Davis contrived to get the first wagon ever introduced into Montpelier, as described in a former chapter. When the first passable wagon road was wrought along here, a part of this ledge had been blasted out along the face of the rock, which descended perpendicularly about sixty feet to the bed of the river; but the road thus made was barely sufficient for one team to pass at a time, while no railing had been provided, and a long, steep pitch succeeded down the rocky road beyond. As the stage was on the descent, and at the narrowest part of this shelf road, with the wheels on one side within a yard of the precipice, the iron ring confining the pole of the stage to the neck-yoke of the horses suddenly broke, giving a cant and direction to the now fast moving carriage, which in a second or two more must have run it off the brink, and proved the destruction of all and everything aboard. At that critical instant, Mr. Blaisdell suddenly leaped on to, and over the near horse, and landing before him in the road, seized the falling pole with one hand and the neck-yoke with the other, gave the carriage the right direction, and, as swiftly as it was going, guided it safely to the bottom of the hill.

During the war of 1812, Mr. Blaisdell ran another, and, to him, a much more costly risk. The two rival parties, Democrats and Federalists, were celebrating the 4th of July, on different sides of the same field in Williamstown, when Mr. Blaisdell, who was engaged in firing a cannon, and probably urging the process hotly in order to outdo that of the other party in quickness of loading and firing, had one arm wholly blown away by the premature discharge of the piece, and lost the sight of one of his eyes.

CHAPTER XIV.

INTELLECTUAL AND MORAL STANDARDS AMONG THE PEOPLE. LITERATURE, AND OFFICES HELD IN TOWN, WITH CONCLUDING REFLECTIONS.

The prevailing feature of Montpelier village has ever been of a business character. The examples of the enterprising and energetic founder of the town, Colonel Jacob Davis, and the spirit he infused into his sons-in-law, and those whom he had in various ways assisted to start in life, all of whom became leading and influential men in the place, continued to operate until its whole society assumed the established tone, which has ever, to a greater or less degree, peculiarly marked it—a tone in which the desire of activity in business and its acquisitions, has largely predominated—in which the useful took precedence of the ornamental; and matters of fact the precedence of matters of taste and speculation. Under such prevailing influences, therefore, intellectual excellence has not found, perhaps, the same relative position here as in many other places; and general intellectual improvement, even of the young, has not engrossed the first thought of the people. As the world is made up wherein the few are rich and the many are not, and as the most pressing wants will ever naturally govern the views and actions of the many, wealth is omnipotent; and it was not the blessing of Montpelier to have her wealthiest men the most liberally educated, else a different appreciation of intellectual character might have here obtained, and a different standard of superiority might have been here established.

And yet, to the credit of the wealthiest men of Montpelier, it may be truthfully asserted, that they have been generally very public spirited and patriotic, in all that related to the material improvement of this village; and even for its intellectual advancement, indeed, they may have been always sufficiently liberal according to their appreciation of the object. And that appreciation has always extended to the necessity of a common education, and, in several instances, to the full advantages of the liberal education of both sons and daughters. These instances, together with those of the less wealthy, but in this respect more ambitious class, have been the means of furnishing, during the last forty years, over a dozen College graduates, and as many young ladies, who have received the best of female educations, at institutions abroad. The views and tastes of the young gentlemen and ladies, thus educated and returning to their native village, have latterly been producing a very perceptible effect in modifying and elevating the general tone of our village society. Montpelier, indeed, has *never* been wanting, when compared with other places of the size, of a full proportion of intellectual power, however much its inability to command the means for its developement may have prevented the fulfillment of its highest mission. The character of the legal profession of the village has been second to that of none in the State. The medical profession has been ever highly respectable for the skill and talents of practitioners, and the clerical, at times, quite distinguished for ability and eloquence. Montpelier, also, has had much more than an ordinary share of indigenous literature, and some of its several native authors have made themselves known far beyond the limits of the State. And as a list of these authors and their respective works seems necessary to make up a full history of the town, we will proceed to enumerate them, with the dates and places of publication:

"*The Indian Captive*," by Horace Steele, containing the fullest account of the *Burning of Royalton* ever written, was published in Montpelier in one thin volume about the year 1812.

"*Baylies' Index*," a law work in three volumes, embracing brief digests of the decisions of English and American Courts, by the Hon. Nicholas Baylies, was published in Montpelier, in 1814, and widely circulated among the profession.

Mr. Baylies also published in Montpelier a work on "*Free Agency*," of 216 pages in 1821.

"*The Battle of Plattsburgh*," a pamphlet poem of some merit by Samuel Woodworth, nephew of Ziba W., was published in 1815.

"*The Gift*," a volume of 172 pages, of highly creditable miscellaneous poems by Miss Sophia Watrous, was published in Montpelier in 1840.

The Reverend Chester Wright published in Montpelier previous to 1830, several sermons delivered on different occasions, all marked by pathos, earnest thought, and a spirit of deep devotion.

The Reverend John Gridley, published in Montpelier in 1843, a discourse delivered on the preceding thanksgiving day, embracing a succinct, but valuable "History of Montpelier."

The Reverend Wm. H. Lord has, within the last few years, published at the request of his people and others, the following sermons:

A funeral sermon on the death and character of Hon. John McLean of Cabot, Feb. 1855.

A fast day sermon on National Hospitality, April 1855.

A funeral sermon on the death and character of Lucretia Prentiss, wife of Samuel Prentiss, June 1855.

A funeral sermon on the death and character of Gen. E. P. Walton, Nov. 1855.

A funeral sermon on the death and character of Hon. Samuel Prentiss, Jan. 1857.

A semi-centenial sermon, on occasion of the Fiftieth Anniversary of the organization of the church in Montpelier, July 1858.

A funeral sermon on the death and character of the Hon. F. F. Merrill, May, 1859.

And besides these he is the author of the extensively known Biographical sketch of the life of the Hon. Samuel Prentiss, which appeared some years ago in Livingston's Law Magazine in New York, and also of an address delivered before the Literary Societies of Vermont University at Commencement, Aug. 1852, and an address delivered before the Phi Beta Kappa Society, at Dartmouth College, at Commencement, July 1857.

All these have met with a most flattering reception, and some of them particularly exhibit a clearness of thought, discrimination and scope of mind, as well as literary taste, equalling those of some of the most successful writers of the day.

The Reverend F. F. Shelton, Rector of the Episcopal Church in Montpelier, has been quite a voluminous writer, having published the following works:

"*Salander and the Dragon*," an allegorical moral tale, in 1848.

"*The Rector of Bardolph*," a social and religious tale, in 1849.

"*Chrystalline*," a tale, in 1850.

"*Up the River*," a volume of miscellaneous papers first contributed to the N. Y. Knickerbocker, in 1850.

"*Peeps from the Belfry*," another picture of social and religious life, in 1855.

Mr. Shelton, as a writer, is original, piquant and instructive, and his works are well written, and all involving a high moral purpose, have deservedly given him quite a wide-spread reputation as an author.

"*Poems*, by Charles G. Eastman," were published in Montpelier in 1848, in a volume containing 208 pages, but embracing only a part of what he had before and what he has since written. Most of these poems, are of a pastoral and descriptive character, delineating rural scenes, and the every day character and events of country life, all entirely original in conception and style of execution, and many of them, such as *The Home Picture*, commencing with "The farmer sat in his easy chair," "*The Town Pauper's Burial*," and the "*Scene in a Vermont Winter*," are scarcely excelled, in kind, by any American poet. These effusions of Mr. Eastman, though only the fruits of his leisure hours, have well established his reputation as a descriptive poet, in this country, and have even met the favorable consideration of English critics.

D. P. Thompson has written and published the following works:

"*May Martin, or The Money Diggers*," a newspaper prize published in Montpelier, in book form, in 1835.

"*The Green Mountain Boys*," 364 pages, was first published in Montpelier in 1840, afterwards stereotyped and published in Boston.

"*Locke Amsden, or the School Master*," 231 pages, stereotyped, was published in Boston in 1847.

"*The Rangers, or the Tory's Daughter*," 329 pages, stereotyped, was published in Boston in 1851.

"*Tales of the Green Mountains*," &c. including *May Martin*, 380, stereotyped, was published in Boston in 1852.

"*Gaut Gurley, or the Trappers of Umbagog*," pages 360, stereotyped, was published in Boston in 1857.

"*The Doomed Chief, or Two Hundred Years Ago*," pages 473, stereotyped, was published in Philadelphia at the commencement of 1860.

Of the above named works, two, at least, "*May Martin*," and "*The Green Mountain Boys*," and, it is said, some of the others, have been republished in England. None of them except the last, now but just out, have passed through less than six editions, while the Green Mountain Boys has passed through fifty, and May Martin a still greater number of editions.

This town has also been the residence, for greater or less periods, at different times, of several distinguished men, who subsequently became widely known for their successful authorship, in the honors of which this place may, perhaps, justly claim some participation. The principal of these are: the Reverend Samuel Hopkins, the settled Congregational Minister and resident of the village from 1831 to 1835, who has recently published a very able and learned work of Ecclesiastical history in relation to the Seceders and Puritans; the Reverend John S. C. Abbott, who resided and preached here in the summer of 1835, and who has since become a very prolific author of both religious and historical productions; and lastly, the Honorable Isaac F. Redfield, for the last twenty-five years a member of the Supreme Court, and for nearly the last decade its Chief Justice, who resided here over a dozen years following 1835, and who has recently written and published a "Practical Treatise on the Law of Railways," which has been pronounced, both in this country and England, to be the best work on the subject extant, and which has at once given him rank with the first of American Jurists.

In addition to the productions of more regular authors, and the volumes of Court Decisions which might be collected from the administering of the Chief Justiceship of the Hon. Samuel Prentiss and the Hon. Isaac F. Redfield, we should perhaps mention another kind of literature, of which Montpelier has probably been more prolific than any town in the State—we allude to its newspaper literature. For the last fifty years the town, with its surroundings, has sustained two, and for the last twenty years four weekly journals on the average, which have been among the best conducted of country newspapers. These journals have been the "Vermont Watchman," the old Democratic "Free Press" and its successor, the "Vermont Patriot," the "State Journal," the "Voice of Freedom" and its successor, the "Green Mountain Freeman," the "Christian Messenger," and the "Christian Repository." The editors of the "Vermont Watchman" have been successively Samuel Goss, Ezekiel P. Walton, and E. P. Walton, Jr.; of the "Free Press" and "Vermont Patriot," Derrick Sibley, George W. Hill, J. T. Marston, and Charles G. Eastman; of the "State Journal," C. L. Knapp; of the "Voice of Freedom" and the "Green Mountain Freeman," C. L. Knapp, Joseph Poland, Jacob Scott, D. P. Thompson and S. S. Boyce; of the "Christian Messenger," Rev. E. J. Scott and Rev. A. Webster; and of the "Christian Repository, "Rev. Eli Ballou.

Montpelier village, also, from first to last, has been honored with its full proportion of State and National offices. Besides numerous minor State officers, it has furnished, at different times, three State Treasurers, E. P. Jewett, George Howes and John A. Page; six Secretaries of State, David Wing, C. L. Knapp, Timothy Merrill, Ferrand F. Merrill, D. P. Thompson and C. W. Willard; three Clerks of the House of Representatives, Timothy Merrill, F. F. Merrill and George R. Thompson; three Judges of the Supreme Court, Nicholas Baylies, Samuel Prentiss and Isaac F. Redfield; two U. S. Senators, Samuel Prentiss and William Upham; two Members of Congress, Lucius B. Peck and E. P. Walton; one U. S. District Judge, Samuel Prentiss; one U. S. District Court Clerk, Edward H. Prentiss; and one Purser in the Navy, Charles C. Upham. Of County officers, and those of County appointment, Montpelier has furnished ten Judges of Probate, Salvin Collins, Jeduthan Loomis, Joseph Reed, George Worthington, R. R. Keith, D. P. Thompson, Azel Spalding, J. T. Marston, Joseph Poland and Jacob Scott; six High Sheriffs, George Worthington, R. R. Keith, Isaiah Silver, A. A. Sweet, Geo. W. Barker and Joseph W. Howes; nine States Attornies, Timothy Merrill, Nicholas Baylies, William Upham, Azel Spalding, Homer W. Heaton, Oramel H. Smith, Charles Reed, Stoddard B. Colby and Ferrand F. Merrill; five Side Judges, David Wing, Cyrus Ware, Joseph Howes, John Spalding and Daniel Baldwin; five County Clerks, George Rich, Joshua Y. Vail, Stillman Churchill, D. P. Thompson and Luther Newcomb; two Councillors elected on the State ticket, Nicholas Baylies and George Worthington; and six Senators elected on the County ticket, Araunah Waterman, Oramel H. Smith, Wooster Sprague, Charles G. Eastman and Joseph Poland.

Having thus far glanced at the intellectual condition of the society of Montpelier village, let us now briefly advert to the moral standard that has generally obtained in this community. We do not here use the word *moral* in contradistinction to the mere vices, or mean to apply it to the personal habits of the people, virtuous or otherwise. But we intend by the term to designate the sense of right and wrong, of justice and injustice, which generally prevails in community, and to which, in cases of disagreement, men may appeal as a sort of generally acknowledged and established standard, that is to govern all men conducting the various transactions of life. In this sense, if we except the period of about a dozen years immediately succeeding 1800, when the new elements of village society, which had been brought together by the prospects of gaining wealth by trade or of realizing other objects of ambition, were in a transition state, and permitted a more unchecked action—in this sense, the moral standard predominating among the people of Montpelier village has always been, when compared with that of other country villages, a sound and healthy one. Not one in a hundred will commit *direct* frauds in a trade; and if a larger proportion commit them *indirectly*, or enter on practices familiarly known by the appellation of *gouging*, they are so quickly exposed, denounced, and made to lose caste in respectable society, as to prevent any frequent repetition of such practices by them, and to operate as a constantly restraining example on those of like secret propensities, as well as on the still larger class who naturally possess only a weak moral sense to guide and govern them in their business transactions, and in the character of their dealings and conduct among their fellow-men. Transient dealers, it is true, have, from time to time, here established themselves, and apparently flourished for a brief period while acting in violation of these wholesome morals of trade , and then, perhaps, finding eventual success impossible under their loose or dishonest practices, have failed, in order to make what regular and honest courses would have brought them. But finding themselves marked men, and seeing no prospect of gaining any permanent footing in good society, they have generally, like other temporary embodiments of evil, soon passed away, leaving their places to be filled by better men. And attempts at success in trade of this kind will doubtless continue to occur, at intervals; but those making them need never expect from them either wealth or reputation ; and the fewer they make of such attempts the better for them and the community.

We have before spoken of an essential reformation in trade as occuring during the period immediately following the years 1809 and 1810. That reformation was permanent, and was a most important one for the interests of the place, while the system of general and often long credits was continued. But another, and perhaps equally important reformation, has, during the last dozen years, been evidently in rapid progress. This consists in the short credit system with the responsible, and the *pay down*, or ready cash system, with all others. By this system, all temptations for overcharging on book, and false promises of lenity in mode and time of payment, are taken away on the part of the seller ;—the desire of fast living, or the thoughtless running up of ruinous debts, obviated, on the part of the purchaser, and habits of frugality and industry continually promoted on the part of all. And perhaps it will not be too much to say of this or any other community, that generally the more limited the credit system among them, the less will mortifying poverty, social contentions, neighborhood quarrels, and vexatious and impoverishing litigation abound, and the more systematic domestic economy, regular habits of industry, and happy pecuniary independence prevail, to the continual advantage of individual weal, social advancement and the public welfare.

In all the agricultural portions of the original township of Montpelier, the standard of general intelligence, morals in contradistinction to the vices, and moral honesty in dealing, having been mainly exempt from the fluctuations which we have named as marking our village society, have ever been, from the first settlement to the present day, quite as high, and every way as creditable to the proverbially industrious and thrifty occupants, as those prevailing among the people of the best farming towns of the State. We have before spoken of the general taste for reading, and the consequent diffusion of general intelligence among our farmers, growing, mainly, as we supposed, out of the wise and provident provisions of the first settlers for libraries and schools. That taste and intelligence they have ever since nobly maintained. The common schools have generally been supplied with the better class of teachers, and the schools themselves maintained always in as good, and often in a better state of forwardness, than our village common schools. They have furnished their full proportion of professional men. In the profession of law, William Upham, Shubael Wheeler, Humphrey Bennett, and Nahum Peck, Esqs., were all of their rearing. In the medical profession they have furnished a still greater number, consisting of Dr. Philip Vincent, Dr. Eleazer Hamblin, Dr. Stephen Peabody, Dr. Nathaniel C. King, Dr. Daniel Corliss, Dr. Charles Clark, Dr. Milo L. Burnham, Dr. Isaac Putnam, Dr. Sumner Putnam, Dr. W. H. H. Richardson, and Drs. James Templeton and his son. They have furnished at least two College graduates now holding high positions abroad—Marcus Tullius Cicero Wing, a son of the Hon. David Wing, now an Episcopal clergyman and Professor in Kenyon College, Ohio, and Nathaniel George Clark, son of Dr. Charles Clark, and now a Professor of the Vermont University at Burlington. They have likewise supplied a fair proportion of county officers, among the most prominent of whom are Royal Wheeler, State Senator for the county, Addison Peck, High Sheriff, Israel Goodwin, a side Judge and also subsequently a County Commissioner, and Shubael Wheeler, side Judge and County Clerk.

As regards general wealth, the part of the township now known as East Montpelier, when reckoned per capita, or averaged among the people, has, till within a recent period, taken the precedence of the village part of the original town, and would doubtless now do so, but for the recent large additions to the village capital, made by wealthy new comers, among whom were some from East Montpelier itself, who have consequently been the means of changing the relative amounts of the wealth of the two divisions against the latter at a double ratio. But with all its liabilities to constant depletion from its wealthy and influential men to build up the village, and with all its lack of advantages for rolling up large individual fortunes by trade, this portion of the old township, in the productiveness of its soil, in the number of its independent, and even wealthy farmers, and in the general thrift, intelligence, patriotism and stable character of the great mass of its inhabitants, has ever been reckoned among the very best agricultural towns in the State.

To sum up all, then, in conclusion, we may safely, as we can proudly say, that in point of healthiness, both the village and the town of Montpelier at large, as we think we have before shown by something more reliable than mere assertious, must be allowed to stand at least among the most favored locations to be found, not only in our generally favored Vermont, but in all the Northerly States of the Union.

In point of fertility of soil and general productiveness, the heavy growths of luxuriant and never failing grasses—of themselves an exhaustless mine of wealth—the thickset, exuberant maize, the yellow fields of waving wheat, oats and other cereals, which, in their season, richly clothe the meadows and uplands of this noble township; and the rare and beautiful horses, the herds of fat or fair-looking neat cattle, and the flocks of thriving sheep, that graze upon, and whiten its "thousand hills," all combine to prove it one of the most productive places ever appropriated by culturist or herdsman.

And, finally, in point of solid, spare capital—the best, perhaps, of all proofs of the productiveness of a given section of country—the village of Montpelier, which may be considered the monied reservoir of the whole original township, has probably,—as demonstrated in the essential aid it furnished in the construction of the Vermoat Central Railroad, and especially in the rebuilding of the State House—no equal of its size, in the State, and few or no superiors in any interior town in New England.

Such has been, and such still is, in all its parts and legal divisions, the noble and important town of Montpelier. We are indeed placed in a cold and rough country, far in the interior, with no great marts of commerce, manufactures or trade. But we all have, among these green hills, the high health and contentment, which combine to make up almost the sum total of all animal happiness. We have the habits of industry and frugality, which best ensure us pecuniary independence as a separate community, and, at the same time, best assure, with our admitted intelligence and virtue, *our* part of the duty of perpetuating our great national blessings of freedom and equal rights. Why, then,—while other and apparently more favorably situated States and communities are, at short intervals, swept by the commercial revulsions that are scarcely felt by us, or torn by political dissensions, or deeply affected in their essential interests by the political changes and fluctuations frequently occurring in the administration of our general government, but only nominally affecting our interests—why then, should we not say with the poet—

"Dear is the lot to which our souls conform,
And dear the hills which lift us to the storm;
And as a child, when scaring sounds molest,
Clings close and closer to the mother's breast,
So let the torrent's and the whirldwind's roar,
But bind us to our native mountains more."

BIOGRAPHICAL SKETCHES.

COLONEL JACOB DAVIS.

Colonel JACOB DAVIS, the first permanent settler of Montpelier, and emphatically the chief of its founders, was born in Oxford, Massachusetts, in the year 1739. Unfortunately his descendants have preserved no memorials of his youth, and only know that he had received no advantages of education except from the poor and insufficient common schools of the times. In 1754 the part of the town, in which his father's family resided, was set off from Oxford, and incorporated into a new town by the name of Charlton; and in this newly created town, he continued to remain until he removed to Vermont. Soon after reaching the years of manhood, he married Rebecca Davis, of the same town, a second cousin, and an intelligent, amiable and every way estimable young lady. Mr. Davis must have been a man of considerable property and standing in his town. He likewise must have become noted in the community around him for intelligence and energy of character; and he probably passed through all the lower grades of military office in the militia of Worcester county, to which his town belonged, and became widely known as an active patriot in the cause of the American Revolution. For in 1776, we find him in the public service of his country, acting under a Colonel's commission of one of the regiments of the Massachusetts detached or drafted militia, subject to the call of Congress or the Commander-in-Chief, whenever the occasion might require. How much he was in active service is now not known; but the traditions of his family make him to have been with his command in the little army of Washington in the memorable crossing of the Delaware to attack the Hessians at Trenton in December, 1776. He was subsequently under contract to carry the United States mail over one of the mail routes in his part of Massachusetts, and for some years continued to execute the duties of the undertaking. Another event, which occurred a few years after, and with which his name stands honorably connected, here deserves to be especially mentioned, in proof of his public spirit, and of the interest he took in the cause of education. There was an old Jew engaged in some kind of traffic, who owned a large house, or ware-house, in the neighboring town of Leicester, and Colonel Davis, in conjunction with another gentleman of the vicinity, purchased this building, had it fitted up for a select high school, and soon caused a school therein to be put in operation. This was the small beginning of the afterwards well known Leicester Academy in Massachusetts, the founding of which its history places in 1774; and that Colonel Davis was considered one of its founders is shown by the fact, that since his death, his family have received a letter asking for his portrait that it might be placed in the Academy building, with that of the other founders of that institution.

Early in the year 1780, Colonel Davis had turned his attention to the selection and purchase of wild lands, in the new State of Vermont; and he was among the most active in procuring the granting and chartering of the township, which he caused to be named Montpelier, at the October session of the Legislature of Vermont in that year, though the charter, on account of the delay caused in the collection of the fees required by the State, from the different proprietors, was not issued until the following August. From that time to the commencement of the meetings of the proprietors in the winter of 1786, which he attended, Colonel Davis appears to have been energetically engaged in his private business, at Charlton, or in public enterprises, like the one above mentioned. But from the date last named, and perhaps the year before, he was obviously employed in disposing of his quite handsome property in Massachusetts, and arranging all his affairs for removal to his newly elected home in the wilds of Vermont; and accordingly, in the winter of 1787, after having made, during the previous summer and fall, several journeys into the State to attend the meetings of the proprietors, commence the survey of the new township, in which he had secured three rights, or about one thousand acres, and make selection of *Pitches* for the occupation of himself and sons, he removed his family to Brookfield, then the nearest settled town to Montpelier; and early in the following spring, still leaving his wife and daughters at Brookfield, till a comfortable home could be provided for them, he came with his sons and a hired man to make his opening in the dark forests of Montpelier. But as his career, for the next twelve or fifteen years, involved, to a remarkable degree, the history of the town, during that period, which we have minutely given in the first chapters of this work, and which, better than anything we could here add, displays the leading features of his truly remarkable character, we will pass over these years, and hasten to the concluding incidents of his eventful life,

Somewhere near the year 1800 he became involved in several large and vexatious lawsuits, growing out of disputed land titles or the sales of lands he had effected through his agencies under foreign landholders. In one of these, for want of his ability to make legal proof of payments that the distant proprietors had received, a large judgment was obtained in the United States

Circuit Court against him, which was considered by himself, his family and friends, so unjust that he, with their concurrence, resolved never to pay it. And in pursuance of this determination, he conveyed to his sons and sons-in-law, the principal part of his attachable property, and, removing his family to Burlington, so as to be within the limits of Chittenden county jail yard, invited the service of the execution taken out against him on his own person. Here in Burlington, he led a quiet life for over a dozen years, during which frequent offers of compromises were made him by the plaintiffs in the suit, which he steadily rejected till the winter of 1814, when they made an offer so nearly amounting to a relinquishment of their whole claim, and so virtually involving an admission of its injustice, that he accepted it, and the whole matter in dispute was amicably settled. But before he became prepared to remove, as he was about to do, to his beloved Montpelier, he was attacked by an acute disease which terminated his active and eventful life on the 9th of April, 1814. His remains were brought to Montpelier for interment and a broad tomb-stone marking the place where they repose may now be found in the old village grave-yard.

In person, Col. Davis was six feet high, broad-shouldered, compactly formed and well proportioned, with unusually large bones and muscles. His face was round favored, and handsomely featured, and his whole appearance dignified and commanding. Of his great physical powers we have previously given one instance in his ability to slash one acre of forest land in a day. Let one other suffice. Old Mr. Levi Humphrey, one of the first settlers, who died in this town, August 1859, at the age of ninety-three years, told us, about a fortnight before his death, that he well-remembered being one day at Col. Davis' log house, when the latter requested two of his strongest hired men to go into the yard and bring in, for a back-log for their long open fire-place, a cut of green maple four or more feet long and nearly two feet in diameter. In compliance, they took each hold of an end, but reported that they were unable to bring it in, and were preparing to roll it up to the door with handspikes, when the Colonel, having noticed their failure to take up the log, came out, motioned them aside, and grasping the ends with his long arms, lifted, marched into the house with it, and threw it on to the fire, pleasantly remarking to them as he did so, that "they did not appear to be any great things at log-lifting." But Col. Davis's physical powers were of small account in the comparison with the other strong traits of the man. Of his enterprise, energy, judgment and far-reaching sagacity, we have already sufficiently spoken. But even they were not all the good qualities of his character. No needy man ever went empty-handed from his door. He ever gave employment of some kind to all who asked for it. And so well he rewarded all his employees, that no reasonable man in the whole settlement was ever heard to complain of the amouut of wages he paid or any unfair conduct in his dealings.

REBECCA DAVIS.

The efficient help-meet of the energetic man whose life and character we have been briefly sketching, is most surely deserving of a separate mention to be passed down to the posterity of the first settlers of Montpelier, with the sketch of her husband.

She was born in Oxford, Massachusetts, in the year 1743, married about the year 1765, and died on the 25th of February, 1823. She lies buried by the side of her husband, in this village, where she peacefully passed the last as well as the middle portion of her useful and exemplary life. She early united with the Congregational Church after it was established in this village, and had long been considered a Christian in works, as well as faith, which would have well warranted an earlier public profession of religion. Unusually comely in person, with a sweet smile ever on her lips, kind in disposition, intelligent and discreet, she was the never failing friend of the needy and distressed, the judicious adviser of the young, and the universal object of the love and respect of all classes of the people of the settlement. Of the more than half score of her cotemporaries in this town of whom we have made enquiries respecting her character, all most cordially united in affirming, in substance, what we will only quote as the warmly expressed words of one of them: "*Mrs. Colonel Davis was one of the best, the very best, women in the whole world!*" Indeed she must have truly been a mother in the early Montpelier Israel, and she has left behind her a name bright with blessed memories.

THE HONORABLE DAVID WING, JUNIOR.

DAVID WING, Junior, was born in Rochester, Massachusetts, on the 24th of June, 1766, removed with his father and family to Montpelier in about the year 1790, and settled down with them on a farm adjoining what is now known as the old Clark Stevens place, in the east part of the town. He had doubtless received a rather superior common school education, though the educational accomplishments, which he almost at once exhibited after coming into the settlement, were probably mainly the fruits of his native taste and scholarship, which is strikingly conspicuous in all the memorials, social or civil, that he has left behind him. He taught the second school of the town, which was opened, it is believed, in the same year in which he became one of its inhabitants. Within about two years after his arrival he was elected Town Clerk. And during the next dozen years, the offices of Town Agent, Town Representative, Judge of the County Court and Secretary of State, seem to have been crowded upon him in regular and rapid succession. As an evidence of his great populaiity among his townsmen, the fact may be cited that while he was holding the office of side Judge, and Chief Judge of the County Court—ten fold the best office held by any other inhabitant of the town—he was elected the Town Representative four years previous to his election as Secretary of State; and not content with that, for the several years during that time, they threw their entire vote for him as State Treasurer. Considering the jealousies usually existing among the numbers found in every town who believe themselves qualified for office, and who generally raise a clamor against bestowing an office on a man who is already holding another good office, perhaps nothing could be adduced, which shows so strongly as this fact, the unbounded respect and personal regard in which David Wing was universally held by his almost idolizing townsmen.

In 1792 he married Miss Hannah Davis, the second daughter of Colonel Jacob Davis, and a young lady of many personal attractions, and of much moral excellence. From this marriage sprang eight children, whose names we give to show the classical tastes of the father, and the estimation in which the different noted personages of history were held by him:—Debby Daphne, Christopher Columbus, Algernon Sidney, Marcus Tullius Cicero, Maria Theresa, David Davis, Caroline Augusta and Maximus Fabius. The two first named of these daughters died in infancy; and the remaining five children arrived at maturity and took highly respectable positions in society, though only one of them appears to have fully inherited the tastes and native scholarship of their father—the Rev. Marcus T. C. Wing, a Professor in Kenyon College, Ohio.

As in the case of Colonel Davis, the most prominent acts and traits of character of David Wing have already been brought too fully to light in the first part of this history of the town to need here any repetition; and we will draw this sketch to a close with a few personal observations.

In person Judge Wing was of medium height, of a good form, fine head, shapely features and an animated countenance, all made the more attractive and winning by the dignified affiability of his manners. As an instance of the quickness of his perceptions, his ready business capacities and the versatile character of his talents, several of his yet surviving cotemporories have named to us the fact, of which they were frequently cognizant, that he would correctly and rapidly draw up any kind of document, report, despatch or legal instrument in writing, and at the same time maintain a connected and lively conversation with those around him.

He was elected Secretary of State in the fall of 1802, and while still holding the office, and in the midst of his usefulness and high promise, was suddenly swept away by a malignant fever, on the 13th day of September, 1806. And rarely, indeed, has ever a death occurred in this section of the State which produced so profound a sensation in community. His death was mourned as a great loss, not only to the town but to the whole State ; and the remark was then everywhere made that, had he lived, no man within its limits was more sure than he of soon being promoted to the highest offices within the gift of the people.

CLARK STEVENS.

Unlike others among the leading first settlers of Montpelier, there was one who has occupied scarcely space enough in its public affairs to make himself known even to all his fellow townsmen, but who, nevertheless, possessed a mind, a heart and a general character, of which the best of them might well be proud, and whose examples of moral purity, wisdom and goodness, deserve to be forever remembered and cherished. That man was CLARK STEVENS, a member and leader in the Society of Friends.

CLARK STEVENS was born in Rochester, Massachusetts, on the 15th of November, 1764. At the age of eighteen he was drafted as a soldier, and served in that capacity several months during one of the last years of the American Revolution. After leaving the army, he engaged himself as a seaman at the neighboring port of New Bedford, and spent several years in the ventures of the ocean. But the perils he had here encountered in the whaling and coasting trade, not only revived the religious impressions formerly experienced, but led him to resolve on the quiet pursuits of husbandry, and to remove, with that object in view, to the new town of Montpelier in Vermont. Accordingly he immigrated into this town in 1790, in company with David Wing, the elder, and his sons, purchased and at once began to clear up the valuable farm near Montpelier East Village, which has ever since been the family homestead. After effecting a considerable opening in the wilderness, and building the customary log house and barn, he returned to the land of his fathers, and, on the 30th of December,, 1793, married Miss Huldah Foster of his native Rochester, brought her immediately on and installed her as the mistress of his heart and household.

Soon after his marriage, Mr. Stevens appears to have been more deeply than ever exercised with his religious convictions; when soon, by the aid of some neighbors who, like himself, had previously united themselves with the Society of Friends or Quakers, he built a log meeting house on the bank of a little brook a short distance to the north-west of his dwelling. And here, under his lead, that little band of congenial worshipers established in the wilderness the first altar for the worship of the living God ever erected in Washington County. Subsequently this band was received into membership with the New York Society of Friends, who held monthly meetings in Danby, in the south-western part of Vermont, which meetings were eventually established at Starksboro', in this State. Of the latter he became a regular monthly attendant, and in 1815, having, besides being the leader and teacher of his Society at home, travelled, each year, hundreds of miles to attend monthly, quarterly and yearly meetings in Vermont, New York, and in the different States of New England, and everywhere evinced his faithfulness as a laborer, and his ability as a religious speaker and teacher, he was publicly acknowledged by the Starksboro' Association as a regular annd accepted Minister of the Gospel. Years before this, through his instrumentality, and that of his worthy and perhaps most energetic fellow-laborer in the cause, the late Caleb Bennett, his Society at home had been considerably enlarged, and a commodious meeting house erected a half mile or more distant from the first primitive one above mentioned.

But if Clark Stevens was a man of the intelligence and virtue which caused him to be placed in such a prominent position in his religieus connections, why was he not, as well as other citizens of his town of the same grade of capacity, promoted to posts of civil trusts, or other worldly honors? It was because, after having been made the second Town Clerk of the town, and reluctantly consented to serve in that capacity one year—it was simply because he ever uniformly declined to accept them. Time and again would the town gladly have made him their Representative in the Legislature. But all movements of that kind were by him promptly discouraged and stopped at the outset. On the organization of the new County of Jefferson, in such high esteem were his worth and abilities held by the leading men of the County at large that, on their united recommendation, he was, without his knowledge or consent, appointed by the Legislature to the more important and tempting office of a Judge of the Court. But this he also promptly declined, and gave the public to understand that civil honors had so few charms for him that it would thereafter be in vain for them ever to offer them for his acceptance.

Thus, "he had wrought out his work, and wrought it well." Thus he lived, and thus, at the ripe age of nearly ninety, he peacefully passed away, at his old residence, on the 20th of December, 1853, with the characteristic words on his lips:— "I have endeavored to do what I apprehended was required of me. I have naught but feelings of love for all mankind; and my hope of salvation is based on the mercy of God through his Son Jesus Christ."

Personally, CLARK STEVENS was one of the finest looking men of his times. Full six feet high, and nobly proportioned, with a shapely contour of head and features, dark eyes and a sedate, thoughtful countenance, his presence was unusually imposing and dignified. He was a prince in appearance, but a child in humility. He was unquestionably a man of superior intellect, and that intellect was, in all its traits, peculiarly well balanced. But it was his great and good heart which shown out the most conspicuously through all the actions of his long and beneficent life. In fine, CLARK STEVENS, in the truest sense of the term, was a great man; for

"The good are great, the great not always good."

ELDER ZIBA WOODWORTH.

Ziba Woodworth, a man whose character was marked by so many peculiar qualities, and whose life was checkered by so many peculiar events as to have caused him to have occupied a sufficient space in the public mind during the early settlement of Montpelier, to deserve a place among our individual sketches, was born in April 1769, in the town of Bozrah, situated about a dozen miles northerly of New London and Groton, Connecticut. He was a connection of the gallant Colonel Ledyard, who married his aunt, and who afterwards won immortality by his martyrdom at Fort Griswold during the Revolutionary War. It might have been, perhaps, through some of the influences growing out of this honorable connection, which induced Ziba, with his two brothers, Joseph and Asahel Woodworth,—all young men, and Ziba the younger, but seventeen,—to become soldiers in Col. Ledyard's regiment. At any rate they all did so; and when that revengeful and conscience-chafed devil incarnate, Benedict Arnold, led the British against New London, and utterly desolated it with fire and sword, Ziba and his brother Asahel, were, with their brave uncle in command, in Fort Griswold, on the Groton side of the Thames, Joseph being with another detachment some miles distant, but hastening on to the rescue. While the infamous Arnold was devastating New London, he sent out a detachment of several hundred British troops under Colonel Eyre, to carry Fort Griswold. The resistance of Colonel Ledyard was gallant but unavailing. Part of the works were dilapidated, and the British, after being kept at bay about an hour, and suffering the temporary loss of their Colonel, who was badly wounded, and the unqualified loss of their second in command, Major Montgomery, who, with many of the soldiers, was killed, poured into the Fort, in overwhelming numbers, under the lead of the third officer in rank, the vindictive and brutal Major Broomfield. Colonel Ledyard now at once surrendered the Fort, and, as every child in America has heard, while presenting his sword, hilt first, to the British commander, was murderously run through the body by his own weapon. Thereupon the British commenced an indiscriminate butchery of the Americans by the rapid volleys of their musketry and the busy use of their bayonets. Among the first discharges, Ziba and his brother Asahel were prostrated,—the former by a bullet, shattering the bones of his knee, and the latter by some head wound, which rendered him insensible. But they had not yet done enough for the already desperately wounded Ziba. One of them made a heavy lunge with a bayonet into his bowels, the wound, however, owing to the strength and thickness of the new tow shirt he had on, not proving mortal. Another struck him with the butt of a musket on the head, and, for the time, stretched him senseless on the ground. The massacre was intended to be universal, but it was not wholly unavenged. On the instant of the fall of Colonel Ledyard, two of his exasperated followers rushed from opposite sides upon his murderer, and instantly impaling him through the body with their pikes or strong spontoons, lifted him writhing on their points, and threw him over the pickets to die the death he so well merited.* After all were slain, or supposed to have received their death wounds, the British, in their wanton ferocity, dragged out a dozen or so of those who exhibited the most signs of life, piled them into a detached cart, and sent it rolling down a steep bank till it struck a large apple tree, by which it was stove to pieces in the shock, and made a

*As the above account which was had from the lips of Uncle Ziba in his life time appears to violate history, it will be contended by some that he mistook some other British officer there slain for the murderer of Ledyard.

sudden end of its groaning victims. Most of these personal particulars were had from the lips of Ziba Woodworth himself, who witnessed them before or after his fall. And they are all confirmed in history except what relates to the just fate of the savage Major Broomfield. And even that is not left wholly unauthenticated; for the British return of the slain included two field officers; and as Colonel Eyre was reported only as wounded, Broomfield must have been one of them. But the fact of the manner of his death rests, we believe, wholly on the testimony of the two Woodworths, who were present. In the name of Heaven's justice, we hope it is true.

After a long and distressing sickness, Ziba Woodworth recovered, except in the use of his knee, and, in a few years, came with his two brothers, and perhaps other members of his family, to settle in Montpelier. His first pitch was made on the lot lying about a mile east of the village, which he soon sold to James Hawkins, and purchased another on the Branch, about a mile and a half above the village, where he continued ever after to reside, till the occurrence of his death by some acute disease, on the 27th of November, 1826.

He married and lived some years with his wife in Connecticut, but on account of some domestic trouble, they were divorced; and soon after coming here, he married for a second wife, Miss Lucy Palmer from Canaan, N. H., and had by her five children, all of whom, but their son John, who is still living, died in childhood.

Ziba Woodworth came into Montpelier about 1790, was present at its organization and became its first Town Clerk. He probably experienced religion in Connecticut; for ever after coming here, he was accounted a religious man of the Free Will Baptist persuasion. In about 1800, he began to exhort in public meetings; and, in January 1806, he was licensed and ordained at a Quarterly Meeting of Freewill Baptists held at Danville, Vt., to go forth to preach the gospel and administer all its ordinances. He did not, however, preach statedly anywhere, but mostly confining himself to his farm, divided his spare time between politics and religion, and became as ardent a partizan as he was a Christian.

Elder Woodworth was a man of a small stature, limping in gate, but of a wonderfully animated manner and conversation. His heart seemed ever absolutely overflowing with the gushing feelings of his love and benevolence. As an instance of his kind and sympathetic nature, may be cited the fact, that on learning that a poor man from his neighborhood, who had moved to Ohio, had fallen sick and died there, leaving two or three unprotected children, he left his business, journeyed all the way to Ohio, at his own expense, in a single wagon, and brought all the children home with him. And still uncle Ziba had enough faults to mingle with his virtues, to make him sometime the subject of curious or doubtful remarks among the less charitable of community. He was quite energetic in all he did or said, and the ardor of his temperament often led him into some extravagance of speech or action. But, take him all in all, he was a man of the kindest of impulses, a hearty friend, a charitable opponent, a good neighbor and a good citizen.

JOHN TAPLIN, ESQUIRE.

Although the subject of the following sketch was, at the commencement of the settlement of Montpelier, and for many years afterwards, a resident within the borders of the adjoining town of Berlin, yet, as he was ever closely connected with our first settlers, both in their private relations and public affairs, was the first officiating magistrate of the place, was associated in that capacity with the organization of the town, was a member of its first Congregational Church, and one of its citizens during the last years of his life, it has been deemed proper, in view of the public positions he occupied, and the worthiness of his general character, to place a brief sketch of his life among those of our prominent first settlers.

JOHN TAPLIN, who, though by common usage he was entitled to the military appellation of Major and the civil one of Honorable, was yet generally known by the more unpretending designation of Esquire Taplin, was born in Marlborough, Massachusetts, in the year 1748. In about 1764 he removed with his father, Colonel John Taplin, to Newbury, Vermont, and soon after to Corinth, of which town his father was one of the original proprietors. His father, who was one of the most noted men of his times, had been a Colonel in the British American Army, under General Amherst, and actively engaged with Rogers, Putnam, Stark, and other distinguished American officers, in reducing the fortresses of the French on Lake Champlain, and fighting their red allies, then prowling through the entire wilderness territory of Vermont. And young Taplin, after receiving a fair common school education for his years, was, from the age of twelve to fifteen years, out with his father in this French and Indian war, being generally stationed at Crown Point and Ticonderoga.

Soon after his removal to Vermont, Colonel Taplin was appointed, under the jurisdiction of New York, Chief Judge of the Court of what was then called Gloucester County, but afterwards became Orange County; and young Taplin, then designated as John Taplin, Junior, was, though then but barely twenty-one years of age, appointed High Sheriff of the same Court and County. Kingsland, now Washington, was at first fixed upon as the shire town of this new County, and the new Court was once actually opened there, though the town was then wholly an unbroken wilderness. We have already, while treating of the New York grants in this section, alluded to the singular opening of a Court in the woods of this place; but as the record of this curious transaction, which has but recently come to light, cannot fail to be regarded as an interesting antiquarian document, we will venture to copy it entire, *verbatim et literatim*:

"KINGSLAND, GLOUCESTER COUNTY,
Province of New York, May 29, 1770.

"Court met for the first time, and the ordinance and comitions Being Read

JOHN TAPLIN, SAMUEL SLEEPER, THOMAS SUMNER — Judges being appointed by the Government of New York

were present, and the Courts opened as is usual in other Courts—Also present

JAMES PENNOCK, ABNER FOWLER, JOHN PETERS — Justices of the Quorum

JOHN TAPLIN, Jr., Sheriff.

"N. B. these Courts were the Courts of Quarterly sessions and the Court of Common Plea for Said County.

"Court adjourned to the last Tuesday in August next to be held in said Kingsland.

"Opened accordingly, and appointed four Constables, Simeon Stevens for Newbury, Jessee McFarland for Moretown, Abner Howard for Thetford, and Samuel Pennock for Strafford, and adjourned to the last Tuesday of Nov.

"Nov. 27, Court opened at Kingsland. Called over the docket of 8 cases only, put over and dismissed them, and appointed Ebenezer Green Constable for Thetford, and Samuel Pennock, Ebenezer Martin & Ebenezer Green and Samuel Allen Surveyors for the County, and adjourned to February next last Tuesday.

"Feb. 25 }
1771 } Sett out from Moretown for Kings Land, travelled untill Knight there Being no Road, and the Snow very depe, we travelled on Snow Shoes or Racats, on the 26th we travelled Some ways, and Held a Council when it was concluded it was Best to open the Court as we Saw No Line it was not whether in Kingsland or not. But we concluded we were farr in the woods we did not expect to See any House unless we marched three miles within Kingsland and no one lived there when the Court was ordered to be opened on the spot, present

John Taplin, Judge
John Peters of the Quorum
John Taplin Jr., Sheriff.

all Causes Continued or adjourned over to Next term
the Court, if one, adjourned over untill the last Tuesday in May Next at which it was opened and after disposing of one case of bastardy, adjourned to August next.

"JOHN PETERS Clerk."

Thus ends this curious specimen of judicial records. It will be seen by it that at the first Court nothing is hinted about the Court being held in the woods and snows. It was probably held at the nearest house in Corinth, and, by a judicial fiction, treated as a Court at Kingsland. But it does not appear that the Court was ever called at Kingsland after the so called August Term, 1771, having the next term met at Newbury, where it continued to hold sessions till the breaking out of the Revolution. The Court did not, however, give up the idea of making Kingsland the Seat of Justice, for they ordered their young Sheriff, John Taplin, Jr., to build a log jail there, which order he promptly executed, and made return to the Court accordingly, though it is believed that the jail, as such, was never occupied. This singularly originated log jail was situated a mile or two south-east of the present village of Washington, near the sources of the brook which, running northerly into Stevens Branch, thenceforward took the name of Jail Branch.

On the opening of the Revolution, Colonel Taplin, declining to take sides against the King who had distinguished him, retired during the war into Canada, leaving our John Taplin, Jr., on the paternal property in Corinth, where he resided until many years after Vermont had become a State had elapsed, and was so much esteemed by his fellow-townsmen as to have received from them at least two elections as their Representative in the Legislature. In the summer of 1787 he removed to Berlin, having purchased that excellent farm, on the lower part of Dog River, since known as the Old John Haden place, and became the first Representative of Berlin, and for several years the first officiating Justice of the Peace in all this vicinity.

At the age of twenty he married Miss Catharine Lovell, daughter of Colonel Nehemiah Lovell of Newbury, who was grandson of the celebrated hero of the Lovell Pond Indian battle. And this wife dying in 1794, he married, for a second one, the following year, Miss Lydia Gove of Portsmouth, New Hampshire. By his first wife he had twelve children, and by his last nine, making twenty-one in the whole; and what is still more remarkable, they all except one which was accidentally scalded to death in infancy, lived to reach years of maturity, marry and settle down in life as the heads of families—thus furnishing an instance of family fruitfulnes and health which, perhaps, never had a parallel in the whole State of Vermont.

Mr. Taplin's practical knowledge of men and the ordinary affairs of life was, from his varied opportunities for observation, quite extensive; and his natural intellectual capacities were, at least, of a highly respectable order. But probably what are called the sentiments, or moral affections, should be considered as constituting the predominant traits of his character. At all events, kindness to all, and active benevolence and charity to the poor and distressed, were very conspicuous elements of his nature; and his house and his hands were ever alike open to relieve the wants of those who might solicit his hospitalities, or more substantial assistance. And, as is too often the case, the sharp and selfish world failed not to take advantage of these over amiable traits of character. The free horse was at length almost ridden to death; and in consequence, at the age of fifty, he found himself badly involved in pecuniary embarrassments, growing out of his general system of benevolence in a good degree, but mainly out of his acts of accommodation in becoming bondsman for others. These so sadly reduced his property as to compel him to part with his valuable old homestead for a less costly one, which, from growing infirmities, he was also at length induced to abandon for a residence with one of his sons in this village. But although the last years of his life were thus clouded and embittered, he was, to the last, yet held in the estimation of all as one of the most amiable and best of men and christians, and as one of the most enlightened and useful of citizens.

He died in Montpelier, in the month of November, 1835, at the advanced age of eighty-seven years; and his memory is still warmly cherished, not only by his numerous descendants, but by all who remember his tall, comely person, the mild dignity of his deportment, and the never varying amenity of his manners towards all classes of people.

DOCTOR EDWARD LAMB.

Dr. EDWARD LAMB was born in Leicester, Massachusetts, in the year 1771. His father being a mechanic, and not in such circumstances as would warrant him in sending his son abroad for the advantages of a full public education, put him, as he began to advance towards manhood, into the Academy, which was growing up in that town, and in which the classics were then beginning to be taught. After attending this institution a few years, and adding a respectable knowledge of Latin and Greek to his acquirements in the English branches, young Lamb entered himself as a medical student in the office of Dr. Fisk, in the neighboring town of Sturbridge, now Southbridge. Here he remained till he had acquired his profession, continuing his connection with Dr. Fisk's office until he had attended a course of medical lectures in Boston and Cambridge, when, at the age of about twenty-four, he removed to Montpelier, where his elder brother, Colonel Larned Lamb, had some years preceded him, and settled down in his profession for life.

In 1799 he was chosen First Constable and Collector of the town, and retained in the office for the two following years.

In 1803 he married Miss Polly Witherell of Montpelier, who died in 1822, leaving no issue. In 1804 he was elected the town representative in the Legislature, and again elected to that office in the years 1814 and 1815, and thus made in all, three years the representative of Montpelier. And what should be esteemed a still greater honor, he was one of the Presidential electors when Gen. Harrison was run in 1836.

Although he was not much of a public speaker, yet that he acquitted himself well in his public stations was generally acknowledged, as it certainly might be safely inferred from his rare good sense, general knowledge and unusually extensive practical information. He was a man of wonderful memory and he had stored it with a vast fund of all sorts of knowledge and learning.

Such were the principal events, public and private, which marked the life of Dr. Lamb; and we know of but two public performances of his, not connected with the above named offices —one the delivery of an original oration at the first celebration of the fourth of July ever held in Montpelier, in 1806, the other his valuable address on the "*Science of Medicine*," delivered before the Vermont Medical Society some fifteen years afterwards.

But it was in his profession that Dr. Lamb was best known to the public, and in that he *was* known more favorably and more extensively than generally falls to the lot of a local physician. His opinions among his professional brethren, in this section of the State, were widely sought and as widely respected. In a knowledge of the technicalities, or the true signification of the terms of medical science, he scarcely had a superior anywhere. In *all* the ordinary diseases, his skill was equal to that of other good physicians—in *fevers* it was so obviously preeminent as to place him with the very ablest practitioners of Vermont. The high estimation in which his knowledge and skill were held, in this respect, by his professional brethren, is sufficiently attested in the significant fact, that during the general and fatal prevalence of malignant fevers in 1813 and 1814, he had at one time, during that period, no less than fourteen sick physicians under his immediate care in this part of the State.

During the run of that fearful epidemic, the spotted fever, in this village and its outskirts, Dr. Lamb had the principal care of seventy cases, and lost but three out of the whole number. His practice, indeed, in his own town, was, through all the active period of his life, which should be set down at at least forty years, as full as it was successful; while for difficult cases, and for consultations, his attendance was constantly sought in all the surrounding country.

So much for Dr. Lamb as a physician. As a man he had some unfortunate deficiences of character; but, what can be said of few others, those deficiences hurt nobody but himself, and affected no interest unfavorably but his own. In all his own pecuniary affairs, he was singularly careless and remiss. More than half the time, it is believed, he made no charges for his services at all. He rarely dunned any man; and if he did, it was when he happened to be hard pressed for money to keep up his unusually plain and cheap way of living. Then often he would go to some abundantly responsible customer, owing him honestly, perhaps, fifty dollars, ask for fifteen or twenty, and on receiving it, hand back a receipt in full of the whole account. In fact, he was one of the most unselfish men in the world, and could not be brought to care any more for money, except for supplying his absolute present wants, than so much dirt beneath his feet. And in all his extensive practice among all classes of community, in this section, it probably never once entered his head to make the least distinction between the richest and the poorest, in the promptitude and faithfulness of his attendance. And the consequence of all this was, that while his just and honest earnings, would have made him, if well managed, worth fifty thousand dollars, he died worth scarcely one hundredth part of that amount.

Thus he passed his long and useful life, in which he was everybody's servant, and everybody's friend but his own; and being at last seized with one of the ten thousand fevers he had so successfully managed in others, he at once predicted its fatal termination, and, in sad realization of his but too correct prediction, he, in a few days passed peacefully away, on the 4th day of November, 1845, at the age of about seventy-four years, universally regretted and universally respected.

Dr. Lamb personally was of medium height, rather stocky, moderate in his motions, slightly limping in gate in consequence of a fever sore on one of his legs in his youth, and very neglectful in all matters of dress and outward appearance. But all these were at once forgotten, when we confronted his massive and noble head, manly features, pleasant blue eye, and thoughtful, impressive countenance. Socially, he was one of the most kindly and agreeable men, full of instructive remarks, which were generally aptly illustrated by the fund of piquant and amusing anecdotes, which, in the course of his various reading and experience, he had treasured in his remarkably retentive memory, and which were always at his command.

If ever a people had cause to remember a man—if ever they owed a great and unequivocal debt of gratitude to any one man, the people of Montpelier and vicinity have such a cause, and rest under such an obligation to Dr. Edward Lamb. Let his descendants never utter his name without breathing a blessing on his memory.

GENERAL PEARLEY DAVIS.

Among those who came to Montpelier with its first settler, Colonel Jacob Davis, or soon followed him, were three brothers, his cousins, Pearley Davis, Nathaniel Davis and Hezekiah Davis. Nathaniel settled on a fine farm in the vicinity of the present North Montpelier village, after some years opened a store there, and amassed a handsome property, which was subsequently lost in the large factory he had erected at the falls on Kingsbury's Branch, in the neighborhood of his residence. Hezekiah settled on a farm on East Hill, and became one of the most independent of our farmers. Both these were men of character and intelligence, and reared fine families of children to sustain the family reputation, but were both of a retiring disposition and so little ambitious to mingle in public affairs that their names do not figure largely on the records of our town transactions. Not so, however, with Parley, whose energy, public spirit and capacities for public business caused his name to become greatly identified with the history of the town, and have furnished good reasons to its historian for placing him among its benefactors and its most noted early settlers.

PEARLEY DAVIS, a son of Nathaniel and Sarah Davis, was born in Oxford, (in the part afterwards becoming Charlton,) Massachusetts, on the 31st of March, 1766, and, after receiving rather an unusually good English education, at the then new Academy in the neighboring town of Leicester, including a knowledge of Surveying, he came into town with Colonel Davis, bringing his set of Surveyor's instruments, and at once engaging in the original surveys of the township, first as an assistant and finally as a principal Surveyor of the town and county.

It was while thus employed, as he once told the writer of this sketch, that, coming on to the splendid swell of forest land then crowning the elevation at the center of the town, he was so struck with the general indications of the soil and the natural beauty of the location, as seen beneath the growth of stately maples, cumbered with little underbrush, that he resolved he would here make his pitch, feeling confident that this must be the seat of town business, and then believing even that it would become the site of its most populous village.

The mistake of General Davis, so far as regarded the growing up of much of a village on the highlands of the town, appears to have been quite a common one with our early settlers. Impressed at first, as he was, with the inviting appearance of the higher parts of their respective townships, when contrasted with the forbidding aspect of the dark and tangled valleys, the most able and enterprising of them, for a general thing, made their pitches accordingly, as in the instances of the settlements of Randolph, Danville, and dozens of other towns in this State. But they soon found their anticipated villages slipping down into the valleys, to leave them, in that respect, high and dry on the hills, with the most travelled roads all winding along the streams. First, there must be mills; then a place near to shoe horses; then a place for refreshment of both man and horse: and while all this is going on, it is a convenience and a saving of time to be able to purchase a few family necessaries; thence, to meet these calls, first comes the blacksmith's shop, then the tavern, then the store; and you have the neucleus of a continually growing village already formed; while people soon find out it is easier going round a hill than over it, and build their roads accordingly.

So far however, as regarded the seat of town business, Gen. Davis' predictions were fulfilled; for he, having pitched on a tract of three hundred acres of land at the center and built a commodious house, had the satisfaction of seeing it the receptacle of all town meetings till a public house was erected; and the latter was the place of such meetings, either for the whole town or his part of it, up to the day of his death. At all these town meetings he was always an active and influential participator. And in looking over the records of the town for the first half century of its corporate existence, we can scarcely find a page on which his name does not appear coupled with some of its most important trusts or offices.

In 1794 he was elected Captain of the first military company ever organized in town; and before the year had closed he was promoted to the office of Major of the regiment formed from the companies of the different towns in this section. In 1798 he was elected a Colonel of the regiment; and in 1799 he was still further promoted to the prominent post of General. In 1799 he was also honored by his townsmen with a seat in the Legislature, and received from them two elections as their Representative in the General Assembly.

In 1794 General Davis married Miss Rebecca Peabody, daughter of Colonel Stephen Peabody of Amherst, N. H., the lady of whose medical skill and general usefulness we have particularly spoken while treating of the incidents and characters of the early settlement. From this union sprang seven daughters, most of whom lived to connect themselves with the best families of this or other towns; and one of them, (now deceased,) Mrs. Truman Pitkin, whose family occupy the old homestead, was the mother of Pearley P. Pitkin, Esq., the present Representative of East Montpelier; while of the surviving, one, endowed with high gifts of poesy, is the widow of the late Hon. S. Pitkin, and another the wife of the Hon. Royal Wheeler.

General Davis, in the expanded benevolence of his mind, appeared to take an interest in the welfare of all his fellow-men, and particularly so of the young, for whose improvement in knowledge he labored earnestly and always. He was one of the most active and liberal in establishing a Town Library. He was ever anxious to see our common schools supplied with competent teachers; and in subscriptions, and in the education of his daughters, he largely patronized our Academy. He was one of the most pleasant, animated and instructive of companions, one of the best of neighbors, and one of the most public spirited and useful of citizens. In short, with his strong, massive person, prepossessing face, intelligent eye, genial and hearty manner, and earnest tone of conversation, he was one whom the world would unite in calling a grand old fellow, and as such he will be remembered till the last of the generation who knew him shall have followed him to the grave.

He died April 14, 1848, at the age of a little over eighty-two years.

His relict, Mrs. Rebecca Peabody Davis, died February 5, 1854, aged about eighty-three years and six months.

THE REVEREND CHESTER WRIGHT.

CHESTER WRIGHT was born in Hanover, New Hampshire, November 6th, 1776; and his father was one of the first settlers of that town, a farmer, a highly respectable, pious man, and long a Deacon of its Congregational Church. His mother being also a pious and exemplary woman, these worthy parents gave their son, Chester, the best of moral and religious trainings. On reaching the age of twenty-one, he purchased a farm and commenced the occupation to which he had been reared; but within a few years, his attention becoming deeply engrossed in the concerns of experimental religion, he sold out his property and commenced fitting for a Collegiate education to prepare him for what he believed to be a call to enter the higher field of laboring for the salvation of his fellow men. In 1802 he entered Middlebury College, then but recently established, and after a creditable College career, was graduated in 1806, at the late age of thirty. Soon after this, he commenced the usual course of theological studies with the Rev. Dr. Burton of Thetford, Vt.; and, having completed his course, he was licensed to preach in 1808, when he immediately began preaching in Montpelier, where, within the year, he was ordained the pastor of the Congregational Church and Society of the place, and where he sustained that relation till his dismissal in 1830, a period of over twenty-one years.

Mr. Wright was a small, spare man, in person, and apparently deficient in physical powers. But he was a person of active temperament, of great moral energy, and of intrepid bearing in leading the way wherever the finger of Duty pointed. When a good deed was to be performed no lions were ever found in the way to turn him back or disturb him. Indeed he was a man of strength, but his strength was in his soul. In disposition, he was mild, pleasant, affectionate and most unselfishly benevolent. He knew nothing, he cared nothing about the calculations of the worldling, not even enough to keep him within the bounds of the ordinary prudence required to ensure the common comforts of a family; and if he had but one loaf of bread in his house, he would any day, if asked, cut it in two and give one half to a needy neighbor.

In regard to his grade of intellect, Mr. Wright was naturally inferior but to very few. But he did not begin to cultivate his mind to any but a very limited extent, till he had arrived at maturity, and then he was hurried through a college at that time affording few advantages over an ordinary Academy; and then, again, he was hurried through a brief course of exclusively theological studies, to be put at once into the harness of hard professional duties and constant parochial labors. In fact, he never had any time for the patient mental training so indispensable to high intellectual efforts; and the only wonder is that he rose so far above mediocrity as he did as a preacher. But what he fell short in learning and compass of thought, he amply made up in moral force, and that certain pathos, which, when coming from the heart of an honest, earnest man, tinges all his thoughts and experiences, quickens them into power for touching our sympathies and then bringing the willing conviction to our otherwise indifferent minds. He had, in fine, that happy combination of qualities that made him seem great and powerful to his hearers, while they scarcely knew how or why his words had produced such an effect. And such, indeed, should be all who undertake to point men the way to eternal life. A preacher of a listless, unsympathizing heart, and consequently a cold deliverer of mere head-work sermons, can touch nobody's feelings—can never make a convert, and should never be suffered to enter a pulpit in the land.

Mr. Wright's success, as a preacher, however, is best attested by the evidence so unmistakably exhibited in the frequent and extensive religious revivals that occurred under his preaching, and in the numerous and influential church that grew up in the place under his efficient ministrations ; while was equally well attested the high respect in which his character and talents were held abroad in the fact, that he was the far-sought counsellor and assistant of all the ministers and churches in this and other parts of the State, and often their chosen delegate to the most important ecclesiastical conventions in other States.

But he was more than a mere preacher. He was one of the most active of our citizens in striving for the moral and intellectual elevation of his people, and even in entering zealously into the spirit of all the more public enterprises which looked to the material advancement of his village. He was always a live man; and when anything occurred affecting the individual or public interests of the place, he was sure to be about, showing him to be a judicious adviser, or an able assistant. When the first great fire—that of the burning of the Cotton Factory—happened at Montpelier, we well recollect running two miles to be present, and that when we reached the burning fabric, the first man we noticed was Mr. Wright, standing on the reach-pole of a rear endangered building, dripping with water, handling buckets, and, with the voice and energy of a young lion, giving orders to the crowd below. And, within this very month, we heard the old first Engineer of our Fire Department, remark that "Parson Wright was the best man at a fire he had ever seen in Montpelier."

We have already, in a previous chapter, commented at considerable length on the great and salutary reformation which

Mr. Wright, through his untiring efforts, effected in the moral condition of the people of Montpelier village. In that respect he did all that was there said of him, and all that his greatest admirers ever claimed for him. While he knew of a wrong, a vice or injurious habit among any of his people, he gave himself no rest till he saw the wrong righted, the vice overcome and the habit corrected. He was everywhere found exhorting men individually as well us collectively. Though often rebuffed, he was never discouraged, but persistently returned again and again to the work of accomplishing his object, till even the most obdurate began to look upon it as a matter of course that they must hear from their misdeeds and delinquencies, and at length to consider that the cheapest thing to be done was, at least outwardly, to reform themselves.

It is not every man and minister, to be sure, that could have pursued such a course with such success. But the subjects of Mr. Wright's labors were all fully conscious, that he was perfectly honest and unselfish in his motives, and that his heart was grieved and yearning for their good; and in some way or other, they all yielded—some perhaps to git rid of him—some to oblige him, but more in consequence of the sincere convictions which the magnetic influence of his affectionate voice, tearful eye and well conceived arguments, had planted permanently in their hearts.

It was thus, with his earnest and efficient labors in the pulpit, that Mr. Wright accomplished the reformation he did in the moral and religious condition of Montpelier village, while having at the same time the gratification of seeing its temperal keep pace with its spiritual prosperity.

But if Mr. Wright was such a man—if he labored so much and effected so much for the good of his people and his town, why was he dismissed in his old age, and, with broken health compelled to go abroad or starve? This question is more easily asked than answered. Admitting there was fault on both sides in the unhappy controversy that resulted in his dismissal, still the fact stands out, and always must stand out, that Mr. Wright, after having done almost everything for his people, and wore out nearly all the energies of his life in their behalf, was virtually driven to vacate his sacred post among them.

His dismission, as will probably be generally admitted, grew out of the agitation then going on respecting the merits and demerits of the Masonic Institution, to which many of his people, and quite a number of the leading members of his church, belonged. It was claimed by the friends of that order that Mr. Wright had been found to entertain opinions adverse to the institution, and that he persisted in openly expressing them. On the other side, it was admitted he might entertain the alledged opinions, and have expressed them in conversation, but never voluntarily introduced them into the pulpit, and therefore had only exercised a common right of every citizen, and, of course, had done nothing worthy of censure. The members of the church, who were members of the order, did not take any part in the controversy, but left the battle to those of the order outside the church, and probably said nothing against Mr. Wright worse than to express their regrets that he had destroyed his influence by expressing the obnoxious opinions; and even they probably *did* nothing worse than, when the annual subscription paper came round for his support, to put down ciphers against their names instead of their usual dollar marks. In this state of things Mr. Wright very properly called a Council to take cognizance of the subject of his dismission. The Council met, patiently heard the complaints, and by way of decision, in substance said: If Mr. Wright must go, we must dismiss him, but "we find no fault with the man; see ye to it."

Mr. Wright was blessed in his domestic relations. In April, 1811, he married Miss Charlotte Whitney of Royalton, Vermont, a very estimable lady, by whom he raised a family of children, all destined to highly respectable positions in life. After his dismissal from Montpelier in 1830, he was soon settled as a minister in Hardwick, Vermont, where he continued his professional labors eight or nine years longer, when he returned to his old homestead at the lower end of Montpelier village, to relieve his worn out system by a little rest—to sicken and die in the spring of 1840, at the age of about sixty-three-and-a-half years.

What more can we now say of that rare man, Chester Wright? Nothing, that will make him appear greater or better than has already been represented; and we will now only recapitulate the substance, as we may justly do, in the lines which Cowper wrote of Whitfield:

"He loved the world that hated him: the tear
That dropp'd upon his Bible was sincere;
Assail'd by scandal and the tongue of strife
His only answer was, a blameless life,
Paul's love of Christ, and steadiness unbribed
Were copied close in him, and well transcribed."

COLONEL JAMES H. LANGDON.

JAMES HOOKER LANGDON, the successful and widely known merchant of Montpelier, was born in the town of Farmington, Connecticut, March 3d, 1783. While yet quite a youth he entered the store of General Abner Forbes, then the leading merchant of Windsor, Vt., to acquire a knowledge of the mercantile profession, which he had determined to make the business of his life. And such was the progress he made in that knowledge, such the confidence he inspired, and such, at the same time, the tact and good judgment he displayed in all the details of trade, and the more important transactions of business coming within the scope of his action, that his employer, General Forbes, even before he reached the age of twenty-one, unhesitatingly took him into partnership, and established him in business at the head of a branch store in the village of Montpelier. This was in 1803; and for the next half dozen years he continued to do business under the firm of Langdon & Forbes; when justly believing he had accumulated capital enough and friends enough in this place to warrant the movement, he bought out Gen. Forbes' interest in the store, and thenceforward conducted the business in his own name, and entirely on his own responsibility.

From this time, alone or in company with different partners—the first and longest continued being the systematic and clear headed John Barnard, who was prematurely cut down by an acute disease in 1822; and the next the Hon. John Spalding, still surviving—from this time, for the next twenty years, Colonel Langdon seemed to be wafted forward on one unvaried tide of prosperity and success. But having in the main body of this work, in the chapter on the progress and reforms of trade, fully descanted on the great public benefits that grew out of his commercial career,—shown how instrumental he was in reforming the irregularities of trade, which up to his day custom had sanctioned, and in placing it on a just and honorable basis, and how, while thus conferring untold benefits on his town by what he did, and by the force of his salutary examples, he so conducted his dealings as well to deserve all the remarkable success which attended him,—we need not here enlarge on his noble characteristics as a merchant; and we shall therefore confine the remainder of our sketch to that which particularly marked him as a man and a citizen, and gave him that strong hold on public feeling, and that high place in the public estimation, which he retained through life.

In 1809 Colonel Langdon married Miss Nabby Robbins, of Lexington, Massachusetts,—a union from which sprang five children, Amon who died in childhood, John B., James R. and Caira R. Langdon, all still living.

Colonel Langdon ever manifested a proper interest, and often took an active part in the public affairs and official business of the town, having at various times filled with acceptance its most important offices. He also entered, and was rapidly promoted, in the military line, till he gained the title by which he is here designated. In the year 1828, having removed over the river on to his beautiful meadows within the borders of Berlin, he was elected with unusual unanimity by the people of that town, as their representative in the Legislature; and in the following year re-elected to the office still more unanimously; and by the application of his excellent judgment and great practical knowledge in the business of legislation, he well justified the choice of his constituents. In 1828 he was elected, on the retirement of the Hon. Elijah Paine, the first to hold the office, President of the Bank of Montpelier, which responsible office he continued to hold to the time of his death.

In person Colonel Langdon was well-formed, and his features were all shapely and handsome; while his countenance was lighted up by one of the most kindly and winning smiles that enlivened the human face. Nor did his countenance belie his heart, which was inherently sincere, sympathetic and humane. And, while in all the movements and enterprises of public benevolence, his liberality was commensurate with his means, in private charities and individual assistance, he went, as he wished, far beyond what was ever generally made known to the public; For he was extremely averse to making any parade of his benefactions, and his favors were very generally conferred under injunctions of secrecy. And thus it was, that the extent of his private charities and pecuniary assistance to the distressed and those laboring under business embarrassments, were never known except through the irrepressible outgushings of gratitude from the lips of those whom he had relieved.

His lenity and forbearance towards all who were indebted to him were remarkable; and, to the credit of human nature be it said, as remarkable was the gratitude of those thus favored, and their determination that he should never be the loser by the kindness he had conferred. After he had retired from business, expecting to be much absent, he placed his demands, over one hundred thousand dollars in amount, in the charge of a confidential agent, who was an attorney, strictly enjoining him to sue nobody and distress nobody, but use all kindly, and charge him for all the expense and trouble incurred in the collections. And though this great amount of miscellaneous demands remained in the hands of that attorney for nearly three years, and though a large number of the debtors failed during that time, yet in all that period never was a single dollar lost out of the whole collection. On the eve of their failures, or when they had any fears of failure, the debtors would come privately to the agent, and, with the remark, that "Colonel Langdon had been too good to them to be injured," voluntarily placed in his hands the fullest securities they had in their power to offer. Within one week after such transactions, perhaps these debtors would fail; sheriffs would be scouring the country for property; and almost every creditor would suffer loss except Colonel Langdon. He, to the wonder of all, was always found secure.

The last characteristic incident of his life occurred, when he was on his death bed. Finding his end drawing near, he sent for his attorney, and ordered him to make a life-lease to an old revolutionary soldier, of the farm he occupied, but of which the Colonel held a mortgage for more than its value. This was the last business transaction of his life. He died January 7th, 1831. As he was the idol of the people when he lived, so at his death he was lamented by more friends in the community at large than falls to the lot of but few to have numbered among their real mourners.

THE HONORABLE JEDUTHUN LOOMIS.

JEDUTHUN LOOMIS originated in the town of Tolland, Connecticut; and, as we copy from the record in his old family Bible, entered with characteristic method and exactness, he was born January 5th, 1779. After receiving a good common school, and a fair academical English education, he studied law with the Hon. Oramel Hinckley, of Thetford, Vermont, and having there been admitted to the bar, he came to Montpelier and established himself in his profession in about the year 1805.

In 1807, March 11th, he married Miss Hannah Hinckley, daughter of Colonel and Judge Oramel Hinckley, of Thetford, who died very suddenly December 24th, 1813, leaving no issue.

In 1814, October 10, he married Miss Charity Scott of Peacham, who died June 13th, 1821, leaving two sons, Gustavus H., the late Dr. Loomis, and Chauncey Loomis, still living, having buried a son in infancy.

In 1822, October 8th, he married Miss Sophia Brigham, of Salem, Massachusetts, who died in 1855, leaving two daughters and one son, Charity, the present Mrs. Dana, of Woodstock; Mrs. Joseph Prentiss of Montpelier, and Charles Loomis, Esq., of Cincinnati, Ohio. Judge Loomis himself died Nov. 12, 1843.

In 1814 Mr. Loomis was appointed Register of Probate, for the District of Washington, but held the office only one year.

In 1820 he was elected the Judge of Probate for this District, and had the very unusual honor of receiving ten successive elections, the greatest number of elections of any other man being five, given to the Hon. Salvin Collins.

From 1807, up to his death, there is scarcely a year in which he did not receive, and, what is better, well and faithfully execute, some one of the trusts or offices of town appointment. And for the last twenty years of his life at least he was, besides being an efficient friend of common schools and popular education generally, always a laboring trustee, often the head prudential committee, and always the treasurer, and indeed the chief pillar of Washington County Grammar School. And it was in the latter capacity, to considerable extent, and to that of being so long the admitted model Judge of Probate of all this part of the State, to a still greater, that he was mostly known to the public abroad.

There was once extant an old book called "*The Minute Philosopher.*" We mention it not on account of the contents of the book, but on account of the name, because it is so suggestive of the character of Judge Loomis. He was really a very carefully reasoning and philosophic man, and carried his every day philosophy into all the minutia of business, and all the ordinary transactions of life. Any of the little offices, trusts or commissions growing out of a town, school district, highway district, or neighborhood, or family affairs, which the more ambitious or selfish would disdain to accept, or, if they did, only half execute, he would cheerfully accept, and always execute with the most scrupulous care and faithfulness. Indeed he seemed to consider it his duty to do every thing asked of him, if, in performing it, he thought he could benefit his fellow men individually or the public at large. It was so with him in his profession, so in the the church of which he was a very active member and an officer, and it was so everywhere.

Being a tall, dark complexioned man, of formal manners, with a grave and rather austere countenance, he might be taken by the unacquainted, for a cold, harsh man, with few sensibilities; but break through the apparent atmosphere of repulsion, and approach him, and you would find him as mild and playful as a lamb and as affectionate as a brother.

Being extremely strict in all moral and religious observances, and seemingly rather set in his opinions, he might sometimes be taken for a bigot; but get at his real views and feelings, and you would find him absolutely liberal, and willing to make all the allowance for errors which the largest charity might demand.

A man of legal knowledge, ordinary good judgment, and of known good motives, who is willing to perform the duties of every small needful office, as well as great one, and who is ever ready to act the part of adviser, assistant and friend, in adjusting town difficulties and neighborhood dissentions, is always a great blessing to a village community. Such a man, most certainly, was Jedathun Loomis. And more than will ever be justly apreciated, probably, is Montpelier village indebted to him for his untiring and self-sacrificing exertions to advance her best interests.

THE HONORABLE TIMOTHY MERRILL.

Timothy Merrill was emphatically a public man, and as such we shall describe and trace him in his official career. His origin, different residences and domestic relations, however, should be mentioned in the connection; and they are briefly as follows:

Timothy Merrill was born in Farmington, Connecticut, March 26, 1781, where, having received little more than a common school education, he, when becoming of age, shouldered his pack and travelled on foot to Bennington, Vermont, in which town his older brother, the Honorable Orsamus C. Merrill, had some years before established himself in the legal profession. Here he studied law; here, in due course of time, he was admitted to the bar, and commenced practice in partnership with the afterwards noted Robert Temple, in Rutland. But not feeling very well satisfied with his prospects or situation here, he dissolved his connection with Temple in less than a year, and removed to Montpelier in the year 1809, and established himself alone in his profession. In 1812 he married Miss Clara Fassett, daughter of Dr. Fassett of Bennington, a surgeon in the army of the Revolution. From this union were born five children—a son who died in infancy, Ferrand F. Merrill, our late well-known fellow citizen; Edwin S. Merrill of Winchendon, Mass, but formerly Post Master of Montpelier; Clara Augusta Merrill, a young lady of much excellence who died in 1842, and Timothy R. Merrill, our present Judge of Probate elect.

In 1811 Mr. Merrill was elected the Town Representative of Montpelier in the Legislature, and was re-elected to the same office the following year. In 1811, also, he was elected the first State's Attorney of the new County of Jefferson, and in 1815 he was again elected to the same office, which office, the name of the county being now changed to that of Washington, he continued to hold through seven successive elections, being eight in all, and two more than was ever received in that office by any man in the county, Dennison Smith having received but six. In 1815 he was elected Engrossing Clerk of the General Assembly, and received seven successive elections to the office. In 1822 he was elected Clerk of the House of Representatives, and received nine successive elections to that office. In 1831 he was elected Secretary of State, which office he retained till his death, having received in it five successive elections.

In his profession, Mr. Merrill took at least a very fair rank, and was sustained by as fair a patronage. But his public employments required too much of his time and attention to permit him to reach the position in his profession to which his admitted talents whould have otherwise doubtless raised him. He was ever considered, however, a safe legal adviser; and in his appeals to juries, as well as in his addresses to public assemblies, he often warmed up into genuine eloquence, the effect of which was heightened by one of the most clear toned and melodious voices which it was ever the good fortune of a public man to possess.

But if Mr. Merrill did such a fair professional business, to bring him money, in addition to his receipts from his public offices, why need he have died worth so little property, two or three thousands being found to be the whole amount of his estate? The question was often asked, and what added pertinency to the enquiry was the known fact that he and his family ever dressed and lived, for their position, with great plainness and frugality. The answer is probably to be found in another fact: he never charged anything at all for advice, though his office was thronged by those seeking it; and, being naturally a peace man and very conscientious, he would advise three men out of lawsuits where he would one into them. Again, he never charged for his legal services much more than half what was usually charged by other lawyers of the same professional standing. And, yet again, of what he did charge he would, in any event, often remit a part, and, if his client was unsuccessful, he would, in his sympathy for him, be quite likely to give in nearly the whole of it.

Mr. Merrill, in person, was below the medium height, but had a fine head, good features and a very intelligent and prepossessing countenance. He was one of the most affectionate of husbands and fathers, one of the most agreeable of neighbors, and one of the most correct and enlightened of citizens.

THE HONORABLE FERRAND F. MERRILL.

Although FERRAND F. MERRILL has but very recently departed from life, and at his death was comparatively a young man, whose life and character might be thought better to be left to some writer of a more distant period, yet there seems a fitness in placing a brief sketch of him along side of that of his father. And, when placed in that connection, brief only it need be; for, to a most singular extent, the public history of the father was the history of the son. Like the father, and for about the same number of years, though at a much younger age, the son was Clerk of the House of Representatives. Like the father, was the son at once transferred from the Clerkship to the office of Secretary of State, to be therein retained, we believe, exactly the same number of years during which the former lived to hold the office. Like the father, the son was State's Attorney for Washington County, though, through the altered rules of rotation, not so long; and, like the father, was the son, for the now customary term, the Representative of Montpelier in the Legislature.

And Ferrand F. Merrill, by his education, great readiness in all matters in form acquired under his father's trainings, advantages of personal appearance, and great courtesy of manners, was unusually fitted to do well and appear well in public life. And accordingly, as might be expected, he was an accomplished and popular officer. In the Legislature he became a prominent member; and in the difficult position in which he found himself placed, in the keenly contested question relative to the removal of the seat of government from Montpelier, he displayed an ability and tact which met the full approval of his constituents, and which, had he consented to be again a candidate, would have ensured him further elections.

In private life he was blameless, in all his social relations much esteemed. In the furtherance of the interests of religion, morals and education, he took a conspicuous part. And, in fine, he began to be looked upon as one of the most capable and useful of our citizens, who could not, therefore, but greatly deplore his early exit. He died very suddenly, of apoplexy, on the 2d of May, 1859, in the meridian of his usefulness, and when his prospects for professional eminence were the brightest, and the probabilities of his eventual promotion to high judicial or civil posts the strongest.

THE HONORABLE ARAUNAH WATERMAN.

ARAUNAH WATERMAN was born in Norwich, Connecticut, November 8th, 1778. He sprang from good Revolutionary stock, his father having been at first a subaltern officer, and then commissary, in the continental army, and his uncles either officers or soldiers. His advantages for education were so extremely limited, that, at the utmost, six months schooling, and that before the age of twelve years, was all that he received. At the age of about thirteen, he was apprenticed to a carpenter, of his town, and served till he was twenty-one, working steadily by day and studying at night by the light of pine knots, to make up the deficiences of his education. Soon after acquiring his trade, he, by some means, had the good fortune to be recommended as a master mechanic, to General Pinkney, of South Carolina, who was wishing to build somewhat extensively on his several large plantations. He accordingly accepted General Pinkney's offers, and, for the first year devoted himself exclusively to the superintendency of erecting the various structures contemplated, among which was a fine Summer House on Sullivan's Island, and the next year, having, by his capacity and integrity, gained the fullest confidence of his employer, General Pinkney, who was then appointed U. S. Minister to England, and consequently compelled to be absent, he was made steward and chief supervisor over all the General's estates. After leaving General Pinkney's employment he returned to Connecticut, but not long there to remain; for, in 1801 or 1802, he came to Vermont, with his brothers, the present Judges Joseph Waterman and Thomas Waterman, and other brothers and sisters, and with them, settled in the town of Johnson. In 1804 he married Miss Rebecca Noyes, daughter of Oliver Noyes of Hydepark, and sister of the Hon. David P. Noyes. By this wife he had several children, among whom is the Hon. Vernon P. Noyes of Morristown.

His wife dying in 1812, he, in something over a year afterwards, married Miss Mehitable Dodge, of New-Boston, N. H., now deceased, but long known among us, as a pious and most estimable woman. By her he had seven children, two of whom, daughters, are still living on the old homestead in Montpelier. After residing in Johnson about a dozen years, engaged in farming, constructing the machinery required about the different mills of that brisk village, and particularly by the carding and clothing works with which he became connected, he removed to Montpelier, about the beginning of the year 1814, and purchased the farm and a portion of the water privilege, lying on the west bank of the North Branch, above and around the falls, on the borders of this village. Here, besides carrying on his farm, he soon engaged in erecting, improving and carrying on carding and clothing works, and before many years, in connection with Seth Persons, erected, and put in operation, the comparatively extensive woolen factory, which was burned March 1826, and at the burning of which, as mentioned in the body of this work, he came so near losing his life. After this catastrophe, he mainly employed himself in improving his farm, which, with his house soon brought considerably within the village by its gradual extension in that direction, he continued to occupy until his death, coming, at the age of eighty to close his unusually varied, active and laborious life, on the 31st of January, 1859.

In 1821 Mr. Waterman was elected town representative of Montpelier, and re-elected in the two succeeding years of 1822 and 1823. In 1826 he was again elected by his townsmen for a fourth term of the same office. When the new State Senate was established, in 1836, Mr. Waterman was triumphantly elected as one of the two first Senators of Washington county, and, on the following year, as triumphantly reelected, to complete the Senatorial term, which, in what is called the *Two Year Rule*, had been previously adopted. In 1840, he was elected by the Legislature, to the office of Judge of the County Court, which office, however, being unsought and unexpected by him, he declined to accept. As a representative and senator, he never spoke for the sake of talking, and never except to support some measure, which he believed calculated for the public good, or to subserve some cherished political interest; and then his extensive practical knowledge, and accurate political information enabled him to speak with effect.

We find Mr. Waterman's name on our town records often associated with the most important of our town offices and trusts. But he was not much known in these, because, doubtless, he was almost constantly in posts requiring a higher order of capacities, and consequently attracting a more general notice. Being esteemed, both theoretically and practically, the best surveyor in this section of the country, he was, after our old surveyor, General Davis, began to retire from the field, much employed on difficult surveys of land plots, disputed lines, boundaries and the laying out of new public roads. And, in about 1830, when on the completion of the great canal in New York, the feasibility of canals across this State began to be agitated, he was appointed, under an appropriation from the General Government, to conduct a survey for a canal from Burlington up the valley of the Winooski, and over the heights to Wells River, running into the Connecticut. This he accomplished, and, in doing it, was the first man to ascertain the altitude of Montpelier above Lake Champlain, and the altitude of Kettle Pond on the eastern border of Marshfield, the lowest summit level of the heights between Montpelier and Connecticut River. And in proof of the accuracy of his survey, as imperfect as were his instruments, may be cited the fact, that when the surveys of the Central Railroad were perfected, it was found that the Engineers, with their greatly more perfect instruments, and their everyway better equipments and means, had made the level of the top of the dam across the river at Montpelier, to vary but between three and four feet from the altitude recorded in Mr. Waterman's survey made a dozen years before.

Mr. Waterman was ever the steadfast friend and supporter of the interests of science and popular education. He was an active man in sustaining and improving our common schools, and, for many years one of the most efficient of the trustees of our Academy. And while favoring all these interests in others, he always, in despite of the multiplicity of his cares and employments, was a close student himself, and found time to keep himself well posted in all matters of general science and literature. He was probably the most reliable geologist in Montpelier. In a knowledge of the principles of mechanics and their practical applications, he had few superiors anywhere. His knowledge of history was extensive, and of our national politics, singularly ample and accurate. The late Jonathan Southmayd, who was twelve years the preceptor of our Academy, and who was in the habit of often conferring with Mr. Waterman, in the solution of difficult problems in the higher branches of mathematics, mechanics and other sciences, once remarked, that he had never met a man, not educated in a College, who could compare with him in the extent of his general, and the accuracy of his scientific knowledge.

As a citizen, as a man and a neighbor, his usefulness, kindness and practical benevolence, were universally admitted, and, indeed sufficiently proved in the fact, that the assistance he was frequently rendering others, always, through their bad returns for the favors conferred, kept down to a simple competence, what would otherwise have been a handsome property for the inheritance of his family.

Among all those of an active life, a man's capicities and character, are best accurately measured by what he accomplishes. By this rule, what Mr. Waterman accomplished would place him far above the level of ordinary men. In the first place he made himself—no common achievment where such a man is made, and made under such disadvantages; and then he achieved for himself, for his family and for the public, all that we have related of him. And let all that stand as the simple record of his life, to be left for the contemplation of his descendants and friends. What cause have they to ask for a better monument to his memory?

THE HONORABLE CYRUS WARE.

The old war horse that has done good work is too often, after he can no longer be of much more public use, turned out to grass, to become the object of the scorn or neglect of those whom his services had benefited, to be kicked and dogged round the pasture, and finally to be knocked in the head, buried out of sight and be forgotten.

Let us not imitate this graceless example in these our brief mementoes of those who, in early days, did good service in the building up of the town of which we have undertaken to give the history.

CYRUS WARE, son of Jonathan Ware of Wrentham, Mass., was born May 8, 1769. Though left fatherless at the age of three years, he continued with his family, attending the common schools of the place, till somewhere near the age of fourteen, when he went to Hartford, Vt., to learn the blacksmith's trade, in the shop of a Mr. Billings, who had married his sister. In this shop he worked faithfully at the trade till he was twenty-one; and then, with no other education than what he had received at the common schools in his boyhood, and the general knowledge he had contrived to pick up by reading during his apprenticeship, he soon went to studying law with the once well known Hon. Charles Marsh of Woodstock. After remaining here a year or two, he went to Royalton and completed the prescribed course of legal studies with Jacob Smith, Esq., of that town. He was here admitted to the bar in 1799, and the same year came to Montpelier and opened an office in the village. His capacities appear to have early attracted the attention of his townsmen; for within about one year after he came into town, we find him figuring in town offices, in some one of which, he was retained until the September State election, 1805; when he was elected to represent Montpelier in the General Assembly; and so acceptably did he acquit himself, and so much to the satisfaction of his constituents, that they gave him five annual successive elections, a number never exceeded in the case of any Montpelier representative, and never equalled except in the case of Colonel Davis. While still representative of his town he was, in 1808 made chief Judge of Caledonia County Court, to which office he received three successive elections, being continued in that responsible and highly honorable public trust, until the organization of the new County of Jefferson, which on account of his residence within it, made him ineligible to any further elections to the bench of Caledonia County. And in addition to these offices, he was annually appointed what is called the law and trial justice of the peace, for the last forty years of his life, doing, through a large portion of that period, the greater share of the justice business of the place, and making its profits the main means of his livelihood.

There can be no doubt that Judge Ware, at the time he was the Judge of the Caledonia County Court and the Representative of Montpelier, and for many years afterwards, was one of the most influential men in the State. That his rulings and decisions while Judge, met the approbation of the bar and the people, is perhaps sufficiently attested in the fact, that he was annually elected to the bench, as long as he was eligible, at the instance of the people of the county where his judicial ministrations were best known. That his general course as town representative, was approved by his constituents, is shown by the same token; and that he secured them, by his talents and skillful management, at the time of the location of the seat of government here particular and untold advantages, need not rest on his testimony, nor that of his family traditions. The late Hon. John Mattocks, who was an active participant in what was called the "first State House struggle," was, in his life time, heard by more than one person in this village to declare that, however strongly right and policy demanded the location of the seat of government here at the centre of the State, yet so keen was the rivalry for the honor by the older villages of the State, that it would never have been conferred on Montpelier but for the unwearied exertions, and able and exceedingly skillful management of its Representative, Judge Ware.

For the last twenty years of his life, through improvidence, careless management of his affairs, and the growing expenses of a large family, but not through personal vices, he appears to have sunk into comparative poverty, and into the public neglect that too often accompanies it. But even in his lowest state of poverty, he was always a philosopher.

"I hope you don't call *me* poor," he would say to those who attempted to commiserate him on his poor circumstances. "I consider it settled that a white child is worth two negro children, which are held at five hundred dollars apiece. And therefore as fast as I had children born, I put them down on my inventory, at one thousand dollars each, till my estate reached the handsome amount of six thousand dollars. And, thank Heaven, I have the same property yet on hand."

In structure of mind, in thought, words and ways, Judge Ware was probably the most perfectly original character we ever had in Montpelier. And his shrewd observations, and quaint and witty sayings were, in his day, more quoted than those of any other man in all this section of the country. Though clear, discriminating and patient in investigating all important cases, which he conducted by a silent process of mind, yet the result was generally made known in terms and phrases which nobody else would think of using. His brain was most singularly creative and futile ; and it seemed to be his greatest recreation, if not happiness, to indulge in its half serious, half sportive frolics. We have it from a lady of this village that, when a small girl, she and her mate used to resort to his house, night after night, to hear him improvise an original novel, which, for their gratification, he would begin one evening, take up the next where he left it, and so carry it on, in good keeping, through a succession of hearings, till it was finished, making probably a more instructive and amusing tale than many that have been published.

Judge Ware married Miss Patty Wheeler, daughter of Gardner Wheeler, Esq., of Barre, May the 26th, 1803, who still survives him. They had six children—Gardner W. Ware, now deceased ; Patty Militiah, now wife of Samuel Caldwell, of St. Johns, Canada East ; Cyrus Leonard Ware, of the vicinity of New York ; Henry Ware, of Ohio ; George Ware, of parts unknown ; Mary Ware, the wife of Joel Foster, Jr., of the firm of Hyde & Foster, and Louisa Ware, now residing with her mother and sister, at Mr. Foster's.

Judge Ware died at Montpelier, February 17, 1849, at the age of nearly eighty.

THE HONORABLE SALVIN COLLINS.

Among the men of political and official prominence, in the earlier period of the History of Montpelier, was the Honorable SALVIN COLLINS.

He was born in Southboro', Massachusetts, March 6th, 1768, where he remained until he reached the age of about twenty-three; when he emigrated to Berlin, Vermont. Though coming a year or two later than the earliest, yet he may be reckoned among that remarkable band of the early settlers of Berlin, consisting of Zachariah Perrin, Jabez Ellis, Eleazer Hubbard, David Nye, Elijah Nye, Solomon Nye, James Hobart, James Hobart, Jr., John Taplin, Hezekiah Silloway, Jacob Black, William Flagg, John Stewart, Matthew Wallis, James Sawyer, Aaron Strong, James Perley, Ira House, Nath'l Bosworth, Simeon Dewey, James Braman, Cyrus Johnson, Major Jones, and others, than whom, a more hardy, enterprising, industrious, virtuous and long-lived set of men never entered the wilds of Vermont. All these but two, during the last twenty or thirty years, have been, year after year, and one after another, dropping into the grave, at very advanced ages, and the two excepted, the Rev. James Hobart, the venerable Simeon Dewey, Esq., only survive, the former at the age of ninety-your and the latter at the age of ninety, as the representative of those departed founders of that excellent town.

On coming to Vermont, Mr. Collins purchased the farm adjoining those of Zachariah Perrin, on the east, and Zabez Ellis, on the south, which to this day is known as the old Collins farm.

About the time of his settling in Berlin, he married Miss Rebecca Wilder, of Lancaster, Massachusetts, by whom he had three daughters and two sons, the oldest being the wife of the Hon. John Spalding of Montpelier. After clearing up and cultivating his farm fourteen or fifteen years, he sold it to Zachariah Perrin, and took up his residence at Berlin Corners, which was then becoming something of a village, containing a store, a tavern and several mechanics' shops.

In 1805, he was elected by his townsmen, as their representative to the General Assembly. In 1806 he was re-elected to the same office. In 1811 he was elected second Assistant Judge of the County Court, of the new county of Jefferson, and during the same year took up his residence in Montpelier village. In 1812 he received a second election as County Judge. In 1815 he was elected the Judge of Probate for the District of Washington, and so well acquitted himself in the responsible duties of that office, that he had the honor of receiving five successive elections, a greater number than ever was received in this District by any man except Judge Loomis. For the last twenty years of his life, at least, he was constantly in the commission of the office of Justice of the Peace, and for a great portion of that time, did a large share of the Justice business of the village.

Mr. Collins was one of the earliest and most exemplary members of the Congregational Church of Berlin, and, on removing to Montpelier, united himself with the Congregational Church of this place, of which, in a few years, he was chosen a deacon, and as such, officiated through the remainder of his life.

Judge Collins, his first wife dying in 1816, married Mrs. Lucy Clarke, who survived him about eight years.

Unobtrusive, unassuming, quiet, social and intelligent, few men were better calculated to make friends than Judge Collins, and few men ever had more of them. As a man his abiding integrity and honesty of purpose, were never doubted ; while the important trusts and offices, to which he was time and again elected, sufficiently show in what estimation his intellectual powers, though unaided by any but the commonest of educations, were held by the public.

He died November 9th, 1831, at the age of sixty-three years, with an extensive circle of friends and relatives, and the public at large, for his mourners, all uniting in the expression that a good and useful man, an exemplary christian and an enlightened citizen had departed.

CAPTAIN TIMOTHY HUBBARD.

To be numbered with those, who, by their business capacities and energy of character, contributed most to the wealth and prosperity of Montpelier, were three brothers, Timothy, Roger and Chester Hubbard, who came here before, or about the beginning of the present century. They were all enterprizing, clear headed men, and, while they remained in trade, successful merchants, especially Chester Hubbard, who confined himself extensively to trade, and died in 1832, leaving, though then only in middle life, a very handsome property. But as the elder more particularly identified himself with the public offices and institutions of the town, and moreover posessed characteristics which more largely attracted public attention, we have selected him as their representative in the sketch which follows :—

Timothy Hubbard was born in Windsor Parish of Winterbury, a short distance from the city of Hartford, Connecticut, on the 17th of August, 1776. He lived with his father and worked on his farm till the age of twenty-one, getting all the education he ever had at the poor common schools of the place. After continuing to work on his father's farm, on stipulated wages, probably, about four years after he was of age, he came, in June 1799, to Montpelier, and established himself in trade with Wyllis J. Cadwell, Esq., a connection of the Lymans of Hartford, Connecticut and Hartford, Vermont. In 1801 he married Miss Lucy Davis, the third daughter of Colonel Jacob Davis, and a very estimable woman. In 1803, he dissolved his connection with Mr. Cadwell, and went into partnership in trade with his distinguished brother-in-law, the Hon. David Wing. After the death of Judge Wing, in 1806, he soon associated with him in trade his *own* brother, Roger Hubbard, and continued in business with him till about 1816, when he ceased to be any further engaged in mercantile affairs, and thence forward employed himself in supervising the cultivation of his different valuable farms in Berlin, and particularly the very eligible one on the southern borders of Montpelier Village, which he soon made his homestead for the remainder of his life.

In 1810 he was elected Captain of the fine military company, called the Governor's Guards, of which Isaac Putnam was the first captain; and though he was taken almost from the ranks, he soon showed himself to be one of the best military officers that ever paraded a company in the streets of Montpelier; and when the news of the invasion of Plattsburgh by the British, in September, 1814, reached Montpelier, he sallied, cane in hand, into the streets, summoned a drummer and fifer, one of them at least, his own hired man, to his side, and with them, marched the streets all day, beating up volunteers, to start at once for the scene of action. And so efficient were his bold appeals, and such was his fired energy throughout the whole occasion, that before night, he had enlisted three-fourths of his fellow citizens, who chose him their Captain by acclamation. Being now in authority, and at the head of perhaps the largest and best company of all the Vermont Plattsburgh volunteers, with the staunch Joseph Howes for his second in command, he decisively gave his orders for the next day; and accordingly, at an early hour, the next morning, they were all seen pouring along, in hot haste, for the seat of war, by night they were in Burlington, and the next day embarking on sloops, and crowding all sail for Plattsburgh, where they arrived in season to take their place in the line of battle.

Captain Hubbard was often chosen to fill the most important town offices, especially if there happened to be pending any financial difficulty, growing out of conflicting interests, which others were unwilling to touch. These he always straightened out without fear or favor to clique or party, but often at the expense of another election, though when another such difficulty occurred they were all for calling him back again; when he would, in his singularly frank and independent way, give them to understand, that it was all the same with him, whether they elected him or not, but if they did, they might depend on it, he should not fear to do his duty. And there can be little doubt, that, had he been willing to condescend to keep down this marked trait of his character, or play even a little of the demagogue, we should have seen him in higher civil offices.

Captain Hubbard was sometimes harsh in rebuking the faults of others, or in defending himself, when he unexpectedly met opposition in the path of what he considered his right and duty. But he seemed to give no lasting offense; for the offended knew that as soon as he found himself in the wrong, he would be the first to rectify it. He was liberal to the poor and always gave freely to forward all educational, religious and benevolent objects. Let us advert to a single instance, which, besides illustrating these traits of his character, discloses a fact which interests the public. When, in what had been before called the Barre street school district, was built a new school house, some twenty years ago, the Captain bought and caused to be hung in the cupola of this school building, a valuable new bell. And the district thereupon, at a regular meeting unanimously voted that their school house should thereafter be called "*Hubbard Street School House*," and the street on which it stood be changed from Barre Street to ***Hubbard Street.*** And this is still the only name that can be legitimately applied to it.

Captain Hubbard's business and financial talents, and trust, worthiness for all, not excepting even the most important posts, were widely admitted in his day, and can hereafter always be made to appear on public records, the records of the numerous estates, of which he was the efficient administrator, and the records of the Bank of Montpelier which, for years, he skillfully managed in the capacity of its President.

At the age of about fifty he reached a point which few wealthy men *ever reach*, the point, when he thought he had property enough, and that he had better be bestowing it where it would do the most good. Accordingly he began giving it to the most needy of the numerous circle of his relatives, and continued the good work, till a full third of his estate had been bestowed on them. His first wife dying in 1839, he shortly married Miss Anner May, who, as his widow and legatee, still survives him on the old Homestead.

He died on the 28th day of October, 1850, leaving no issue that long survived him.

GENERAL EZEKIEL P. WALTON.

In the incipient stages of the growth of every country village there are nearly always two different personages who occupy the largest space in the thoughts of the people—the Minister and the Editor. And in proportion as these are faithful, intelligent and able, so, to an almost unappreciable extent, will be its moral, social and intellectual advancement. It was the good fortune of Montpelier, for the first twenty years after the place could fairly lay claim to the dignity of a village, to have the right kind of a man for her Minister, and the right kind of a man for an Editor, in the persons of Chester Wright and Ezekiel P. Walton. A sketch of the former has already been given; one of the latter remains to be furnished.

Ezekiel Parker Walton was born in the year 1789, in Canterbury, N. H., in which town his father, George Walton, formerly resided, but from which he at length removed to Peacham, Vt. There was a good Academy at Peacham, and young Walton, previous to reaching the age of fifteen, attended it a few terms, studying the ordinary English branches, and completing all the school education he ever received.

There was, at this time, a small newspaper, of Federal politics, published at Peacham by Mr. Samuel Goss, a practical printer and Editor of his own paper, which was called the *Green Mountain Patriot.* Into this establishment the boy Walton often found his way, and at length began to feel so much interest in the business he saw going on that he offered himself as an apprentice to the trade; and Mr. Goss, as he has recently told us, so liked the looks of the bright little fellow that he concluded to take him in that capacity, and in despite of the opinion of others, who believed that little could ever be made of him. As Mr. Goss had predicted, however, the boy turned out a well behaved, faithful apprentice, and made good proficiency in his trade. After serving three years at his trade in Peacham, he came, in 1807, to Montpelier, with Mr. Goss, who bought out the *Vermont Precursor*, a paper established here the year previous by the Rev. Clark Brown, and changed the name to that of the *Vermont Watchman*. Here he served out the remainder of his apprenticeship, which expired in 1810; when, being of legal age, he, in company with Mark Goss, a fellow apprentice in the office, bought out Mr. Samuel Goss; and the paper was then, for the next half dozen years, conducted by the firm of Walton & Goss, Mr. Walton discharging the chief duties of editor. In 1816 Mr. Mark Goss went out of the establishment, and Mr. Walton became its sole proprietor and editor, and so continued nearly twenty years; when, as his sons became of age, he took them into partnership, and the business, to which book-selling and paper-making were at length added, was conducted in the name of E. P. Walton & Sons until 1853, during which he wholly gave up the proprietorship of the newspaper to his oldest son, the present Hon. Eliakim Persons Walton, who still owns and conducts it. Though the editorship had been entrusted to this son for many years previous to 1853, General Walton continued to assist in editing and in writing for certain departments of the paper, even into the last year of his life.

At an early period he passed rapidly along the line of military promotion till he reached the rank of Major General, when he threw these kinds of honors aside and thought no more of them. Mr. Walton was never an office seeker, nor was office, as much as was due to him as a man and a politician, nor half as much as was due to him from his party, ever bestowed on him. He was, however, several times the candidate of his party for town Representative, but never when that party happened to be in the majority. In 1827 he was elected one of the Council of Censors, and served with credit to himself and his electors, among a board of the most distinguished men in the State, Judges B. Turner, D. Kellogg and S. S. Phelps being included among the number. In the Presidential election of 1852 he was elected one of the Electoral College for Vermont, when the vote of the State was thrown for General Scott. In 1854, he was nominated as candidate for the office of Governor of Vermont by a large mass State Convention, and could the people have had their way, would have been triumphantly elected.

But out of an ardent desire to consolidate the political sentiments of the people in one controlling organization, as well as out of high personal regard for the venerable Chief Justice, Stephen Royce, who had been previously named for the executive chair by a Convention of the Whig party, General Walton cheerfully yielded his place on the ticket. The name of Judge Royce was substituted by the State Committee, and he was heartily supported by the people; and thus was organized the present Republican party of the State. For that organization, a large measure of credit is due to Gen. Walton.

We have named the circumstances connected with Mr. Walton's nomination to the office of Governor, for the double purpose of showing the remarkable lack of even well-warranted assumptions, in the man, and his patriotic readiness to submit to any personal sacrifice which he was led to suppose public good required him to make, as well as of showing how his party, while so generally admitting his qualifications for office, and the merit of his services in their behalf, so strangely overlooked him, when they so often had the power to reward and honor him. That he was ever honorable and just in his treatment towards his political opponents, the writer of this sketch, who was for many years one of them, can, and here does most cheerfully attest; and the late Araunah Waterman, who was ever a staunch political opponent, was often heard frankly to admit that "General Walton was both an honorable man and an honest politician." That he, in his long, persistent, judicious, and able editorial labors, was eminently instrumental in establishing the ascendency of his party and keeping it in power, is a fact too well known to be questioned. Probably, indeed, that man has never lived in Vermont, who did so much toward building up the old Whig party of the State, and its successor, the Republican party, which he lived to see become, from the minority in which he found it, one of the most overwhelming majorities ever recorded in the history of party warfare. But while it was his lot to do so, and see all this, it was his lot also to be often compelled, like many another political editor, "to make brick without straw," or, in other words, manufacture great men out of small patterns, who, when made, carried their heads so high as generally to entirely overlook their political creator.

Mr. Walton's style of writing was, for his advantages, unusually correct, and unusually well calculated for enforcing his sentiments and enlisting the sympathy of his readers. During the first years of his residence in Montpelier, he, in company with other young aspirants of the village, got up an association for mutual improvement in knowledge and literature, called the "Franklin Society." In this Society, in which theme writing was a leading exercise, he probably made much progress in forming his style, which was evidently modelled on that of Dr. Franklin, so generally the great oracle of the printer boy. The *bon homme* of "Poor Richard," however, can never be successfully imitated by a man without a good heart. But Mr. Walton had that heart; and, through the force of finely blended emotional and intellectual qualities of his heart, he gradually formed a style of his own, which, with the vein of good common sense that pervaded it, gave him rank with the most pleasing and instructive of our editorial writers. As before intimated, he continued to write for his old paper to the last; and in so doing, besides his instructive articles on farming and domestic economy, he wrote and published in the Watchman, the year before his death, sixteen numbers on the events of the Olden Times in the Valley of the Winooski, over the signature of Oliver Old-School, which deserve to be republished in pamphlet, for public reading and preservation.

In the political world, Gen. Walton was ever a person to be consulted—among men he was always a man—in the Church an influential officer—in the social circle a dignified, but a very courteous and kindly companion, and in his family an exemplary husband and father. His integrity, whether in business or politics, appears never to have been doubted, by either friend or foe; his general intellectual capacity was always conceded, and his frank and generous disposition known to the utmost limits of his extensive personal acquaintance.

On the 28th of April, 1811, Mr. Walton married Miss Prussia Persons, daughter of Eliakim D. Persons, of Montpelier, by whom he had eight children—Eliakim P., now in Congress; Harriet Newell, wife of the Hon. H. R. Wing, a lawyer of standing at Glen's Falls, N. Y.; George Parker, a very promising young man who died at the age of about twenty-four years, at New-Orleans; Nathaniel Porter, for some years the accountant of the firm of E. P. Walton & Sons; Chauncey, now an invalid; Samuel M., the book-binder in Montpelier; Ezekiel Dodge, who died at the age of about twenty-five years, at Philadelphia; and Mary, wife of George Dewey, a merchant of New York city.

This sketch would not be complete without a brief notice of the religious character of Mr. Walton. He was an earnest, frank and sincere christian, always warm and generous in the utterance and support of his religious principles. He combined the wisdom of the serpent, the boldness of the lion and the harmlessness of the dove, in his whole christian course. He was a devoted member and an honorable office bearer in the Congregational Church for many years. His piety irradiated his household, his secular cares and his place of business. Everywhere, at all times, he was the admirable type of a christian gentleman. In the Conference, in the Sabbath School, in the support of charitable and religious institutions, none surpassed and few equalled him. The young men in his office felt his influence very strongly. Of the many who graduated from his office, and came to fill afterwards, with honor, public stations in the councils of the State and in the halls of Congress, and in the Courts of Justice, twelve have been members of churches, and two have become useful and respected Ministers of the Gospel. And none could bear higher testimony to the invariable and elevated religious character of Mr. Walton than they.

Gen. Walton died on the 27th of November, 1855, leaving, as might be expected from one of his liberal views, not much property, indeed, but that "good name" which is better than riches.

CALVIN JAY KEITH.

CALVIN JAY KEITH, a son of the Hon. Chapin Keith, late of Barre, was born in Uxbridge, Massachusetts, April 9, 1800, and before he was a year old came with his father's family to Barre, Vermont. At the age of sixteen, having shown himself a good and industrious scholar in the English branches taught in the common school of his home village, he commenced fitting for college at Randolph Academy, in the spring of 1816. In 1818 he entered Union College, at Schenectady, N. Y., and in 1822 was graduated from that institution, with a good reputation for scholarship and moral character. He then, for a year or two, taught in the State of Virginia in capacity of a private tutor in the family of a wealthy planter; when he returned to the North, and commenced the study of the law in the office of the Hon. William Upham in Montpelier. Having completed the usual course of legal studies, he was admitted to the bar in 1826, and commenced practice in this village, at first alone, and afterwards, for three or four years succeeding 1830, in company with Mr. Upham. In about 1837 a brother of C. W. Storrs of Montpelier died in St. Louis, Missouri, leaving considerable property, and Mr. Keith was employed by the relatives of the deceased to go to St. Louis and gather up and settle the estate. After executing this commission to the advantage and satisfaction of all concerned, he returned to Montpelier, not however to resume his profession, but to accept the office of Treasurer in the Vermont Mutual Fire Insurance Company, which was tendered him by the Directors. But after acceptably executing the duties of this office a year or two, he resigned the post to accept another and far more important commission to settle an estate of a deceased Vermonter in the South. This was the estate of one of the brothers Elkins, from Peacham, Vt., who had been in business as cotton brokers in the city of New Orleans. The estate was found to be large, and its affairs in so complicated a condition as to require the labor and attention of years to bring to a close. For the next ten or twelve years, therefore, Mr. Keith took up his residence in New Orleans, and remained there through all but the hot and sickly months of the year, which he spent mostly in Montpelier, having generally brought with him, at each annual return, such sums of money as he had been able to collect out of the different investments of the estate, for division among the Elkins heirs. After pursuing this course some ten years, assiduously engaged in the difficult, and, in many respects, dangerous position, he succeeded in bringing the affairs of the estate mainly to a close, except in the case of the large quantity of Mexican scrip which was left on hand, and which was considered only of doubtful or chance value. That same scrip, however, was eventually to make up the great bulk of the fortune Mr. Keith was fortunate enough to acquire by means of his southern trust. He agreed on a division of this uncertain property between the heirs and himself, the consideration offered to them being his promise to make no charge for any future services. In a year or two after this bargain, the General Government decided to redeem this Mexican scrip ; and Mr. Keith, being fortunate enough by means of arguments made potent by some of the existing cabinet, to get his claims rather promptly allowed, realized for his share of the venture the snug sum ef $35,000—which, with his previous accumulations, made him a man of fortune.

The year 1852 was mostly occupied by Mr. Keith in making the tour of Europe, and, having returned to Montpelier the following year, he was seized with what was supposed to be a brain fever, which terminated fatally on the 23d of September, 1853.

Mr. Keith, was in some respects, rather a peculiar man—in nothing more so, perhaps, than in his likes and dislikes, and these again were generally as peculiarly manifested. The former might always be known by his open commendation, and the latter by his entire silence, when the names of the objects were respectively mentioned. This seemed to grow out of his constitutional sensitiveness, which was often affected by what would have affected few others, which he could not help, but which his natural conscientiousness enabled him so to correct as never to make the matter worse by detraction. He was most constant and faithful to those who had his esteem ; while to those who had not, he manifested only a negative conduct. But with his few peculiarities, Mr. Keith had many virtues. He was, in all his deal, one of the most strictly honest men in the world. His views of life, society and its wants, were just and elevated, and he was patriotic and liberal in contributing to the advancement of all good public objects. His character, indeed, was well reflected by his singular will, to which we alluded in a description of our new Cemetery. By this will he notices a whole score of such as had gained his esteem, by bequests of valuable keepsakes or small sums of money, and then goes on to bequeath handsome sums for various public objects, among which was one thousand dollars for a Cemetery for Montpelier village, and five hundred dollars for a library for its Academy. And thus he has identified his name with the public interests of the town where he longest resided, and should thus be remembered among its benefactors.

HEZEKIAH HUTCHINS REED.

Among the business men who have lived and died in Montpelier, and who have made fortunes by their tact and enterprise, and left them for their families and for public purposes, it is but justice to give a place to HEZEKIAH HUTCHINS REED.

He was born at Hamstead, New Hampshire, May 26, 1795, and came with his father, Captain Thomas Reed, and family to Montpelier in 1804. From 1804 to about 1812 he, for the greater part of the time, attended the Academy in Montpelier, and made such good proficiency in all the branches of English education, and exhibited promise of so much executive talent, that, at the early age of sixteen, he was employed, and successfully fulfilled his engagement, in teaching one of the largest and most forward winter district schools in his town. Soon after this he went to Fort Atkinson, or French Mills, on the northern frontier in New York, and became a clerk in the store of Mr. Gove, while the American Army was wintering there in 1813. When the army retreated southward he followed it to Plattsburgh, where it took its final stand, and remained with it in the capacity of sutler till the battle of Plattsburgh, September, 1814, at which he was present. The following winter he taught school in Grand Isle County; and then soon after commenced the study of the law in the office of the Hon. Dan Carpenter of Waterbury. In the spring of 1819 he was admitted to the Bar, and during the following summer he went west, and finally settled down for the practice of the law in the town of Troy, Miami County, Ohio. Here he remained about five years, when he collected in his earnings, and invested the whole of them in flour, which he put on board one of the so-called *flat boats* of the *Ohio*, and sailed down the river with it to Natches, where he sold it, and then with the proceeds in his pocket, returned on horse-back through Tennessee, Kentucky and Pennsylvania to Philadelphia, and then by other conveyance to his old home in Montpelier. Here he went immediately into partnership with his brother, Thomas Reed, Esq., who had already opened a law office in the village. This partnership lasted about twenty years, and was attended throughout with unusual pecuniary success. The Messrs. Reed did a very large business, mostly in collecting and in honorable speculations, acting as advocates in the courts but little more than in the management of their own cases. They invested largely in the stock of the first and second Bank of Montpelier, and bought out nearly all the stock of the old Winooski Turnpike, which they eventually sold out at a good bargain to the Vermont Central Railroad Company. They also became extensive land owners in this and several of the Western States, and their purchases of this character all turned out, in the aggregate, very profitable investments.

Mr. Reed was elected, by general ticket, a member of our Council of Censors in 1841, and in that office—his first public one—acquitted himself with credit to himself and the section of the State he was understood to represent. He was one of the Delegates of Vermont to the National Convention which nominated General Winfield Scott for President, and was for many years considered as one of the most active and influential politicians in the State. In 1851 he was chosen, by a large majority, as the Representative of Montpelier in the Legislature; and the following year he received a second election to the same office, and here also acquitted himself handsomely, and to the very general satisfaction of his constituents. On the establishment of the Vermont Bank, in 1849, he was chosen its first President, and was continuously retained in the office to the day of his death.

Mr. Reed was an unusually stirring, energetic and enterprising business man; but business and money-making were evidently not the only objects of his life. He was ever patriotic and public spirited, entering into, and often leading in, all enterprises designed for the public good and the social, religious and educational interests of his town, with his usual zeal and energy; and was always quite ready to help on all such movements by liberal subscriptions in the way of pecuniary assistance. He perhaps should be considered the foremost in bringing about our present Union School, and gave one thousand dollars towards the building to be erected on its establishment.

He died suddenly, and almost in the prime of his life and energies, of inflammation of the lungs, while on a journey to the West, on the 15th of June, 1856, and now sleeps in our new Green Mount Cemetery, which he took so much pride in planning and ornamenting.

DOCTOR JAMES SPALDING.

Doctor JAMES SPALDING, who, for forty years was a successful practising physician of Montpelier village and vicinity, died at his residence, on the 15th day of March, 1858, at the age of sixty-six years, and still in the midst of his professional usefulness.

A few months subsequent to his death, the following accurate and deserved sketch and tribute of his life and memory appeared in the Boston Medical and Surgical Journal, which we cordially adopt and endorse, as doing more ample justice to his character than we should be able, with our means, to contribute on the subject:

Doctor SPALDING was born in Sharon, Vermont, March 20th, 1792. His father, Deacon Reuben Spalding, was one of the earliest settlers in the State, whose life was not more remarkable for his toils, privations and energy, as a pioneer in a new country, than for his unbending integrity, and for the best qualities of the Old New England Puritanism. James was the third son of twelve children, all of whom reached maturity and were settled in life with families. At the age of seven years, he received a small wound in the knee joint, which was succeeded by an accute inflammation and suppuration, confining him for more than six months, and attended with extreme suffering. During this sickness Dr. Nathan Smith, of Hanover, was called; the knee had been opened at several points, but still there was no improvement. This eminent surgeon discovered matter deeply seated in the ham, and made a free incision, after which the limb healed, leaving the knee partially anchylosed, to recover from which required years.

It was while confined, that he entertained the idea of becoming a physician and surgeon, probably in consequence of his estimation of Dr. Smith, which was retained through life. Hence he received from his companions the title of Doctor, and retained it until, by his scientific and literary attainments, he became justly entitled to it. His early advantages were limited, having never attended a high school or Academy ; but still his love of study enabled him to obtain a good common school education, besides storing his mind with much general knowledge. Alone and without instruction, he had acquired that mental discipline which so highly distinguished him in after life. He commenced his studies at the age of seventeen years, with Dr. Eber Carpenter, of Alstead, N. H., stipulating that the expenses of his education should be defrayed by his practising one year with the Doctor after he had graduated. He applied himself with uncommon assiduity to his medical studies, taking, at the same time, private lessons in Greek and Latin. At the age of twenty years he graduated at the Dartmouth Medical Institution, having heard the lectures from those celebrated teachers, Smith and Perkins.

It may not be improper to remark, that while a student, his opportunities for practice were very extensive. It was then that the *Spotted Fever* prevailed so generally throughout New England. This epidemic was truly appalling in Alstead and the neighboring towns. Dr. S. had an opportunity of studying the disease under its varied aspects, and brought his discriminating mind to the subject, with all the candor and close observation of a veteran in the science, and arrived at the same conclusions as to its pathology and treatment as others who had the best opportunities for observation, and stood the most eminent in the profession. His position was very embarrassing, being called the "boy physician," having to meet men renowned in the profession, for whom he entertained an exalted opinion. Modesty would hardly prevent him to differ from them, yet he had so studied this epidemic that in most cases his views and treatment were adopted.

After practicing two years in Alstead with Dr. Carpenter, he commenced business in Claremont; but having friends in Montpelier, he was induced by their urgent solicitations to remove to that place. Though but a boy, he had seen much practice, and performed many surgical operations, and therefore it required but a short time for him to gain general confidence as a physician, and more especially as a surgeon, which he retained without abatement through life. His fixed purpose seemed to be improvement in his profession, having never engaged in any other business or sought any political preferment. Others may have done more, under other circumstances, yet by his example, integrity, industry, communications for the medical journals, and dissertations before the County and State Medical Societies, from time to time, it may with propriety be said he added something to the general stock of knowledge in his profession. As a Surgeon Dr. S. was successful above most others. The distinguishing trait of his mind was a sound judgment, based upon a careful and discriminating examination of all the evidence which gave to each individual case its peculiar characteristic. Being well informed in books and in the general principles of his profession, and having an extensive intercourse with his medical brethren, he was well prepared to impart to others the results of his extensive experience. With propriety it may be said he was an original thinker, as was not only manifested in his medical and surgical practice, but in other departments of science. Few men had occasion to change their opinions, when formed, so seldom as Dr. Spalding. Others might have come to conclusions more readily, but when his opinions were formed, the evidence on which they were based was in his own mind ; and for this reason he was much sought for in consultations. It was a maxim with him that there should be no guess-work in his profession, and more especially in surgery. In consultations, due respect was paid to the opinions of his professional brethren, but still he would suffer his judgment to be influenced only as the evidence in the case affected his own mind, never evading responsibility, and always governed by his own independent conclusions.

Dr. Spalding retained through life the confidence and respect of his professional brethren. From his commencement in practice till his death, he was much engaged in consultations. Though differing from others, in his diagnosis and treatment of disease, yet he succeeded in leaving the confidence of patient and friends in the attending physician unabated, and thus discharging his duty to his patients without injury to the feelings or reputation of any one. It was a settled maxim of his life, that strict integrity was the true and only policy which should govern every man who desires his own interest or that of others ; and therefore he never sought to appropriate to himself what justly belonged to them.

For more than forty years, he was an active member of the Vermont State Medical Society, and, through it, he labored to advance the best interests of the profession he so much loved. He thus became acquainted with most of the distinguished physicians of the State, among whom he had many personal friends. In 1819 he was elected Secretary, which office he held for over twenty years. In 1842 he was appointed chairman of a committee to draft a petition for a Geological survey of the State. He was elected Vice President in 1843, Treasurer in 1844, Chairman of the committee on the History of the Society in 1845. He read a thesis in 1846, " On Nature as manifested in Disease and Health," which was highly commended. He was elected President in 1846-7-8, and delivered a dissertation on

Typhus Fever in 1848, which was published by a vote of the Society. He was elected a corresponding Secretary in 1850, and Librarian in 1854, which office he held until his death. He was also a member of the Board of Fellows of the Vermont Academy of Medicine, besides holding many offices connected with science, literature, temperance, &c. But few men in the country have seen such an amount of disease and so carefully observed the peculiarities of the various epidemics occurring for nearly half a century; and it is to be regretted that so little is left on record of his extensive observations and experience both as a physician and surgeon.

Not only as a professional man would we lament our departed friend; but as a christian, father, citizen and philanthropist would we remember him. His life was that of the good Samaritan, a life of toil, prayer and sympathy for others. His principles were deeply rooted in the heart, and his faith manifested by works. We love to contemplate his character, and hope his mantle will fall on many who will as faithfully devote their lives to the best interests of their fellow beings, and as highly honor their adopted profession."

In 1820 Dr. Spalding married Miss Eliza Reed of Montpelier, by whom he raised six children, James R. Spalding, an editor in the city of New York; William C. Spalding, a physician at the West; Martha E. Spalding, an estimable young lady who died at about the age of eighteen years; Jane Spalding, George Spalding, and Isabella Spalding. Mrs. Spalding, a woman of many virtues, died in 1854, and about two years after, Dr. Spalding married Mrs. Dodd, a daughter of the late Wyllys Lyman, of Hartford, Vermont, who died in 1857.

In private life Dr. Spaulding was a man of much amenity of manners,—of great worth and purity of character—of enlarged benevolence and of high minded purposes in all that goes to make the enlightened christian and good citizen.

COLONEL JONATHAN P. MILLER.

While drawing these personal sketches to a close, we have been glancing back over the list; and though we find exhibited in them almost every shade of practical character, yet not in one of them any thing that fillls the popular idea of the character of a hero. But for the gratification of those inclining to regret the lack of a full variety, we are happy to present them a sketch of Colonel Miller.

JONATHAN PECKHAM MILLER was born in Randolph, Vermont, February 24th, 1797. His father, who died in 1799, had given him to his uncle, Jonathan Peckham, who, dying about 1805, appears to have commended the boy to the care of Captain John Granger of the same town. And with that gentleman he resided till 1813, when he went to Woodstock, Vt., to learn the tanner's trade. He did not remain long there, however, before sickness compelled him to return; and his illness settling into protracted feeble health, he made Mr. Granger's house his home for the next four years. But during this time the invasion of Plattsburgh by the British occurring, and Captain Libbeus Egerton of that town having raised a company of volunteers to go to the rescue, young Miller, sick or well, determined on joining the expedition, which nevertheless turned out to be a bloodless one; for the company had not quite time to reach the scene of action before the battle was over, and the enemy had beat a retreat; when they all returned to Randolph, with no other glory than that which arose from this good showing of their patriotic intentions. Whether this incident started in Miller a taste for miliitary affairs, or whether he began to feel that farming would prove too tame an occupation for him, is not fully known; but certain it is that, as early as 1817, he resolved to change his mode of life. And accordingly during that year he went to Marblehead, Mass., where a company of United States troops were stationed, and enlisted as a common soldier in the army. He continued in the service about two years, being a part of the time stationed on our northern frontier; when his health again failing, he procured a discharge, and returned to Randolph, where he attended the Academy of that town, and soon began to fit for College. After dilligently prosecuting his studies here till the summer of 1821, he entered Dartmouth College; but, for some reason, left in the course of a few weeks, and joined a class, of like standing as the one he had been in at Dartmouth, in the University of Vermont. At Burlington College he steadily pursued his studies, advancing with the rest of his class, to almost the last year of the prescribed course of collegiate requirements, when, on the 24th of May, 1824, the College buildings accidentally caught fire and were totally consumed, and with them a portion of the public library and the private books of the students, among which were those of Mr. Miller.

Mr. Miller was now afloat again; but he does not appear to have long hesitated in making up his mind upon a course of action for his immediate future. The struggles of Greece for liberty had by this time become the theme of every American fireside, and the appalling woes her people were suffering from the remorseless cruelties of their turbaned oppressors, had already enlisted the sympathies of every American heart that could feel for anything. As might be expected of one of Miller's warm and patriotic nature, his feelings had been among those of the first to be aroused at the recital of these tales of outrage. But heretofore he had been engaged in the accomplishment of the task before him—the completion of his College course. He thought it hardly worth his while now, however, at his age, to enter a new College for this purpose; and if not, his time was on his own hands. Why, then, should he not go to succor the oppressed, as well as other patriotic Americans who had already sailed for Greece, or were intending shortly to do so? With the question, came the decision that he would go.

He knew there was in Boston an association of wealthy and influential gentlemen, styled the *Greek Committee*, who had been selected to receive and appropriate contributions for the Greek cause, by purchasing needed munitions, or by furnishing the means of transit to those who, without such means, were willing to volunteer their personal services in behalf of the oppressed. But he must first obtain an introduction to them; and for this purpose he went to Governor Van Ness, at the destruction of whose house by fire, a short time before, he knew he had performed an important and dangerous service in rescuing valuable property from the flames. The Governor, who never forgot a benefit, wrote a letter, not only of introduction, but of warm recommendation of Mr. Miller, to the Hon. Thomas L. Winthrop, and the Hon. Edward Everett, the President and Secretary of the Greek Association, who, in their turn, gave him letters to the President and leading members of the Greek Government, at *Missolonghi*, and furnished him withal with over three hundred dollars in money, to enable him to pay his passage, equip himself with a good personal outfit, and have money left for exigencies that might arise after he had reached his destination; when he, with other American volunteers, sailed for Malta, on the 21st of August, 1824. After reaching that place, and spending a few weeks, and at some other of the neighboring islands, he proceeded to the fated Missolonghi, and enquired out the house, which Lord Byron, then very late deceased, had made his head quarters, and which had been retained for the ordinary meetings of the members of the Government of Western Greece.

Here he encountered Dr. Mayer, who was a root of the fighting stock of William Tell of Switzerland, and had, for several of the last years, been one of the bravest and most useful of the European volunteers in Greece. Mr. Miller presented his credentials to the Doctor, and was promised an early presentation to members of the Government. He was also invited to take up his quarters in that house, and having been shown a room where he might take a little of the repose he so much needed, he wrapped his cloak around him, threw himself down on the floor and was soon asleep. Before long, however, he was awakened by the entrance of a man already widely known through Europe and America. This was General George Jarvis, a son of Benjamin Jarvis of New York, who held a situation under the U. S. Government in Germany, where the son was born, educated and reared to manhood. He entered the Greek service in 1821, and continued in it through the whole of that memorable struggle, passing through every grade of military office to the rank of Brigadier General of Lord Byron's brigade, and seeing probably more fighting, and undergoing more suffering and hardship than any one of all the heroes of Greece. He and Mr. Miller appear to have almost at once made the discovery that they were congenial spirits; and a mutual friendship and respect sprang up between them, which soon resulted in Mr. Miller's appointment as one of the General's staff officers, with the rank of Colonel in the Greek service.

It is not our purpose to follow Colonel Miller through the various hardships he endured through the next two years of that wild and bloody conflict, nor enumerate those feats of arms, which seem so to have awakened the admiration of the Greeks, and caused him to be known among them by the peculiar name of *The American Dare Devil.* Let an instance or two, which we have had from his own lips, serve as a specimen of his many personal risks and escapes, as well as of his individual daring.

On one occasion, when he was stationed in command of a small band of soldiers in a walled garden a few miles from Napoli, he suddenly discovered the place to be surrounded by a force of some thousand Turkish troops. Knowing that the instant the weakness of his band was discovered they would all be sacrificed on the spot, Col. Miller at once resolved on the desperate expedient of a sally right into the mouth of the lion. Accordingly, calling on his band to follow at his heels, he dashed out into the midst of the closely investing foe, firing his girdle full of pistols, and slashing about him with his sword as he went, with such fury as to astonish the Turks, who supposing, of course, the garden to be full of Greeks, about to scatter death among them from behind the walls, instantly became panic struck and fled.

Another instance of a similar character occurred in a different part of the peninsula, when General Jarvis and Colonel Miller, with a small force, being unexpectedly beset by a large body of Turkish cavalry, were wholly cut off from their companions, and, as their only chance of escaping with life, were compelled to run for a piece of woods at the top of a hill a fourth of a mile distant. But this only resort came near proving a fatal one. A large squad of the mounted fiends pursued them, and were all within pistol shot, while the woods were yet too far distant to be reached by them. They supposed there was but a moment more for them in this world ; but they resolved that that moment should not be passed unimproved. They suddenly wheeled round, drew up their pieces and fired directly into the faces of their pursuers, who, in surprise at the strange act, came to a dead halt, and the next instant turned and fled, doubtless believing that they would not take such a stand, unless there lay concealed in the borders of the woods a force of their foes, from whom it was their wisdom to escape while they could.

The first of these instances, we find in substance related in *Posts' Visit to Greece and Constantinople* in 1827, and also in

Dr. Howe's History of Greece, and the latter, though not named in history, is doubtless an equally veritable incident.

Besides the many personal encounters and skirmishes with the foes of Greece, of the character of those just described, Colonel Miller was an active participant in several important engagements, in which his gallantry appears to have attracted favorable notice. Among these we find one handsomely alluded to in the lately published volume of "*Travels in Greece and Russia*" by Bayard Taylor, as follows :

" *At the end of the Argive plain is the little village of Miles, where Ypsilanti gained a splendid victory over the troops of Ibrahim Pacha, and Colonel Miller greatly distinguished himself.*"

But the most continuous, the hardest and most important of Colonel Miller's military services in Greece, were in the terrible twelve months seige of the ill-fated Missolonghi, one of the most wealthy and populous towns of the Grecian peninsula. We have space only to give a general idea of the character of this siege ; and this idea will perhaps be the best given by a letter from Dr. Mayer, of whom we have before spoken, and who was one of the one hundred and thirty persons perishing in the last defense of the place, written within three days before his death ; and in another letter from Colonel Miller himself to Edward Everett, after Missolonghi had fallen, and he had escaped with the remnant of the beseiged, as he has described, out of the city, but not out of danger.

Dr. Mayer's letter is as follows :

"The labors which we have undergone, and a wound I have received in the shoulder, which I am in expectation is one which will be my passport to eternity, have prevented me till now from bidding you my last adieus. We are reduced to feed on the most disgusting animals, we are suffering horribly from hunger and thirst. Sickness adds much to the calamities that overwhelm us. More than seventeen hundred and forty of our brothers are dead. More than one hundred thousand bombs and balls, thrown by the enemy, have destroyed our bastions and our houses. We have been terribly distressed by cold, and we have suffered great want of food. Notwithstanding so many privations, it is a great and noble spectacle to witness the ardour and devotedness of the garrison. A few days more, and these brave men will be angelic spirits, who will accuse before God the indifference of christendom for a cause which is that of religion. All the Albanians who deserted from the standard of Reschid Pacha, have now rallied under that of Ibrahim. In the name of all our brave men, among whom are Notha Botzaries, Travellas, Papodia Mautopolas, and myself, whom the Government has appointed Generals to a body of its troops. I *announce* to you the resolution, sworn to before Heaven, to defend, foot by foot, the land of Missolonghi, and bury ourselves, without listening to any capitulation, under the ruins of this city. History will render us justice, posterity will weep over our misfortunes. I am proud to think that the blood of a Swiss, of a child of William Tell, is about to mingle with that of the heroes of Greece. May the relation of the seige of Missolonghi, which I have written, survive me. I have made several copies of it. Cause this letter, dear S——, to be inserted in some public journal."

This beautiful and touching letter to a friend has been preserved in the History of Greece. Colonel Miller's letter which was also embodied in the same history, is as follows:—

"NAPOLI DE ROMANIA, May 3, 1826.

EDWARD EVERETT:

Honored and Dear Friend:—It is with emotions not to be expressed, that I now attempt to give an account of the fall of Missolonghi, and the heart-rending situation of illfated Greece. Missolonghi fell into the hands of the Turks, eight days since, after a gallant defense of eleven months and a half. When we take into consideration the means of its defense, and the overwhelming numbers that approached it by sea and land, there cannot be a doubt but that its resistance rivals anything of the kind either in ancient or modern times. The particulars of its fall are enough to draw tears from the most obdurate and unfeeling heart, and will bring into action the energies of the christian world, if indeed such a world can be said to exist. Pardon me, my dear sir; the agonies of my mind cause the expression; for who can believe, that, in an age like this, if there are christians, infidels should be allowed to butcher an entire population?

Missolonghi contained over eight thousand inhabitants, at the time of its surrender, or rather of its destruction. There were no more than three thousand capable of bearing arms; the rest were women and children. We were reduced to the last extremity for provisions, having eaten all the mules and horses, which were in the place, when the gloomy inhabitants were cheered by the arrival of the Greek fleet; but alas! the gallant Mianlis found the Turkish force too strong for his little squadron; after sustaining considerable loss in three attempts to break through the Turkish fleet, he retired. The inhabitants of Missolonghi were now driven to desperation. They knew of the unhappy fate of those who had been taken at Aurtolico, and of the outrages the Arabs would commit if the place should capitulate. They took a horrid but glorious resolution of blowing into the air their wives, daughters and sons. I call it glorious, because the women requested it; and there was no possible way of preventing the Arabs from committing outrage upon the women and boys, if they once should get them into their power. They all assembled at the old Turkish Seraglio. Their husbands and brothers, after laying a train of powder, embraced them for the last time, then giving them matches, left them to set fire to the train. The men then prepared themselves for cutting their way through the

Turkish camp sword in hand. And out of the three thousand, only one thousand are said to have escaped.

There is the greatest sorrow here, women beating their breasts, and asking every Frank they meet "if all the christian world has forsaken them?" I must close this hasty scrawl; for my heart is too full to write more. I lost all my articles of European clothing at Missolonghi. But this is nothing. If I am happy enough to escape I shall go to Smyrna.

My regards to Mrs. Everett, I am thankful it is not for her to endure the distress of the fair, but illfated daughters of Greece.

I am, dear sir, with due respect, your humble servant,

J. P. MILLER."

This was the last of all systematic resistance the poor Greeks were able to make; and they remained in their desolated country, a subdued, but not conquered people, till the Christian nations having been aroused, the naval victory at Navarino secured the independence of their country. But the people, in the meanwhile, were in a starving condition; and Colonel Miller, after lingering there till fall, came here to the United States to arouse his countrymen to the work of contributing for supplying of their wants. Arriving here in November, he lectured through most of the Northern and Middle States with that object; but in February, 1827, while thus engaged, he was appointed by the N. Y. Greek Committee to the agency of going to Greece and superintending the distribution among the suffering inhabitants of that country of a cargo of provisions that had been already collected for them. He went, was gone about a year, and discharged his duty to the full satisfaction of the friends of Greece here, as the proofs, published with his Journal by the Harpers of New York, after his return, abundantly make manifest. The aggregate value of the provisions and clothing distributed by him in Greece was over seventy-five thousand dollars. Yet it was found to be well for the beneficiaries that he could act both in the character of almoner and soldier with equal efficiency. For, when he arrived in Greece he was beset by sharpers and mercenary villains of all kinds, who insolently demanded portions of his cargo in despite all his judicious rules for distribution; and in one instance a scheme was laid to get possession of his whole store, and it would probably have been successful, as well as the less bold attempts of the kind, but for the decisive stand and personal intrepidity of Col. Miller, who, on such occasions, would throw off the character of the almoner as quick as the quaker did his coat, draw sword and pistols, and drive the lying knaves from his presence.

Among the things which were destined to become permanent remembrancers of Colonel Miller's expeditions to Greece, was the adoption and education of a Greek orphan boy, Lucas Miltiades, who, after having received through his childhood and youth from the Colonel all the privileges and affectionate care and kindness which a father could have bestowed, removed West soon after reaching his majority. And Lucas Miltiades Miller has now become, through the advantages thus received, and his own capacity, energy and enterprise, one of the most respected, wealthy and influential citizens of Wisconsin.

Lucas M. was the younger of two brothers brought to this country by Colonel Miller and Dr. Russ, the intimate friend of the former, and one of the most cultivated, noble and efficient of all his compatriots in the Greek Revolution.

Another memento was what now should be considered an antiquarian relic of great interest—nothing less than the veritable sword which Lord Byron wore in his Greek campaign. Lord Byron gave this sword to a young Greek named Loukas, a Captain in his legion, who afterwards was shot dead in a sortie from the Acropilis at Athens; and being found with his sword knotted to his wrist, was carried into the fortress. When the sword and his clothing were sold for the benefit of his sisters by the English Consul of Poros, who was requested to take charge of the effects of the deceased, Colonel Miller, being present at the sale, purchased the sword and brought it home on his second return. He loaned it to Mr. Castanis, a native Greek lecturer, by whom it was carried back to Greece, and for a long time was supposed to be lost. But when, a few years since, Colonel Miller's daughter, who in the meantime had grown to womanhood and married Mr. Abijah Keith of Montpelier, visited Greece with her husband, and while there receiving the flattering attentions of the many who called on her in manifestation of their gratitude for what her father had once done for them, for their relatives and for their country, she learned the wereabouts of Mr. Castanis and this sword, and soon recovered it. And being at the house of the now celebrated George Finlay of Athens, known not only as Lord Byron's early British associate in Greece, but as the learned antiquarian, and historian of the different eras of Greece, he at once identified the sword, and gave Mr. and Mrs. Keith the following certificate, which we copy from the original in their possession:

"Mr. and Mrs. Keith have just shown me the sword which Colonel Miller purchased at Poros, at the sale of the effects of Captain Loukas:—This sword I have seen in Lord Byron's possession, before he gave it to Loukas; and I was present at Poros when it was sold.

GEORGE FINLAY.

Athens, 17 January, 1853."

Dr. Russ who has already been mentioned, and who is still living in New York, will also attest to all the material facts above presented.

The identity of this sword, which has an Asiatic inscription on the blade, with Byron's initial and a crown engraved on the hilt, is thus placed beyond a cavil.

Soon after his second return from Greece, Colonel Miller

came to Montpelier and took up his permanent residence, passed through a regular course of legal studies, was admitted to the bar, and opened a law office in the place in company with Nicholas Baylies, Esq.

In June 1828, he married the daughter of Captain Jonathan Arms, a capitalist. For the three years, 1830, 1831 and 1833, he was elected the representative of Berlin, within whose borders he was then residing with his father-in-law, Capt. Arms. During the session of the Legislature of 1833, Col. Miller introduced the following resolution:

"Whereas, slavery and the slave trade, as existing in the District of Columbia, are contrary to the broad declaration of our Bill of Rights, which declares that liberty is the inalienable right of all men; and whereas they are a national evil, disgrace and crime, which ought to be abolished; and whereas the power of legislation for that District is with the Congress of these United States; therefore,

"*Resolved*, the Governor and Council concurring herein, that our Senators in Congress be directed, and representatives in Congress be requested, to use their endeavors to effect the abolition of slavery and the slave trade in the District of Columbia."

This preamble and resolution, which we have copied at large, not only because Colonel Miller was the mover, but because they constituted the first anti-slavery movement in the Legislature of Vermont, were, after lying on the table some weeks, called up by Mr. Miller, earnestly supported by him, and,—that being long before it was good policy for leading politicians to support anti-slavery resolutions,—opposed by Mr. Foot of Rutland, who moved to dismiss the resolution. The House, however, refused to dismiss it, by twenty majority, but consented to refer it to the next session, when it was finally dismissed by fifteen majority.

From about this time, however, Colonel Miller, gave his almost undivided attentions and sympathies to the cause of anti-slavery, lecturing in all parts of the State, and not only bestowing his time and labors, but a large amount of money for its advancement. And it probably is not too much to say that no man ever did as much as Col. Miller, in building up the anti-slavery party of Vermont, and putting it on that onward march and steady increase, which raised it to a power that made it necessary for the dominant party, as a matter of self-preservation, to adopt its principles and take all its members into political fellowship.

In 1840, Colonel Miller, one of the two Vermont delegates, attended the World's Anti-slavery Convention, in London, where he appears to have been much noticed by Daniel O'Connell, Lord Brougham, and other leading men of the kingdom, to whom he had formerly become known by his championship of oppressed Greece. He took a prominent part in the debates of this celebrated Convention. And, in glancing over the volume of its proceedings, published the next year in London, we are unable to perceive why his speeches do not honorably compare with the majority of those of the many very able men of whom that body was composed.

As a public speaker, Colonel Miller was off-hand, bold and earnest, appearing more solicitous of bringing out his principles with effect, than of draping his thoughts with the graces of oratory. And in his manners in private life, he exhibited the same characteristics by which he was known in all his public actions —a fearless utterance of his opinions, and a straight forward, unstudied frankness, united with a soldierly bearing, which, with the affectedly refined, was considered as approaching the borders of roughness. As a citizen he was public spirited, without vices, and benevolent to a proverb. He always had around him, half a regiment of the poor, or poor tenants, who came not to pay him rents, but to obtain additional favors ; and the fact that both these classes continued to throng him through life is sufficient evidence that they never went away empty handed. He must have given away, during his residence in Montpelier, in private charities, in the furtherence of the anti-slavery cause, and in aidance of educational or benevolent institutions, the largest part of a handsome fortune, receiving in return nothing but the good name he carried to his grave.

He died prematurely, in consequence of an accidental injury to his spine, on the 17th day of February, 1847, leaving a wife and one child, the daughter to whom we have before alluded, Mrs. Abijah Keith; and he now sleeps on the boldest point of yonder Green Mount Cemetery, beneath the massive, square rough granite obelisk, so typical, in many respects, of his Roman virtues and strong traits of character.

THE HONORABLE WILLIAM UPHAM.

WILLIAM UPHAM, son of Captain Samuel Upham, was born in Leicester, Massachusetts, August 5th, 1792, where, while a resident there, he received only the first rudiments of education, being too young to attend the academy in that town. In 1802 his father and family removed to Vermont, and settled on a farm near the Centre of Montpelier. Here, from the age of ten to about fifteen, he worked on the farm, only attending the winter schools of the common school district in which he resided; when he met with an accident, which, at that time, apparently gave a new turn to his destinies for life:—While engaged about a cider mill, his hand was caught in the machinery, and all the fingers of the right hand so badly crushed that they had to be amputated even with the palm. This, unfitting him for manual labor, led his father to consent to what had before been his wish, the commencement of a course of education, preparatory to the study of the law. Accordingly he attended the old academy, at Montpelier, a few terms, and then, with the late Reverend William Perrin of Berlin for a fellow student, pursued the study of Latin and Greek, about one year, with the Reverend James Hobart of the last mentioned town. In 1808 he entered the office of the Hon. Samuel Prentiss, in Montpelier, as a law student; and, after pursuing his legal studies there about three years, he was admitted to the bar, and soon went into partnership in the practice of the law with the Hon. Nicholas Baylies. After continuing in partnership with Mr. Baylies a few years, he opened an office alone in Montpelier; and from that time, until his election to the United States Senate, he, either alone or with temporary partners, continued in the constant and successful practice of his profession, the business of which was always more than ample enough to require his whole time and attention. For the first thirty years of his professional career, Mr. Upham, with the exception of only one instance, steadily declined the many proffers of his friends for his promotion to civil office, though his opportunities for holding such offices included the chance for a seat on the bench of our Supreme Court. The excepted instance was involved in his consent to run as candidate for town representative, in 1827; when, though the majority of his party was a matter of much doubt, he was triumphantly elected. In 1828, he was re-elected, and in 1830 received a third election, serving through all the three terms to the entire satisfaction of his constituents, and therein exhibiting talents as a public debator which gave him a high position in the Legislature. In the presidential campaign, 1840, he, for the first time, took an active part in politics, and, to use a modern phrase, stumped nearly the whole State, making himself everywhere known to the people by the peculiar traits of his popular eloquence, and by doing efficient political service in favor of the election of General Harrison. In 1841 he was elected to a seat in the United States Senate; and in 1847 he was re-elected to the same distinguished office, and died, at Washington, before the completion of his last term, on the 14th of January 1853.

In his professional career, to which the main energies of his life were devoted, he became widely known as one of the best advocates in the State. He was, indeed, what might be called a natural lawyer, and the practice of his profession seemed to amount to almost a passion with him; and, even in his youth, even before he commenced his legal studies, he would often, it was said, leap up from his dreams in his bed, and go to pleading some imaginary law case. And, what he determined to be, that, he became, one of the most successful jury lawyers to be found in any country. Never hesitating for word, and fluent almost beyond example, the style of his speaking was rapid, thoroughly earnest, and often highly impassioned, and so magnetic was that earnestness and seeming confidence in his case, and so skillfully wrought up were his arguments, that bad indeed must have been his side of the question, if he did not command the sympathies and convictions of a good part, if not all, of the jury.

As a statesman it ill befits us to judge him, while those, who spoke by more authority, and from better opportunities, have so well and fully done so. At the time the customary resolutions, on the occasion of his death, were introduced in Congress, Senator Foot, in his obituary address, said of him :

" His impaired health, for some years past, has restrained him from participating so generally and so actively in the discussions of this body, as his inclination might otherwise have induced him to do, or his ability as a public debator might perhaps have demanded of him. Nevertheless his speeches on several important and exciting public questions, have the peculiar impress of his earnestness, his research, his ability and his patriotic devotion to the best interests of his country. A striking example is furnished of his fidelity to the trust committed to him, and his constant and patient attention to his public duties here, in the fact, which I had from his own mouth, that during the ten years of his service in this body, he never absented himself from the City of Washington for a single day, while Congress was in session, and never failed, while the condition of his health would permit, of daily occupying his seat in the Senate."

Senator Seward said :

" WILLIAM UPHAM was of Vermont ; a consistant exponent of her institutions. He was a man of strong and vigorous judgment, which acted always by a process of sound, inductive reasoning, and his compeers here will bear witness that he was equal to the varied and vast responsibilities of the Senatorial trust. He was a plain, unassuming, unostentatious man. He never spoke for display, but always for conviction. He was an honest and just man. He had gotten nothing by fraud or guile; and so he lived without any fear of losing whatever of fortune or position he had attained. No gate was so strong, no lock so fast and firm, as the watch he kept against the approach of corruption, or even undue influence or persuasion. His national policy was the increase of industry, the cultivation of peace, and the patronage of improvement. He adopted his opinions without regard to their popularity, and never stifled his convictions of truth, nor suppressed their utterance, through any fear or favor, or of faction; but he was, on the contrary, consistant and constant

As pilot well expert in perilous wave,
That to a steadfast starre his course hath bent."

Mr. Upham's best known speeches in the Senate are his speech on *Three Million Bill*, delivered March 1, 1847; on *The Ten Regiment Bill, and the Mexican War*, delivered February 15, 1848; on the *Bill to establish Territorial Governments of Oregon, New Mexico and California*, delivered July 28, 1848; on the *Compromise Bill*, delivered July 1 and 2, 1850.

These were all published in pamphlet form, as well as in all the leading political papers of the day, and, at once received the stamp of public approbation as elaborate and able efforts. But besides these, and besides also the numerous written and published reports he made during his Congressional career, as chairman of committee on *Revolutionary Claims*, on the *Post Office* and *Post Roads*, and of other committees, Mr. Upham made many other speeches on various subjects, which, though less extensively circulated perhaps, than those above enumerated, yet received almost equal praise from high quarters. Of the latter may be cited, as an instance, his speech in opposition to the Tariff bill of 1846; and to show the approbation with which it was received, at the time, among distinguished men, we are permitted to copy a characteristic note from Mr. Webster, which was sent Mr. Upham, the evening after the speech was delivered, and which, after his death, was found among his private papers:

"THURSDAY EVE., July 26, 1846.

My Dear Sir:—If you could conveniently call at my house, at eight or nine o'clock in the morning, I should be glad to see you for five minutes. I wish to take down some of your statements respecting the market abroad, for our wool. Following in your track, my work is to compare the value of the foreign and home markets.

Yours truly,

DANIEL WEBSTER.

If I had the honor of being a correspondent of Mrs. Upham, I should write to her to say, that you had made an excellent speech. The point, of the duty of government to fullfil its pledges, so frequently and solemnly made, was exhibited in a very strong light." D. W.

In his domestic relations, Mr. Upham was also fortunate and happy. Near the close of the year 1814, he married Miss Sarah Keyes of Ashford, Connecticut. The fruit of this union were five children, a son that died in its extreme infancy, William Keyes Upham, now a lawyer of talents in Ohio, Charles Carrol Upham, a purser in the United States Navy, Sarah Sumner, the wife of Mr. George Langdon, of this village, and Miss Mary Annett Upham, also a resident of Montpelier.

MRS. SARAH UPHAM.

Mrs. Sarah Upham, wife of the Honorable William Upham, was born in Ashford, Connecticut, October 10th, 1795 ; and, being a connection of the family of Mr. Thomas Brooks, of Montpelier, with whom she was temporarily residing, she became acquainted with Mr. Upham, and, at the early age of nineteen, united her destinies with his for the journey of life.

Many a public man, probably, has been left to regret that he had not a partner who, by her personal appearance, intelligence and conversational powers, was fitted to sustain herself in the refined social circles, into which his high positions often necessarily brought him. Not so, however, with Mr. Upham. His partner, who usually attended him to Washington, found no difficulty in sustaining herself among the best society annually congregated at the National Capital. Mrs. Upham, indeed, was ever, abroad or at home, a very lady like, kindly, vivacious, intelligent and agreeable woman, and was deservedly what might be called a popular favorite. And each successive generation of the young people of Montpelier, especially, were always greatly indebted to her unwearied exertions to promote their happiness, for her unexclusive hospitalities, and for the numerous opportunities she gave them for refining and improving themselves at the frequent pleasant parties, at which, with the full approbation of her liberal and congenial husband, she was delighted to gather them at her house.

After her husband died, she, though of a buoyant disposition, and striving hard to bear her loss with christian resignation, soon began visibly to droop, and on the 8th of May, 1856, followed him to the grave.

THE HONORABLE JOSEPH REED.

JOSEPH REED was a native of Westford, Massachusetts, where he was born March 13, 1766, and where he appears to have resided with his family till he was nearly a dozen years of age. He then, in consequence of a curious circumstances, which will be disclosed in the following pages, left Westford and went to live with an uncle in Plymouth, N. H. Here he resided about six years, receiving only the advantages of common schools for an education. And then, at a little over the age of eighteen, commenced an appenticeship to the carpenter's trade, with James Sargeant, a well known mechanic of Plymouth. After fully serving out the term of his apprenticeship, which brought him to the age of twenty-one, he worked one year for his master, for the sum of one hundred and fifty dollars as his wages, and then continued in the employments of his trade nearly five years longer, working in various places in the vicinity. At the end of this period he wholly relinquished his trade as a means of livelihood, and resolved on merchantile pursuits. And in pursuance of this object, he entered the store of Mr. Mower Russell, a merchant of repute in the same town, served awhile, and settled in Thetford, Vermont, in 1803, opened a store and commenced trade. In June 1804 he married; but having no children by his wife, and domestic difficulties occurring which warranted the step, he procured a legal separation from her in 1811; and during the following year he married Miss Elizabeth Burnap, daughter of Rev. Jacob Burnap, D. D. of Merrimac, N. H., by whom he had two sons, the present Charles Reed, and George W. Reed, Esquires of Montpelier. In 1814 Mr. Reed was elected as the

Town Representative of Thetford in the Legislature, re-elected the two succeding years, and received five more elections to that office during the next seven years. In 1818 he was elected one of the Judges of Orange County Court, and held the office two years successively. Having been very successful in trade in Thetford and closed up business there, he removed to Montpelier in 1827. In 1830 he was elected the Judge of Probate for the District of Washington, and was retained in that office three years. In 1834 he was chosen one of the Council of Censors to revise the Constitution of the State; and in 1840 he was elected one of the Presidential Electors who threw the vote of Vermont for General Harrison. All these offices of honor and trust, together with that of County Treasurer of this county, which he held for almost the last thirty years of his life, were well and ever acceptably filled by Judge Reed during the various periods of his somewhat eventful but almost uniformly successful career both in private and public life.

His second wife, who shared his cares and his fortunes through nearly the thirty years which embraced all the most active period of his life, and during which his fortunes and character had become established, died, leaving behind her the purest and best of memories, on the 18th of March, 1840; and Judge Reed next married her sister, Miss Lucy Burnap. The latter, however, did not long survive; and in the course of a few years he selected a fourth wife, in the person of Miss Frances M. Cotton, daughter of the Hon. John H. Cotton of Windsor, who, with a daughter, still survives him.

Judge Reed, on his death, which occurred on the 6th of February, 1859, left a handsome fortune, and, what is far better, a character which his descendants and connections may always well be proud to contemplate. Of him, his personal peculiarities and general character, it was said, in a tribute from a discriminate source, which appeared in one of our public journals at the time of his death—it was as justly as comprehensively said:—"He was a gentlemen of the Old School, precise and methodical in his habits; of noble presence and demeanor; honest and sinscere in all his dealings; reserved and prudent in his speech, sagacious and comprehensive in his views, of resolute and unflinching perseverance, and wise and ample generosity."

Although this single sentence finely embodies the whole of his general character, yet some of its peculiar traits may, perhaps, with interest and instruction to the reader, be more definitely told and illustrated. Among these marked traits was, besides his general honesty of purpose and unbending integrity, his particular and nice conscientiousness. And there can be no doubt but that, during the latter period of his life, he spent much time in looking over his actions in the past for the purpose of recalling, if such were to be found, any of his individual transactions of so faulty a nature as to seem to require from him restitution or acknowldgment. This, perhaps, could not be more forcibly illustrated than by a relation of the incidents involved in the curious correspondence which appears in the biography of the Rev. Ebenezer Hill, embraced in the recently published history of the town of Mason in New Hampshire.

The correspondence just named is as follows:

"MONTPELIER, VT., Jan. 4; 1848.

"REV. EBENEZER HILL,

"*My Dear Sir:*—I noticed not long since your name as a clergyman in Mason, in a New Hampshire Register. My object in writing to you is to ascertain if you are the person that taught a district school in Westford about the winter 1788. Will you be so kind as to inform me by mail; and if I find that you are the same person, I will then inform you of my object in asking for this information.

"Yours with great respect,

"JOSEPH REED."

To this letter Mr. Hill replied as follows:

"Mr. JOSEPH REED,

"*Sir*:—I received a line from you requesting information whether I am the person who taught a district school in Westford in the winter of 1788.

"In answer to your question, I say, I graduated at Cambridge in the year 1786, and in the autumn of the year took the town school in Westford for a year. This school I kept two years, removing from one district to another. Whether the turn came to the Forge, or Stony Brook district, in the winter of 1788, I I do not recollect. But of this I am sure that there was no school kept in the town in those two years other than was taught by me; and for a season after quitting the schools I remained in Westford, and made that my home; so that I feel confident that no school master of the name of Hill taught a scool in Westford but myself.

"I shall, Sir, with some degree of excited curiosity, be waiting for the promised information respecting the inquiry.

"Respectfully yours,

"EBEN'R HILL."

To this the following reply was received:—

"MONTPELIER, Jan. 18, 1848,

"Rev. EBENEZER HILL,

"*Dear Sir*:—Yours of the 10th inst. is received, in which you say you taught school in Westford two years, commencing in the autumn of 1786. I am satisfied that you are the person I have been anxious to find for the last half century or more. I am the son of Joshua Reed, living in the east part of the town. I attended your school in the winter of 1787, and in the fall of the same year, when you kept in the middle of the town, also the winter school of 1788, when you kept in the district where my father resided. Cols. Wright and Osgood lived in the same district. I think you boarded with Capt. Peletiah, or Capt.

Thomas Fletcher, both winters. All passed pleasantly till the last week in February, when for some trifling fault in—say whispering—being then only eleven years old, you called me up, and ordered me to stand out in the middle of the floor, about an hour before the school closed in the afternoon, and let me stand there, without my reading or spelling, until the school closed for the day, and without your saying a word to me, which I considered a great insult. I therefore remained until you and the scholars had retired, except a young man (Levi Wright) who was to take care of the house. I then thought of revenge, &c., and collected your books, inkstand and ruler with intent to burn them up; but before I could effect the object, Levi Wright discovered what I was doing and interfered, and saved all except the inkstand, ruler and a small book or two, say to the value of from three to six shillings worth. Wright told me I should be whipped to death the next day, which brought me to my senses. I then resolved to leave the country. I had an uncle visiting at my father's, who lived in Plymouth, N. H. I resolved to go home with him, to get rid of punishment; and finally persuaded my father to let me go, though he would not if he had known the reason, and I was off in a day or two; so I escaped the punishment I so richly deserved, without my parents knowing my crime; and I never returned to reside in the town. I have ever regretted my fault and error, and have intended, if ever I could see you or learn your place of residence, to make an apology and satisfaction, though perhaps you have long since forgotten the transaction. I now, sir, inclose to you five dollars, to pay debt and interest, which I hope you will receive with the same kind feelings which I have in sending it to you; and wish you to consider my extreme youth when the error was committed. * * *

"Respectfully yours, with my best wishes for your health and happiness.

"JOSEPH REED."

This letter from Judge Reed needs no comment, except to say that, as might have been expeeted, it promptly brought from the Reverened gentleman a glowing response, claiming that the transaction had entirely passed out of his memory, rejecting all idea of indebtedness on the part of the donor, but accepting the gift as a token of friendship; and then indulging in reflections on the mysterious ways of Providence in making the destinies of his creatures sometimes turn on the seemingly most insignificant circumstances.

But the feature of the life and character of Judge Reed by which he probably effected the most extensive good, and for which, doubtless, he will be the longest, and by the largest number of people, remembered, was that which was involved in the peculiar system of benevolence he early adopted for assisting indigent but promising young men in obtaining an education. When, in about middle life, he found he had accumulated a property which afforded a yearly surplus over the economical support of his family, and the probable expense of educating his children, he, as he once told a friend, began to feel it his duty to bestow at least a good portion of that surplus on objects calculated for public good. And distrusting the wisdom of many of the schemes of benevolence in vogue, on which others were bestowing their charities, he for some time cast about him for a system by which to bestow his money so that it might conduce to the most benefit to individuals, and through them to society at large. And he soon settled on the system above named, which was loaning to any poor young man, showing promise of usefulness, such sums of money as he should need tocarry him through College, without requiring any security for the payment of the amounts advanced, and leaving the payment a wholly voluntary matter with the beneficiary. And having made known his intentions, and finding no lack of applications, he at once put his system in practice, and nobly persevered in keeping it up to the last year of his life, and till the number of young men educated through his means amounted to more than twenty, among whom are to be found some of the most eminent men of the country, ornamenting the learned professions, or adding dignity to the official positions to which their merits have raised them.

Other wealthy men may have been as benevolent, others as patriotic in bestowing money for temporary purposes, but how few can boast of having originated, and so persistently maintained, through all the vicisitudes and changes of feelings and views incident to the human heart, during the period of an ordinary life time, a system of benevolence so wise and noble in conception, and of such wide spread, happy influences in the execution, as must have flowed from the remarkable one which stands associated with the memory of the late Joseph Reed. The benefits he has thus conferred are of scarcely possible computation, for they are self-multiplying, and, only beginning with the first set of beneficiaries, go on extending themselves through generations of descendants, till hundreds and thousands become in some way or other the recipients of the original bounty, and society around them becomes proportionally enlightened and elevated by the ever expanding beneficence.

THE HONORABLE SAMUEL PRENTISS.

SAMUEL PRENTISS, though at an early age he became an adopted son of Vermont, was yet a native of Stonington, Connecticut, where he was born March 31st, 1782. His family, an old and honorable one, is of a pure English and Puritan stock, traceable as far back in England, as A. D. 1318, through official records, which also show the reputable positions occupied by the succeeding branches of the family, till they came to New-England, where the lineage at once took stand among the best in the colonies. In direct descent he was the sixth from his first American, but English born ancestor, Captain Thomas Prentiss, who was born, in England about 1620, became a resident of Newton, Massachusetts, 1752, was a noted cavalry officer in the King Philip war, and died 1710, leaving

Thomas Prentiss, Jr., who died at the age of 36, leaving a son,

Samuel Prentiss, 1st, who removed, in about 1710, to Stonington, and died leaving

Samuel Prentiss, 2d, who was a Colonel in the Revolutionary army, and died leaving

Samuel Prentiss, 3d, who was a physician and surgeon in the army, and the father of

Samuel Prentiss, the subject of this sketch.

Though the whole family stock of the Prentisses was good, yet the branch we have been tracing appears to have been particularly so, both physically and intellectually: Colonel Prentiss of Revolutionary memory, six feet high and weighing over two hundred pounds, without corpulency, was one of the best built and most muscular men of the times; and the different members of the family descending from him, for the last two or three generations, of which those now living have been cognizant, will be remembered to have been, with a more than ordinary uniformity, well formed, shapely and good looking, while they have been very generally noted as possessing, also, an unusual share of intellectual capacity and power.

When the subject of the following sketch was about a year old, he removed with his family from Stonnington, Connecticut, to Worcester, Massachusetts, and from thence, in about three years more to Northfield, on the Connecticut, in the same state, where his father, Dr. Prentiss, continued ever after to reside in the successful practice of his profession till his death in 1818. The son, in the meanwhile, was kept, through all the earlier part of his boyhood, at the common schools of the place, where he made such proficiency in all the English branches of education, that, while he was yet young, he was put, as was quite customary in those days, upon a course of classical studies with the Reverend Samuel C. Allen, the minister of the town. And after pursuing this course a few years, and gaining, together with a reputation of accurate scholarship, an amount of literary and scientific acquirements deemed sufficient to warrant the step, he, at the age of about nineteen, entered himself as a law student in the office of Samuel Vose, Esq., of the same town. He did not, however, complete the prescribed course of legal studies here; but with the object of so doing, he passed over into the neighboring village of Brattleboro', Vermont, entered the office of John W. Blake, Esq., and remained there till December 1802, when he was admitted to the Bar, several months before attaining his majority.

In view of what Mr. Prentiss afterwards became, all will readily understand how well and discriminately he studied the elementary principles of the law before his admission to the Bar; but few, perhaps, are aware how close and extensive, in the meantime, had been his study of all the great masters of English literature, how careful the cultivation of his taste, and how much his proficiency in the formation of that style, which subsequently so peculiarly stamped all his mental efforts, whether of writing or speaking, with unvarying strength and neatness of expression. We recollect of having once met with a series of literary miscellany written by him, probably when he was a law student, published first in a newspaper in consecutive numbers, and afterwards republished by some one in pamphlet form, which were all alike marked by neatness of style, and beauty of sentiment, and which, though only intended, doubtless, for mere off hand sketches, would have favorably compared with our best magazine literature.

Early in the year 1803, Mr. Prentiss came into this part of the State, and opened an office, in the new, but promising village of Montpelier, which was to be ever after his home, and the central point of the field of the splendid professional success which he was destined to achieve.

The legal attainments of Mr. Prentiss, the genius he displayed in developing them, the skill he manifested in the management of his cases, and his peculiarly smooth and happy manner as a speaker, appear almost immediately, after he commenced practice here, to have attracted attention, and given him a distinguished place in the estimation of all the people of the surrounding country, as a young man of unusual promise. But he knew better than to repose on laurels of this kind. He knew that not to advance in his profession, was virtually to recede; and he knew, also, that he could make no real progress without exploring the great field of jurisprudence, within whose portals he felt he had only just entered, or in other words, without devoting himself to study,—careful, close and unremitting study. He soon, therefore, commenced a course of legal research, which, passing beyond the applications of all his own special cases, was as extended as the principles of the law itself, when regarded no less as a science than a system of technicalities. And this course, for the next twenty years, while all the time in active employ as a practitioner, he pursued with an assiduty and perseverance, rarely ever witnessed among lawyers who, like him, have already reached the higher ranks of their profession.

Such a course of legal research, conducted by a mind of the nice discrimination and power of analysis, which characterized that of Mr. Prentiss, could not long remain unattended by fruits made visible to all, and especially appreciable to those whose superior intelligence places them in control of public affairs. And accordingly, we find the Legislature of his State, as early as 1822, proffering him, with singular unanimity, a seat as one of the associate justices, on the bench of the Supreme Court. This honor, however, he declined. But during the years 1824 and 1825, he consented to serve his town as their representative in the General Assembly ; and having been triumphantly elected, he soon gave, in that service, an unmistakable earnest of those abilities as a legislator and a statesman, which were afterwards so conspicuously displayed in the broader field of the Council Chamber of the nation. At the session of the Legislature of the last year in which he was a member, he was elected first associate justice of the Supreme Court so unanimously, and with so many private solicitations for his acceptance, that he did not any longer feel himself at liberty to decline the responsibility of a membership in our State tribunal. Consequently, he now went upon the bench; and so scrupulous, and so ably, did he execute all the duties of his post, during the next four years, that, by almost common consent, he was elected in 1829, to the high and responsible office of Chief Justice of the Supreme Court of Vermont.

In 1830, he was elected a member of the Senate of the United States. In 1836 he was re-elected, or, more properly speaking, perhaps, he was elected a second term to the Senate. And before his term of service had quite expired, he was nominated by the President, and, without the usual reference of his case to a committee, unanimously confirmed, as the Judge of the United States' District Court of this State, in place of the Hon. Elijah Paine then just deceased. And this quiet, though highly responsible office, whose duties were to be discharged so near home, he, in his declining health, decidedly preferred to a seat on the bench of the Supreme Court of the United States, which it was more than intimated here from high quarters, he might soon obtain. He therefore accepted the post, and continued to hold it till his departure from life on the 15th of January, 1857.

Such was the brilliant official career of the Honorable Samuel Prentiss, who, for the last thirty-four years of his life, never passed an hour without bearing the responsibilities of some important public trust, and was never removed from one except to be promoted to a higher one, till he had reached the highest but one within the gift of the American people.

As a Senator, Judge Prentiss won an enviable and enduring reputation in a body embracing almost all the intellectual giants in that highest period of American statesmanship. Among the beneficent measures, of which he was the originator and successful advocate, was the law, still in force, for the suppression of duelling in the District of Columbia. His speeches in support of that measure, were unusually effective, and have taken rank among the best specimens of senatorial ratiocination and eloquence. His speech against the bankrupt law of 1840, was pronounced by John C. Calhoun to have been the clearest and most unanswerable of any, on a debatable question, which he had heard for years. His stand on this occasion attracted the more public notice from the fact, that he had the independence to contest the passage of the bill, in opposition, with only one exception, to the whole body of his party. And there can be but little doubt, that his argument, which was felt to stand still unanswered, had much to do with the repeal of that unfortunate law, a few years afterwards.

Judge Prentiss was obviously held in the highest estimation in the Senate, alike for the purity and worth of his private, and the rare ability of his senatorial character. His equal and confidential relations with Henry Clay and Daniel Webster, were, at that day, well known; while his sterling talents and civic virtues were admitted and admired by all, who, as we were often told at the time, cheerfully joined his more particular associates in conceding him to be the best lawyer in the Senate.

It is in his character as a jurist, however, that Mr. Prentiss will be longest remembered. It is perhaps sufficient praise for him to say, that not one of that series of able and lucid decisions, which he had made while on the bench of our Supreme Court, has ever been overruled by any succeeding tribunal in this State, nor, as far as we are apprized, by that of any other, though those decisions are, to this time, being frequently quoted in the Courts of probably nearly every State in the Union. With the legal profession, facts of this kind involve probably the best evidence of high judicial accomplishment which could possibly be adduced. With those out of that profession, the opinions of other great and learned men respecting the one in question, might be, perhaps, more palpably conclusive. And to meet the understandings of both these classes, therefore, we will close our remarks on this part of our subject by mentioning a curious legal coincidence, which, while it involved an important decision, was the means of drawing forth a high compliment from the lips of one of the most distinguished of all our American jurists:

Sometime during Judge Prentiss' Chief Justiceship of this State, Sir Charles Bell, of the Common Bench of England, made, in an important case, a decision which was wholly new law in that country; and it was afterwards discovered, when the reports of the year, on both sides of the water, were published, that Judge Prentiss had, not only in the same year, but in the same week or fortnight, made, in one of *our* important suits, precisely the same decision, which was also then new law here, arriving at his conclusion by a process strikingly similar to that of the English Justice. This remarkable coincidence, involving the origin of then new, but now well established points of law, and involving, at the same time, an inference so flattering to our Chief Justice, at once attracted the notice of the celebrated Chancellor Kent of New York, who, soon after, falling in company with several of our most noted Vermonters, cited this singular instance in compliment to the Vermont Chief Justice, and after remarking that there was no possibility that either the American or English Justice could be apprised of the other's views on the point in question, wound up by the voluntary tribute:—

"Judge Story, the only man to be thought of in the comparison, is certainly a very learned and able man; but I cannot help regarding Judge Prentiss as the best jurist in New England."

Perhaps there is nothing about which there is more misconconception among men generally than in what constitutes a really great intellect. Most people are prone to be looking for some bold and startling thoughts, or some brilliant or learned display of language, in a man, to make good in him their preconceived notions of intellectual greatness. And should they see him take up a subject in a simple, natural manner, analyze it, reject all the factitious, retain all the real, arrange the elements, and, thus clearly proceeding, at length reach the only just and safe conclusion of which the case admits, they would perhaps feel a sort of disappointment in not having seen any of the imposing mental machinery brought into play, which they supposed would be required to produce the result. Demagogues might indeed make use of such machinery, but a truly great man, never. For it is that very simplicity and clearness of mental operations which can only make an intellect efficient, safe and great. Grasp of thought, penetration and power of analysis, are the expressions generally used in describing a mind of the character of that of Judge Prentiss. But they hardly bring us to a realization of the extremely simple and natural intellectual process, through which he moved on, self-poised, step by step, with so much ease and certainty to the impregnable legal positions where he was content only to rest. And to have fully realized this, we should have listened to one of his plain but luminous decisions, on a case before supposed to be involved in almost insuperable doubts and perplexities—perceived how, at first, he carefully gathered up all that could have any bearing on the subject in hand—how he then began to scatter light upon the seemingly dark and tangled mass—and then, how, segregating all the irrelevant and extraneous, and assorting the rest, he conducted our minds to what at length we could not fail to see to be the truth and reality of the case. That Judge Prentiss possessed, besides his profound knowledge of the law as a science, a finely balanced and superior intellect is unquestionable; and that it became so, in the exercise of those peculiar traits we have been attempting to describe, need, it appears to us, to be scarcely less doubted.

In person, Judge Prentiss was nearly six feet high, well formed, with an unusually expansive forehead, shapely features, and a clear and pleasant countenance, all made the more imposing and agreeable by the affable and courtly bearing of the old school gentleman.

In his domestic system, he was a rigid economist, but ever gave liberally whenever the object commanded his approbation. Let a single instance suffice for illustration: Some years before his death, his minister lost an only cow; and the fact coming to his ears, he ordered his man to drive, the next morning, one of the cows he then possessed, to the stable of the minister.

But strangely enough, the cow selected for the gift died that night. He was not thus to be defeated, however, in his kind purpose; for hearing that the minister had engaged a new cow, at a given price, he at once sent him the amount in money required to pay for it.

Judge Prentiss has gone; but the people of the town which had the honor to be his home will cherish his memory as long as they are capable of appreciating true excellence, and be but too proud to tell the stranger that he was one of their townsmen.

At the October session of the United States District Court, following the death of Judge Prentiss, after a suitable announcement by the District Attorney, and the delivery in Court of eloquent tributes to the character of the deceased, by the Hon. Solomon Foot, and the Hon. David A. Smalley, the new Judge, the following preamble and resolutions were entertained, and ordered to be placed upon the records of the Court, as "an enduring evidence of the high veneration in which his memory was held by the Bar":

"WHEREAS, the Honorable SAMUEL PRENTISS, late Judge of the District Court of the United States for the District of Vermont, having departed this life within the present year, and the members of this Bar and the officers of this Court entertaining the highest veneration for his memory, the most profound respect for his great ability, learning, experience and uprightness as a Judge, and cherishing for his many public and private virtues the most lively and affectionate recollection, therefore

"*Resolved*, That his uniformly unostentatious and gentlemanly deportment, his assiduous discharge of his official duties, his high sense of justice, his unbending integrity, and the exalted dignity and purity of his public and private character, furnish the highest evidence of his intrinsic worth, and of his great personal merit.

"*Resolved*, That the District Attorney, as Chairman of this meeting of the Bar, communicate to the family of the deceased a copy of these proceedings, with an assurance of the sincere condolence of the members of the Bar and the officers of this Court, on account of this great and irreparable bereavement.

" *Resolved*, That, in behalf of the Bar and the officers of this Court, the Honorable the Presiding Judge thereof be, and he is hereby, respectfully requested to order the foregoing preamble and resolutions to be entered on the minutes of the Court."

MRS. LUCRETIA PRENTISS.

MRS. LUCRETIA PRENTISS, the daughter of the late Edward Houghton, Esq., of Northfield, Massachusetts, was born March 6, 1786. After having resided with her father in that town till 1804, and received a good English education for the times, she married Samuel Prentiss, Esq., and settled down with him for life in the village of Montpelier. Here she became the mother of twelve children—George Houghton, Samuel Blake, Edward Houghton, John Holmes, Charles Williams, Henry Francis, Frederick James, Theodore, Joseph Addison, Augustus, Lucretia and James Prentiss.

George H. Prentiss died soon after arriving at maturity and settling down in his profession, which, like that of all the rest of the brothers who reached manhood, was that of the law. Augustus, and Lucretia, the only daughter, died in infancy.

The cares, labors and responsibilities of the wife are generally, to a great extent, mingled with those of the husband. Much less than usual, however, were they so in the case of Mrs. Prentiss. In consequence of the close occupation of the time of her husband in his crowding legal engagements when at home, and his frequent and long continued absences from home in the discharge of his professional or official duties, almost the whole care and management of his young and numerous family devolved on her. And those who know what unceasing care and vigilance, and what blending of kindness, discretion and firmness, are required to restrain and check, without loss of influence, and train up with the rightful moral guidance, a family of boys of active temperaments, of fertile intellects and ambitious dispositions, so that they all be brought safely into manhood, will appreciate the delicacy and magnitude of her trust, and be ready to award her the just meed of praise for discharging it, as she confessedly did, with such unusual faithfulness and with such unusual success.

After a life of unvarying industry and usefulness, Mrs. Prentiss died at Montpelier, on the 15th of June, 1855, in the seventieth year of her age.

It would be difficult to say too much in praise of the character of this rare woman. She was one of earth's angels. In her domestic and social virtues; in the industry that caused her *to work willingly with her hands;* in *the law of kindness* that prompted her benevolence, and the *wisdom* that so judiciously and impartially dispensed it; together with all the other of those clustered excellencies that went to constitute the character of the model woman of the *Wise Man*—in all these Mrs. Prentiss had scarce a peer among us, scarce a superior anywhere. As already intimated, she had done everything for her family. And she lived to see her husband become known as he "sat among the Elders of the land," and her nine surving sons, all of established characters, and presenting an aggregate of capacity and good repute unequalled perhaps by that of any other family in the State, and all, all praising her in their lives. These were her works, but not all her works. The heart-works of the good neighbor, of the good and lowly christian, and the hand-works that looked to the benefit and elevation of society at large, were by her all done, and all the better done for being performed so unobtrusively, so cheerfully and so unselfishly.

"Oh, many a spirit walks the world unheeded,
That, when its veil of sadness is laid down,
Shall soar aloft with pinions unimpeded,
Wearing its glory like a starry crown."

APPENDIX.

LIST OF THE ORIGINAL FREEMEN OF MONTPELIER WHO VOTED AT THE ORGANIZATION OF THE TOWN, MARCH 1791.

Benjamin I. Wheeler,
Jacob Davis,
David Persons,
Pearley Davis,
Ebenezer Dodge,
Solomon Dodge,
Nathaniel Peck,
David Wing,
Lemuel Brooks,
Clark Stevens,
Jonathan Snow,
Hiram Peck,
James Hawkins,
James Taggart,
John Templeton,
Elisha Cummins.
Jonathan Cutler,
Charles McCloud,
Isaac Putnam,
Nathaniel Davis,
Ziba Woodworth,
Jerahmel Bowers Wheeler,
Smith Stevens,
Charles Stevens,
Edmund Doty,
Duncan Young,
Freeman West.

David Wing, Jr., and Larned Lamb, and perhaps one or two others, were freemen of the town, but for some reason were absent.

TOWN REPRESENTATIVES, TOWN CLERKS AND SELECTMEN OF MONTPELIER FROM ITS ORGANIZATION.

DATE.	REPRESENTATIVES.	TOWN CLERKS.	SELECTMEN.
1791	Jacob Davis,	Ziba Woodworth,	James Hawkins, James Taggart, Hiram Peck.
1792	Jacob Davis,	Clark Stevens,	James Hawkins, Benj. I. Wheeler, Rufus Wakefield,
1793	Jacob Davis,	David Wing, Jr.,	Pearley Davis. Benj. I. Wheeler, Rufus Wakefield.
1794	Jacob Davis,	David Wing, Jr.,	Pearley Davis, Benj. I. Wheeler, Barnabus Doty,
1795	Jacob Davis,	David Wing, Jr.,	Jacob Davis, Barnabas Doty, Jos. Woodworth, A. Nealy, J. Putnam.
1796	Jacob Davis,	David Wing, Jr.,	Jacob Davis, Elnathan Pope, Benj. I. Wheeler.
1797	David Wing, Jr.,	David Wing, Jr.	David Wing, Jr., Pearley Davis, Benj. I. Wheeler.
1798	David Wing, Jr.,	David Wing, Jr.,	David Wing, Jr., Pearley Davis, Benj. I. Wheeler.
1799	Pearley Davis,	David Wing, Jr.,	David Wing, Jr., Pearley Davis, Benj. I. Wheeler.
1800	David Wing, Jr.,	David Wing, Jr.,	David Wing, Jr., Pearley Davis, Benj. I. Wheeler.
1801	David Wing, Jr.	David Wing, Jr.,	David Wing, Jr., Arthur Daggett, Benj. I. Wheeler.
1802	Pearley Davis,	David Wing, Jr.,	David Wing, Jr., Pearley Davis, Arthur Daggett,
1803	Joseph Woodworth,	David Wing, Jr..	David Wing, Jr. Pearley Davis, Paul Holbrook.
1804	Edward Lamb,	David Wing, Jr.,	David Wing, Jr., Paul Holbrook, Clark Stevens.

DATE.	REPRESENTATIVES.	TOWN CLERKS.	SELECTMEN.
1805	Cyrus Ware,	David Wing, Jr.,	David Wing, Jr , Clark Stevens, Joseph Woodworth.
1806	Cyrus Ware,	David Wing, Jr.,	David Wing, Jr., Joseph Woodworth, Jerahmel B. Wheeler.
1807	Cyrus Ware,	Joseph Wing.	Joseph Woodworth, J. B. Wheeler, Pearley Davis.
1808	Cyrus Ware,	Joseph Wing,	Joseph Woodworth, J. B. Wheeler, Cyrus Ware,
1809	Cyrus Ware,	Joseph Wing,	Joseph Woodworth, J. B. Wheeler, Cyrus Ware.
1810	Joseph Woodworth,	Joseph Wing,	Joseph Woodworth, Clark Stevens, James H. Langdon.
1811	Timothy Merrill,	Joseph Wing,	Joseph Woodworth, B. I. Wheeler, James H. Langdon.
1812	Timothy Merrill,	Joseph Wing,	Joseph Woodworth, B. I. Wheeler, Ziba Woodworth.
1813	Joseph Howes,	Joseph Wing,	J. B. Wheeler, Jeduthun Loomis, Samuel Rich.
1814	Edward Lamb,	Joshua Y. Vail,	Benj. I. Wheeler, Salvin Collins, Joseph Woodworth.
1815	Edward Lamb,	Joseph Wing,	Benj. I. Wheeler. Timothy Hubbard, Nathaniel Davis.
1816	Nahum Kelton,	Joseph Wing,	Benj. I. Wheeler. Timothy Hubbard, Nathaniel Davis.
1817	Nahum Kelton,	Joseph Wing,	Benj. I. Wheeler, Salvin Collins, Nahum Kelton.
1818	Nahum Kelton,	Joseph Wing,	Benj. I. Wheeler, Salvin Collins, Nahum Kelton.
1819	Geo. Worthington,	Joseph Wing.	Timothy Hubbard, Nahum Kelton, Joel Bassett.
1820	Nahum Kelton,	Joseph Wing,	James H. Langdon, Nahum Kelton, Isaac Putnam.
1821	Araunah Waterman,	Joseph Wing,	James H. Langdon, Nahum Kelton, Araunah Waterman
1822	Araunah Waterman,	Joseph Wing,	James H. Langdon, Joseph Howes, Josiah Wing.

DATE.	REPRESENTATIVES.	TOWN CLERKS.	SELECTMEN.
1823	Araunah Waterman,	Joseph Wing,	Joseph Howes, Pearley Davis, Joseph Wiggins.
1824	Samuel Prentiss,	Joseph Wing,	James H. Langdon, Thomas Reed, Jr., Andrew Sibley.
1825	Samuel Prentiss,	Joseph Wing,	Joseph Howes, Josiah Wing, Samuel Templeton.
1826	Araunah Waterman,	Joseph Wing,	Joseph Howes, Josiah Wing, Nahum Kelton.
1827	William Upham,	Joseph Wing,	Joseph Howes, Josiah Wing, Nahum Kelton.
1828	William Upham,	Joseph Wing,	Joseph Howes, Josiah Wing, Nahum Kelton.
1829	Nahum Kelton,	Joseph Wing,	Timothy Hubbard, Stephen Foster, Samuel Templeton.
1830	William Upham,	Joseph Wing,	Araunah Waterman, Samuel Templeton, Apollos Metcalf.
1831	Azel Spalding,	Joseph Wing,	Josiah Wing, Royal Wheeler, Joseph Reed.
1832	Azel Spalding,	Joseph Wing,	Josiah Wing, Royal Wheeler, Joseph Reed.
1833	Azel Spalding,	Joseph Wing,	Royal Wheeler, Jared Wheelock, Harry Richardson.
1834	William Billings,	Joseph Wing,	Royal Wheeler, Harry Richardson, George Clark.
1835	William Billings,	Lyman Briggs,	Royal Wheeler, Harry Richardson, George Clark.
1836	Lucius B. Peck,	Lyman Briggs,	Harry Richardson, Isaac Cate, William Billings.
1837	Lucius B. Peck,	Lyman Briggs,	Isaac Cate, Lewis Sibley, Alfred Wainwright.
1838	Royal Wheeler,	Lyman Briggs,	John Gray, Joel Bassett, Alfred Pitkin.
1839	Royal Wheeler,	Lyman Briggs,	R. R. Keith, Larned Coburn, Cyrus Morse.
1840	H. N. Baylies.	Lyman Briggs,	R. R. Keith, Larned Coburn, Cyrus Morse,

DATE.	REPRESENTATIVES.	TOWN CLERKS.	SELECTMEN.
1841	H. N. Baylies,	Lyman Briggs,	Charles Sibley, Ira S. Town, John Vincent.
1842	Addison Peck,	Lyman Briggs,	Charles Sibley, Ira S. Town, John Vincent.
1843	Addison Peck,	Lyman Briggs,	John Vincent, Thomas Needham, Lot Hathaway.
1844	J. T. Marston,	Lyman Briggs,	Thomas Needham, Lot Hathaway, Hiram Sibley.
1845	J. T. Marston,	Lyman Briggs,	Hiram Sibley, John J. Willard, Carlos Bancroft.
1846	Charles Clark,	James T. Thurston,	John J. Willard, Carlos Bancroft, Charles Walling.
1847	Charles Clark,	James T. Thurston,	Charles Walling, George S. Hubbard, John G. Putnam.
1848	H. W. Heaton,	James T. Thurston,	George S. Hubbard, S. F. Stevens, Isaac Cate.
1849	J. A. Vail,	James T. Thurston,	Thomas Reed, C. W. Bancroft, S. K. Collins.
1850	J. A. Vail,	James T. Thurston,	C. W. Bancroft, S. K. Collins, William Howes.
1851	H. H. Reed,	Jonathan E. Wright,	Geo. Worthington, John Spalding, B. F. Walker.
1852	H. H. Reed,	W. W. Cadwell,	Joseph Howes, Geo. C. Shepard, Wm. N. Peck.
1853	E. P. Walton, Junior,	W. W. Cadwell,	Joseph Howes, Henry Nutt, Wm. N. Peck.
1854	Abijah Keith,	W. W. Cadwell,	Wm. N. Peck, Henry Nutt, John Spalding.
1855	E. P. Jewett,	Geo. L. Kinsman,	C. W. Bancroft, Charles Reed, A. W. Wilder.
1856	F. F. Merrill,	Geo. L. Kinsman,	Charles Reed, Wm. N. Peck, David W. Wing.
1857	F. F. Merrill,	Geo. L. Kinsman,	Charles Reed, Wm. N. Peck, David W. Wing,
1858	Geo. W. Collamer,	Geo. L. Kinsman,	Charles Reed, R. W. Hyde, Ebenezer Scribner.

DATE.	REPRESENTATIVES.	TOWN CLERKS.	SELECTMEN.
1859	Geo. W. Collamer,	Adams Kellogg,	Charles Reed, R. W. Hyde, Ebenezer Scribner.
1860	Geo. C. Shepard,	Adams Kellogg,	Joseph Poland, Joel Foster, Jacob Smith.

The first Town Treasurer, Jonathan Cutler, elected in 1792, held the office one year. Barnabas Doty held it three years, to 1796; Elnathan Pope one year. Joseph Wing held it continuously seventeen years, to 1814; then J. Y. Vail one year; then Joseph Wing seven years, to 1822; then John Barnard two years; then Joseph Wing five years, to 1828; then Daniel Baldwin one year; then H. N. Baylies one year; then Wm. Hutchins two years; then R. R. Keith two years, to 1836; then Daniel Baldwin eleven years, to 1847; then Carlos Bancroft two years; then Timothy Cross one year; then J. A. Page six years, to 1856; then R. Richardson to 1859; then George W. Scott, present incumbent.

The Selectmen were generally made Overseers of the Poor till about 1840. Since then it has been a separate appointment; and, with only two or three exceptions, Henry Y. Barns has held the office.

TOWN OFFICERS OF EAST MONTPELIER SINCE THE SEPARATION IN 1848.

DATE.	REPRESENTATIVES.	TOWN CLERKS.	SELECTMEN.
1849	Nathaniel C. King,	Royal Wheeler,	J. C. Nichols, B. H. Pierce, Chas. Sibley.
1850	Nathaniel C. King,	Royal Wheeler,	J. C. Nichols, B. H. Pierce, Chas. Sibley.
1851	J. P. W. Vincent,	Royal Wheeler,	J. C. Nichols, Jacob Rich, Cyrus Morse.
1852	J. P. W. Vincent,	Royal Wheeler,	Jacob Rich, Cyrus Morse, Samuel Templeton.
1853	James Templeton,	Royal Wheeler,	Samuel Templeton, Lorenzo Gray, Hazen Lyford.
1854	James Templeton,	Royal Wheeler,	Lorenzo Gray, H. D. Foster, Learned Coburn.
1855	Stephen F. Stevens,	Royal Wheeler,	Edson Slayton, D. R. Gray, T. C. Kelton.
1856	Stephen F. Stevens,	Austin D. Arms,	Edson Slayton, H. D. Foster, E. D. Nye.
1857	Larned Coburn,	Austin D. Arms,	E. D. Nye, Hazen Lyford, M. B. Hamblin.
1858	Larned Coburn,	Austin D. Arms.	Hazen Lyford, M. B. Hamblin, Jas. Bennett.
1859	Pearley P. Pitkin,	Austin D. Arms,	James Bennett, O. F. Lewis, E. H. Vincent.
1860	Pearley P. Pitkin,	Austin D. Arms,	O. F. Lewis, E. H. Vincent, J. T. Putnam.

The first Town Treasurer, Addison Peck, elected in 1849, held the office three years. N. C. King, the present incumbent, elected in 1852, has held the office every year since.

The first Overseer of the Poor, Addison Peck, elected in 1849, held the office three years. Jacob Bennett, elected in 1852, held it eight years, to 1860. Addison Peck is the present incumbent in 1860.

LIST OF ATTORNIES,

Comprising all the Attornies ever Practicing in Montpelier, Arranged in the Order they Commenced.

Charles Bulkley, deceased in 1836,
Cyrus Ware, deceased in 1849,
Samuel Prentiss, deceased in 1857,
Nicholas Baylies, removed 1836, & dec'ed,
William Upham, deceased in 1853,
Timothy Merrill, deceased in 1837,
J. Y. Vail, 20 yrs Co. Cl'k, deceased 1843,
Jeduthun Loomis, deceased in 1843,
James Lynde, removed 1818 and deceased,
Thomas Reed, not in practice,
Azro Loomis, deceased in 1831,
Roswell H. Knapp, deceased in 1835,
H. H. Reed, deceased in 1856,
L. B. Peck,
J. P. Miller, deceased in 1847,
D. P. Thompson, not in practice,
O. H. Smith,
C. J. Keith, deceased in 1853,
Azel Sdalding, removed in 1859,
S. B. Prentiss, now of Ohio,
Nicholas Baylies, Jr., now of Mississippi,
Geo. B. Manser, now a clergymen,
F. F. Merrill, deceased in 1859,
J. T. Marston, now of Wisconsin,
Isaac F. Redfield, remvd & Ch'f Jus. S.Ct.,
H. W. Heaton,
John H. Prentiss, now of Orleans Co.,
Charles Reed,
Wm. K. Upham, now of Ohio,
J. A. Vail,
S. Churchill, Co. Cl'k 1838, not in practice,
R. S. Bouchett, now of Montreal,
Geo. W. Reed, not now in practice,
A. W. Tenney, soon removed,
Charles W. Prentiss, now of N. Y. City,
Timothy P. Redfield,
Luther Newcomb, County Clerk,
Joseph A. Prentiss,
Stoddard B. Colby,
C. W. Willard,
Wm. P. Briggs,
B. F. Fifield.
N. G. Ferrin,
Geo. W. Bailey, Jr.,
C. J. Gleason,

LIST OF PRACTICING PHYSICIANS.

Arranged in the Order they Commenced.

Pierce Spalding, village, removed,
Philip Vincent, town, deceased,
Edward Lamb, village, deceased,
Stephen Peabody, town, deceased,
Jacob P. Vargeson, village, removed,
Stephen Day, " deceased,
Samuel Prentiss, " "
Phineas Woodbury, " "
Nathan B. Spalding, " removed.
Nathaniel C. King, town, East M.,
James Spalding, village, deceased,
Eleazer Hamblin, " "
Julius Y. Dewey, " not in practice,
Benjamin Walton, " removed,
Hart Smith, " deceased,
Seth Field, " removed,
Azel Holmes, " "
F. W. Adams, " deceased,
Zebulon P. Burnham, " removed,

Charles Clark, town and village,
Daniel Corliss, town, deceased,
Milo P. Burnham, removed,
Sumner Putnam, East M., removed,
Thomas C. Taplin, Homeopathist,
J. M. Gregory, Dentist, removed,
Ralph Kilbourn, Dentist, deceased,
M. Newton, and Brockway & Hawley, Den,
O. P. Forbush, Dentist,
Orrin Smith, village, removed,
C. M. Rublee, "
E. Paine, "
G. N. Brigham, " Homeo.,
C. B. Chandler, "
W. H. H. Richardson, village,
James Templeton, East M.,
G. H. Loomis, village, deceased,
F. A. McDowell, " removed,
M. M. Marsh, "
C. M. Chandler, "

CLERGYMEN.

Resident one year or more.

Congregational—Rev. Clark Brown for the year 1805.—Village.
" Chester Wright, from 1808 to 1830.
" Samuel Hopkins, from 1831 to 1835.
" Buel Smith, from 1835 to 1840.
" Sherman Kellogg, from 1835 to 1845.
" John Gridley, from 1841 to 1846.
" Jacob Seeley, from 1845 to 1846.
" John M. Stearns, from 1839 to 1841.
" Wm. H. Lord, from 1846 to 1860 and continued.

Methodist.—John G. Dow, from 1829 to 1831.
Joel Templeton, from 1831 to 1833.
——— Sprague, from 1833 to 1835.
E. Scott, from 1835 to 1837.
Samuel Kelly—hill, from 1837 to 1839.
Eleazer Smith, from 1839 to 1841.
C. R. Harding and A. C. Smith, from 1841 to 1843.
John G. Dow and E. J. Scott, 1843 to 1845.
John G. Dow, E. J. Scott, James Templeton, from 1844 to 1846.
E. J. Scott and A. G. Button, from 1846 to 1848.
A. Webster and A. Holbrook, from 1848 to 1850.
E. J. Scott and I. D. Russ, 1850 to 1851.
S. P. Williams, Schuyler Chamberlain, 1851 to 1852.
E. J. Scott and I. D. Russ, from 1852 to 1854.
E. J. Scott and E. Copeland, from 1854 to 1856.
E. J. Scott, F. D. Hemenway and E. Brown, from 1856 to 1859.
H. P. Cushing and E. Brown, from 1857 to 1859.
W. D. Malcolm E. Brown, and A. Hitchcock, from 1860

Baptists.—Ziba Woodworth to 1826; Philip Wheeler to about 1834; Zebina Young from 1841 about 3 years.

Episcopalians.—Geo. B. Manser from 1843 to 1850.
F. W. Shelton from 1850 to 1851.
Edward F. Putnam from 1851 to 1854.
F. W. Shelton from 1854 to 1860 and continued.

Universalist.—Paul Dean in 1808; John M. Austin in 1835; Eli Ballou from 1842.

Friends.—Clark Stevens from 1815 to 1853.

LIST OF MERCHANTS AND TRADERS,

With Dates of Commencing Business as Individuals or Firms.

1791 Dr Frye
1794 Col Joseph Hutchins
1796 Col. J & W Hutchins
1799 Hubbard & Cadwell
1802 W I Cadwell
Col D Robbins—East part town
Robbins & Freeman
1803 Hubbard & Wing
Langdon & Forbes
1807 Timothy & Roger Hubbard
James H Langdon
Uriah H Orvis
Dunbar & Bradford
1808 Chester W Houghton
Josiah Parks
1809 John Crosby—Drugs, &c
1810 L Q C Bowles, Bookseller, &c
Walton & Goss, Booksellers, &c
French & Dodge, Shoes
1811 J F Dodge
Langdon & Barnard
1813 John Spalding
1814 C Hubbard & J Spalding
D Baldwin & Co
Austin Arms
Emerson & Wilkins
Luther Bugbee
Charles Storey
1815 Wright & Sibley
1816 E P Walton & Geo S Walton
Books, &c
French & Harvey, Shoes
1817 Sylvester Larabee
E P Walton
H Y Barnes, Harness and Saddlery
1821 John Barnard
Langdon & Spalding
Chester Hubbard
Barnard & Dutton
W I Cadwell & Son
1822 C Hubbard & E P Jewett
Roger Hubbard
1823 Dutton & Baylies
W W Cadwell
1824 Hubbard & Kimball
T M Taylor
Warren Swift
Langdon, Spalding & Co
Otis Standish
1825 Baldwin, Hutchins & Co
Cadwell & Goldsbury
Taylor & Prentiss
Dodge & Standish, Drugs, &c
1826 Wiggins & Seeley
Geo W Hill, Books, &c
1827 Luther Cross
Joseph Wiggins
Goss & Wiggins
1828 Luther Cross & Co
Hubbard, Jewett & Co
Spalding, Storrs & Co
Baylies & Hutchins
1829 N Harvey, Shoes

1830 Baldwin & Prentiss
1831 Charles Lyman
J S & G Town, Jewelry, &c
W W Cadwell alone
Hart & Riker
J M & B H Snow
E H Prentiss
1832 W & M P Hutchins
1833 Emerson, Lamb & Co
Snow, Bancroft & Co
Snow & Bancroft
James Pierce & Co
Silver & Pierce
Standish D Barnes
G W Ware
Baldwin & Scott
1834 Jewett & Howes
Burbank & Hubbard
Baylies & Hart
Ebenezer Colburn
S B Flint, Saddlery & Harness
Hutchins & Wright
Wm Clark, Books, &c
1835 H N Baylies & Co
Harvey & Harran, Shoes
John & Chas Spalding
Silver, Pierce & Co
Silas Burbank & Co
Ira Day
Asa Prentiss
1836 Jewett, Howes & Co
Emerson & Russell
Baylies & Storrs
1837 Bancroft & Riker
C & L L Lamb
C Alexander
1838 Spalding & Foster
Langdon & Wright
Town & Witherell, Jewelry
John S Abbott
1839 Baylies & Goss
S P Redfield, Drugs
J T Marston, Books &c
Storrs & Langdon
E P Walton & Sons, Books &c
1840 Charles Spalding
Silver, Lamb & Co
Harran & Dodge
1841 H N Baylies
Jewett & Howes
Baldwin, Scott & Co
Lyman & King
J H Ramsdell
Cross, Hyde & Co, Bakery
1842 Cross, Day & Co
Benj Day & Co
French & Bancroft
Ellis, Wilder & Co
Clark & Collins, Drugs
1843 Silas C French
1844 Augustus Haven
Zenas Wood, Stoves and Tin
Webb, Bancroft & Co
J Booth, Hats
Moses & Rich, N Montpelier
J Huntington, E Montpelier
1845 Z & C Wood
J T Marston, Books &c
Wm T Burnham, Hats &c
Samuel Abbott, Jewelry
N C King, N Montpelier
1846 Bancroft & Riker
J W Howes
L & A A Cross
Erastus Hubbard
1847 Harvey King
1848 Loomis & Camp
Hyde, Dodge & Co, Hardware
E C Holmes
Witherell & Mead, Jewellers
Eastman & Danforth, Books, &c
A A Sweet, Tin and Stoves
Alfred Scott, Hats
1849 Keith & Barker
S K Collins, Drugs
Redfield & Grannis, Drugs

1850 Scott & Field
Geo P Riker
Bancroft & Holmes
Abbott & Emery, Cabinet Work
John Wood "
James Howland, "
L M Wood, Clothing and Tailoring
R R Riker " "
1851 Hubbard & Black, Stoves
1852 Peck & Lewis
Ballou & Burnham, Books, &c
R W Hyde
T C Barrows
1853 Lyman & King
1854 Keith & Barker
Ellis & Bancroft
Gustavus Hubbard
Walker & White
Wilder, Scott & Co
Smith & Pierce
Dr B O Tyler, Drugs
Geo L Kinsman, Hats
N C Bacon
Emery & Brown, Crockery & Furniture
Wm P Badger, Hats
W W Cadwell, Hats
Phinney & Mead, Jewellers
S M Walton, Book Bindery
C G Eastman, Books and Stationery
Ballou & Loveland, "
Wm McCollum
1855 C W Storrs
John S Barker
H S Loomis
Peck & Bailey
Union Store
Fuller & Smith
Jacob Scott
Oliver & Helmer, Hardware
French & Sanborn, Clothing
H B Witt "
Fred E Smith, Drugs
Collins & Pierce, "
Keith & Peck, Leather Dealers
1856 W Corliss, E Montpelier
Chas Sibley, N Montpelier
Palmer & Storrs
Burbank & Langdon, Flour
Hyde & Foster, Hardware &c
A C Field, Clothing
1857 Ellis & Hatch
James G French, Clothing
S C Woolson, Clothing and Tailoring
1858 J P Dewey
Storrs & Fuller
J S Lee, Clothing
L F Pierce, Drugs
D K Bennett, Guns and Pistols
Mercantile Union, J H P Rowell Agent
C & S E Robinson
Adams Kellogg, Hats and Clothing
E Dewey " "
Emery & Field, Crockery and Furniture
Wm Storrs
Herrick & Page, Shoes
A A Mead, Jewelry
T C Phinney "
1859 E C Lewis
S S Boyce, Books &c
S Abbott, Jewelry
Field & Watson
M P Courser
A L Carlton
J R Langdon, Flour
J C Emery, Crockery and Furniture
E. Gunnison, Shoes
Bailey & Brothers
Palmer & Stetson
Wooster Sprague
1860 Eli Marsh
Wm B Burbank
J W Ellis & Co
Jacob Smith, Clothing
Demming & Brooks

THE PUNISHMENTS INFLICTED FOR THE LIGHTER CRIMES IN THE EARLY SETTLEMENTS.

While the settlements were in their infancy, and before there were any jails in this part of the State, the lighter crimes and misdemeanors were punished by fines, whipping, running the gauntlet, and other inflictions of a similar character. The late General Pearley Davis furnished the Rev. John Gridley, for his historical sermon on Montpelier, published in 1843, the following reminiscence of a case of this kind:—

"I recollect, in the very early settlement, that a young man, not an inhabitant, was tried for some petty crime—I think for stealing—at the tavern house, before Colonel Jacob Davis, and was found guilty and fined, which fine he had not the means to pay. A commutation of the punishment was offered him, which he accepted—which was that he should run from the tavern house until he crossed the bridge into Berlin, with a supple man to start behind him at a short distance, with a whip or stick, and apply it on his back if he could come within reach of him, and that he would never again return to Montpelier. This should be in full payment of the fine. Whether the Justice had any hand in this commutation I cannot recollect; but I heard the trial, and saw the punishment inflicted, with many others, with much satisfaction."

About this time, also, a man, for some small crime, was had up in the lower part of Middlesex, tried by a Justice or Judge Lynch, and, in expiation of the sentence pronounced, tied to a tree and received a severe whipping from beech or birch switches, in the hands of a constable, or more probably, as the days of the "Beech Seal" were then yet fresh in memory, in the hands of some patriotic volunteer for this public service.

THE ABORIGINAL INHABITANTS OF WINOOSKI VALLEY.

The question, who were the aboriginal inhabitants of Winooski Valley, together with other parts of Western Vermont, or in other words what Indian nation first occupied and owned it, has never, to this day, been fully settled. This question, it may be borne in mind, has always been involved in that of allowing by our Legislature the claim of the Caughnahwahgah Indians, who, professing to be, as they doubtless are, the only organized remaining representatives of the once powerful confederacy of the Iroquois, or the Six Nations, of New York, have repeatedly petitioned for remuneration for the portion of the State which they allege was formerly owned by their people, and which has never been paid for. The boundaries of the territory on which this claim has been made to rest, have always been defined by them to be Lake Champlain on the West, and the mountain ranges which divide the waters running into Lake Champlain from the Missisquoi, the Lamoille, and the Winooski rivers, from the waters running into the Connecticut, with so much of the land drained by Otter Creek as would be embraced in a line drawn from Ticonderoga to the sources of the Winooski. And although none of the various committees or commissioners appointed to act on the claim of the Iroquois, in any of the repeated applications they have made to our Legislature for remuneration since the year 1798, have made the question of their right to turn on their original occupancy and ownership of the land, yet the alleged fact of such original occupancy and ownership, and the length of that occupancy, if they were not the original occupants, has been often questioned in connection with their applications, and always more or less discussed, but without any settlement of the historical question, which we have stated to be involved in the controversy—a cheaper mode to dispose of the claim being generally resorted to by those to whom the consideration of the subject has been submitted.

The question, who were the first Indian inhabitants of Winooski Valley, since a large part of the State has been placed in the same category by this Iroquois claim, becomes therefore invested with something more than of a mere local historic interest; and this circumstance has induced us to give the subject a more extended investigation than we could properly introduce into the body of this work. But believing that, from the connection of the subject with the locality of our town history, something of the kind should accompany it, we have reserved the discussion for our appendix.

At the time when the French and English began to effect lodgments in Canada and the Northerly parts of the present United States, they found the country in possession of two distinct, and wide spread native people, speaking two different languages, which were varied only, in each, by the different dialects of the tribal divisions. These two peoples or nations were the Abenakis, a name signifying the people of the East, or those first seeing the light of the rising sun, and the Great Western Confederacy of the *Six Nations*, to whom the French gave the general name of the *Iroquois*. The Abenakis, under their various tribal names and organizations, were found in possession and undoubted ownership of all the present New England States bordering on the Atlantic. New Brunswick, Nova Scotia, all *Lower* Canada, East of and around the St. Lawrence up to and some distance above Montreal, and so much of Vermont, at least, as lies East of the Eastern range of the Green Mountains. And all this class of native people have always uniformly claimed, and all the old men of their descendants, who yet keep up, in dwindled remnants, their tribal organizations on the Penobscot, and on other rivers perhaps in Maine and New Brunswick, still continue to claim, that the Western boundary of their territory was originally, and always rightfully, Lake Champlain, and embraced the whole of the present State of Vermont, and that the Iroquois, who, for a period, might have been in possession of Western Vermont, obtained it without treaty, purchase or right, and wholly by aggressive warfare. In confirmation of this we find that the marking or designating lines on the ancient map, published in 1660, by Rev. Father Ducreux, with his history of Canada, places "*Lacus Champlenius*," Lake Champlain, as the Western boundary of the rightful territory of the Abenakis or Eastern Indians. This view of the Western boundary of the Abenakis is fully sanctioned by the Rev. Eugene Vetromile, professor in the Catholic College at Worcester, Mass., who, having spent a long period as a missionary, teacher and Patriarch of the Penobscot Indians, and mastered their language and traditionary history, has recently communicated for the publications of the Maine Historical Society a very discriminating and valuable treatise on the subject of the Abenaki division of the Indians. And we can no where find any authority militating against this view of the case, with a single exception, which, at first blush, might be thought to do so. This was in the conference held by the commissioners sent from Boston, and the Eastern Indians in the presence of the Governor of Canada, in 1725, after those Indians began to carry on their war against New England in alliance with the French. The passage to which we refer, appears in the report soon after published by these commissioners, giving the results of the conference, which had been demanded by the Governor of Canada in relation to the destruction of the Indian village of Norridgewock, in Maine, and other aggressions by the English. In that report the commissioners, in speaking of the "*haughty*" demands of the Indian leaders, say "*they demanded that the English should restore their lands and rebuild their church*," which they had destroyed at Norridgewock; and when asked what land they referred to, said "*their land commenced at Long River, (the Connecticut) which lies to the West, beyond Boston—that this river was formerly the boundary which separated the lands of the Iroquois from those of the Abenakis*," &c. Now although the first glance at this passage might lead us to suppose it indicated the Connecticut river as the dividing line between the Abenakis and the Iroquois, throughout its whole length, yet a second inspection will bring us to perceive that it refers only to the lower portion of the river, which, lying West of Boston and bordering Massachusetts, was, after they had subjugated the Mohicans in truth, in that section of the Connecticut, the Eastern boundary of the Iroquois; and it probably has no application to the river as such boundary, on the upper part bordering Vermont; or, if it possibly has, the word "*formerly*" must refer only to the time when the Iroquois held their *temporary* possession of this part of the country.

To this evidence of the original ownership of Vermont by the Abenakis, should perhaps be added the fact, that the Indian names of the rivers and lakes of Vermont, as far as they have ever become known to us, are all made up of words from the language of the Algonquins, who were the Canadian branch of the Abenakis. This fact, it is true, is not very conclusive, since the Eastern Indians would not have been very likely to retain the names which their enemies, the Iroquois, might have previously bestowed; but it at least *clearly* shows that the former must have been last, and for a considerable period, in possession of this disputed territory.

But here leaving this division of the subject, let us now examine the evidence which has been, or may be produced, to sustain the other, or Iroquois side of the question.

In the first place we have, in the published journal of the expedition of Champlain, when, in the summer of 1609, he discovered and explored the lake that bears his name, full and direct evidence that the Iroquois were in possession of just about the same tract of territory in Vermont to which their descendants have latterly been laying claim as a part of their original domain, being a gore of land bordering on the lake, extending back Eastward between forty and fifty miles, embracing four out of five of the largest rivers, and almost one half of the State. Champlain also found the Abenakis, from which nation he enlisted his attendants for the voyage, at war with the Iroquois—a war probably which grew out of the aggression of the latter in obtaining possession of this very disputed territory, and which had continued up to that time. It was one of the conditions of the attendance of these Abenakis in Champlain's voyage, that he should help them fight their enemies, the Iroquois, whom they would be likely to encounter, as it appears they did, on their voyage through the lake. And he distinctly states, that during this voyage, and while noting the mountains on the East, as he was rowing through the broad lake, he asked his new allies what people inhabited those mountains, when they told him that it was their enemies, the Iroquois, who peopled all the vallies among those mountains, where they raised abundance of corn. In addition to this evidence, that the Iroquois were, at that time, in full possession of the disputed territory in Vermont, may be adduced another fact, which, it appears to us, has a strong bearing on the subject we are discussing. Champlain, on proceeding on his expedition, found the outlet of the lake, the Sorell, bearing the name of the "River of the Iroquois"—a name which the French must have bestowed on one of their first voyages up the St. Lawrence, more than half a century before, when Cartier made his abortive attempts to found colonies at Quebec and Montreal. That this name was bestowed on the outlet of the lake by the French in one of their two first ascents of the St. Lawrence, in 1535 and 1540, we infer from the fact that, after 1540, no French voyagers came up the St. Lawrence till the arrival of Champlain in the beginning of the next century; and had he himself discovered and named this outlet, he would, in his account of it, have doubtless mentioned the circumstance, instead of treating it, as he evidently does, as an old and established name. If this conclusion is correct, it shows that, as early at least as 1540, the Iroquois were in possession of the outlet of Lake Champlain, and, as may very safely be presumed, of the lake itself and the territory bordering both its shores, including the whole of that tract in Vermont subsequently claimed by their descendants. This is the only fact we can find among either the French or English authorities, from which can be inferred the first date, when the Iroquois were in possession of the claimed part of Vermont. And it is probable, from what can be gathered from their general history, that it was about that date, 1540, or not many years before it, that they gained this possession, and gained it by conquest, as it will be our next purpose to show that they did, instead of having been the original possessors and owners.

According to David Cusick, the only native historian of the Six Nations, an educated Iroquois, who has attempted to give, with many of their fabulous traditions, a correct history of their origin, the principal events in chronological order, which have marked their growth and progress as a people. According to Cusick, the Iroquois originated in five families, at first, located on the North Eastern border of Lake Ontario, more than a thousand years before the discovery of America by Columbus. These families at length became large tribes, formed a lasting confederacy, and, adding a sixth to their number, located themselves, at first, around the group of smaller lakes in Western New York, and then, in process of time, spread themselves through the Valley of the Mohawk, and finally, in the last located, the Sixth Nation, over the country further East and North around the upper portions of the Hudson, making war with the Mohegans, on the East side of it, and reducing them to a tributary nation. This last event he makes out to have occurred just before the first coming of the Whites to America. The confederacy then were in the height of their power, numbering 23,000 warriors. Soon after this, they began to extend their conquests Westward and Southward, waged their most important war with the Eries of Ohio and drove them from their country, which opened to the conquerors all the Great West to the shores of the Mississippi, while their conquests South were soon extended to the Carolinas.

Much of this account of Cusick is, doubtless, handed down as it was in traditions from generation to generation, unreliable, especially in respect to the earlier dates, but in regard to the origin of this people, the localities of their residence, and their principal wars and conquests, the successive oral transmitters of their history could hardly fail of being essentially correct. And we may therefore, confirmed as it is by the many circumstances found to exist on the advent of the Europeans, set it down as an established fact that the Iroquois originated in the North West and gradually extended themselves over the South Eastern parts of New York to the upper parts of the Hudson, and finally to Lake Champlain, and some distance at least into the country to the East of it. And we may further pretty safely conclude that they could not have reached and become possessed of Western Vermont much before the French found their way into the St. Lawrence in 1535; since their conquest of the Mohegans did not take place till about the time North America had been discovered by the Whites, and we may reasonably suppose the lapse of a score of years or so, after their conquest and possession of the rich and extensive Mohegan territory South East of the upper part of the Hudson, before they would push Northerly on to Lake Champlain and engage in a new war with the Abenakis, and succeed in wresting from them their territory in Western Vermont.

De Witt Clinton, in his very able and discriminate address on the subject of the Six Nations, delivered before the N. Y. Historical Society in 1825, says, that Lake Champlain was called, by the first French Voyagers, the "*Sea of the Iroquois.*" And he further distinctly states, after quoting Colden, the first Fnglish historian of the Six Nations, and numerous other of the best early English and Freneh authorities, that this lake was one of the many lakes found by the whites in possession of that people. And, in another part of his discourse, while endeavoring to ascertain the limits of their possessions on the East, he also says "the supremacy of the Iroquois probably prevailed, at one time, over the territory as far East as the Connecticut River."

This was when this great and sagacious native Republican confederacy, which claims to have furnished the model of our own, was in the height of its power and glory, extending from within the limits of New England on the East, to the Mississippi on the West, and to South Carolina on the South, and embracing the great body of the present United States. And it must have been, also, about the time of the first French voyages up the St. Lawrence, in 1540. And there is no reason to believe that the limits of their supremacy were in any part circumscribed for the next hundred years, or before about 1640 or 1650, when, on the growing power of the French in Canada, and the increasing inclination of their tribes to move Westward for the occupation of their opening in the more genial climes towards the Mississsippi, it appears quite certain they must have relinquished their Eastern possessions of conquests round Lake Champlain and the upper Hudson, and began to follow the course of their nation Westward.

We arrive at the conclusion, therefore, that though the Iroquois were not the original occupants and owners of any part of Vermont, yet they *did* become possessed of it, or at least the part of it claimed by their descendants, including the Winooski Valley, by conquest, a short time previous to 1540, and that they continued to possess it for about a century afterwards; when they must have voluntarily relinquished it and withdrawn into the State of New York. We say voluntarily, because at the close of that period, and for twenty years afterwards, the Iroquois, or the Mohawks, as they were generally called, were the terror of all the New England tribes, and the latter would never have had the disposition nor power to assail and expel such formidable enemies from the territory, in which they had become so well established by conquest, had the latter any wish to retain it. And that this relinquishment of Vermont by the Iroquois did take place before or about the period we have named, 1640, we may very safely infer from a combination of facts and circumstances which otherwise could not have existed. In the first place, we may infer it from the before cited map of Father Ducreux, published in 1640, making the Western boundary of territory of the Abenakis to be, at that time, Lake Champlain. In the second place we may infer it from many of the well known events of a later date. In the war of King Philip, which occurred in 1675, it became well known that both sides of the Connecticut, from its mouth to its sources and far towards the Hudson on the West, were in possession of the Eastern Indians. For he made alliances with their tribes living on both sides of that river, and drew an important part of his forces from the West side of it, as high up as the portion bordering Vermont. And it appears that about the same time he personally visited the Mohawks, in the valley of the river of that name, to try to draw them into his alliance, but not only utterly failed in the attempt, but, through some mismanagement of himself or attendants, actually brought down a foray of the Mohawks on his Western rear, which was doubtless the true secret of the sudden desertion of his allies and the disastrous turn which all at once mysteriousiy occurred in the fortunes of that great native warrior of New England. Now had the dreaded Mohawks been in possession of any part of Vermont when Philip was mustering his forces, none of the Eastern tribes would have been found round the upper portions of the Connecticut to come forward to join him; nor would he have made the upper part of the Valley of the Connecticut the refuge or fastness, as he often did, to which he withdrew his forces during the war.

In addition to this, may be cited the facts attending the destruction of Schenectady by the French and their Abenakis allies in 1690. The whole valley of Lake Champlain was then evidently entirely clear of Iroquois; for the assailants of that fated village, though not a strong force, passed unmolested through that valley, and even to that village 60 or 70 miles to the South West of it, without attack, or fear of attack, from the Iroquois, who at that time, though in close alliance with the Dutch and English, were located still further up the Mohawk River.

It seems that Capt. Champlain, by his imprudent course in joining the Abenakis, on his first voyage through the lake, and killing two of the Iroquois chiefs in the skirmish that there ensued, roused up the lasting ire of that fierce and proud people, which resulted in a lasting war upon the French, that, at one time threatened the entire expulsion of the latter from Canada. And this led to the close alliance which was then formed between the French and all the tribes of the Abenakis, and which continued uninterrupted till the conquest of Canada by the English in 1760. And not only was the expedition against Schenectady by the French and Abenakis made through the valley of Champlain; but all the subsequent ones by the same allies, or by the Abenakis by themselves, against the frontier settlements of Massachusetts and New Hampshire were made through, or emanated from, some one of the vallies in Vermont embraced in the disputed territory, generally the Winooski Valley; and to this territory they retreated, after their forays, as to the stronghold and home, in which there was no danger of pursuit. This would never have been the case, if there were any trace of the dreaded Iroquois remaining in any part of Vermont. It may be said by some, perhaps, that the Iroquois may have been *expelled* from Vermont by the French and their allies, the Abenakis, as the French power increased in Canada, and that they did not leave it voluntarily as we have supposed. But we have no accounts of any battles or skirmishes between the French and Abenakis and the Iroquois on the borders of Champlain, in which any such expulsion could be effected. Indeed, all our early histories concur in making out the expedition against Schenectady the first one undertaken in this quarter by the French and Eastern Indians, whether to make war against the English or the Iroquois.

There is one more consideration to be presented before closing this branch of the subject, which is this: If the Iroquois were the original owners of this disputed territory in Vermont, how came it about that they, being so powerful a people, should own such a peculiarly marked and located portion of it? Why did they not own the whole of it, including the pleasant vallies of the Connecticut in the Southern part of the State, taking that river against Vermont for their Eastern limit, which would have made one of those natural, national boundaries so generally adopted by the Aborigines of this country? It would be very difficult to give a satisfactory answer even to this question, on the supposition that the Iroquois were the original owners of the territory in question.

The questionableness of the claimed boundary, indeed, is not without confirmation in the admission of these Iroquois claimants themselves. In the Report of the Hon. T. P. Redfield, who was appointed in 1853 by the Governor to investigate this claim, and who embodied in his report of 1854 all our former legislative and executive proceedings on the subject, we find, in the most formal and specific memorial which the Iroquois chiefs ever presented to our Legislature—that of 1812—the following admission: "*In the year* 1683, *our ancestors had a considerable dispute, as to the boundary line of the land we now claim, with the Eastern Indians.*" This at least proves that the Iroquois claim to the disputed territory has never been acquiesced in by the Eastern Indians; and it probably also points to the time when those Eastern Indians, having for the previous forty years been gradually resuming their possession of this territory, now began to be in a position to vindicate their right and title on the ground of their prior ownership and occupancy.

In view, then, of all the evidence on both sides of this question, we think we are well warranted in deducing the following conclusions:—

1st. That the Abenakis, or Eastern Indians, were the original owners, and the first and last possessors of the Winooski Valley and all the rest of Vermont claimed by the Iroquois.

2d. That the Iroquois *did* come in possession of this territory by conquest, some short time previous to 1540, and held it and lived in it till near 1640, when they voluntarily relinquished it to the original owners, the Abenakis, who coming in—perhaps gradually stealing in—took full possession and retained it for the next hundred years, or till the settlement of the State by our ancestors between 1740 and 1760.

[A citizen and native of Montpelier, who, for amusement, sometimes writes but never publishes, has furnished the following lines, composed the morning after the catastrophe they describe, for insertion in our appendix.]

BURNING OF THE STATE HOUSE AT MONTPELIER.

On the evening of the 6th day of January, 1857, the State House at Montpelier was consumed by fire. The night was cold, the thermometer fifteen degrees below zero, and the wind blowing a gale. The coals and cinders were blown for half a mile over the village, setting fires in many places, which were, however, by the vigilance of the citizens, extinguished without damage.

O'er Montpelier, beauteous town,
The shades of night were closing down;
The lovely moon, the queen of night,
Was driving on her chariot bright;
And star on star their influence lent,
'Till glowed with fire the firmament.
The wind was blowing high and strong,
And swept in fearful gusts along;
The piercing cold had cleared the street
Of merry voice and busy feet,—
And gathered round the cheerful hearth,
The smiling face, the social mirth,
Show'd that the night was gaily past,
While outward howled the roaring blast.

What means that wild and startling cry.
To which the echoing hills reply?
First feeble, low, and faint and mild,
Then loud and terrible and wild.
'Tis fire! fire! that awful sound!
Fire! fire! fire! the hills resound!
Now rising near—now heard afar,
The stillness of the night to mar,
Join'd with the wind's wild roaring, hear
The cry of fire burst on the ear!

Forth from the hearth, the shop, the store,
At that dread sound, the myriads pour—
And, gathering as they pass along,
Each street and alley swells the throng.
The rattling engines passing by,
The roaring wind, the larum cry,
The ringing bells, the wild affright,
Still add new terrors to the night.

See younder grand and stately pile,
With lofty dome, and beauteous aisle,
Our village glory, and our pride,
Whose granite walls old Time defied;
Her halls of state, her works of art,
Both please the eye, and charm the heart.

The moon's pale light on those dark walls
  Coldly now is gleaming;
But in her proud and lofty halls
  A wilder light is streaming.
Now gaily dancing to and fro,
  Now upward speeds its flight—
See! on its dome, now capp'd with snow,
The flame doth spread its fearful glow
  Of purple light.

The wind roars loud, the flames flash high,
Leaping and dancing to the sky;
  While in the rooms below,
From hall to hall resistless rushing,
From doors and windows furious gushing—
  Oh! how sublime the show!

Dark clouds of smoke spread far and wide,
And balls of fire on every side
  Fall like the Autumn hail;
Before the fury of the blast,
The rushing flames, that spread so fast,
  The heart of man may quail.

Ah, man, how feeble is thy power,
In that dread and fearful hour
  When flames are flashing free
From lofty spires and windows high,
And clouds of smoke obscure the sky,
As onward, on, the flames rush by,
  In their wildest revelrey!

Roar on, fierce flame; beneath thy power
The works of years, in one short hour,
  Are swept from earth away;
And nought is left of all their pride,
But ashes, scattered far and wide,
And crumbling walls, with smoke dark-dyed,
  Spread out in disarray.

That lofty pile, one hour ago,—
The State's just pride, the Nation's show,
Capp'd with its bright and virgin snow,—
  In beauty shone:
The next, a mass of ruined walls,
Of columns broke, and burning halls,—
  Its beauty flown.

www.ingramcontent.com/pod-product-compliance
Lightning Source LLC
LaVergne TN
LVHW020233110826
845151LV00003B/908